# The Cycle of Life

Also by Erel Shalit

Enemy, Cripple, Beggar:
Shadows in the Hero's Path
ISBN 978-0-9776076-7-9

Requiem:
A Tale of Exile and Return
978-1-926715-03-2

The Complex:
Path of Transformation from Archetype to Ego
978-0-919123-99-1

The Hero and His Shadow:
Psychopolitical Aspects of Myth and Reality in Israel
978-0-761827-24-5

Will Fishes Fly in Aquarius—
Or Will they Drown in the Bucket?
978-1-926715-40-7

# The Cycle of Life

## Themes and Tales of the Journey

Erel Shalit

*The Cycle of Life*

*Themes and Tales of the Journey*

Copyright © 2011 by Erel Shalit
First Edition
ISBN 978-1-926715-50-6 Paperback
ISBN 978-1-926715-51-3 eBook

Published simultaneously in Canada, the United Kingdom, and the United States of America by Fisher King Press. For information on obtaining permission for use of material from this work, submit a written request to:

permissions@fisherkingpress.com

Fisher King Press
PO Box 222321
Carmel, CA 93922
www.fisherkingpress.com
info@fisherkingpress.com
+1-831-238-7799

Many thanks to all who have directly or indirectly provided permission to quote their works, including:

KEELEY, EDMUND; *C.P. CAVAFY*. © 1975 by Edmund Keeley and Philip Sherrard. Reprinted by permission of Princeton University Press.

# CONTENTS

# Acknowledgements

During the years of writing *The Cycle of Life*, a parental generation passed away, leaving its imprint, having, to the best of their ability, passed on the bucket of living waters, and generations of wisdom, for which I am grateful.

And a generation of grandchildren are being born, bringing joy, hope and prospects for what is, axiomatically, an uncertain future, lovingly guided by their parents, attended to by their grandmother.

I want to thank all those who have granted their permission to borrow from the wisdom of their souls, often expressed by the images in their dreams. I am indebted to my colleagues and other professionals who have read and commented on my manuscript, and to you, the reader of my labor. I value and appreciate the time you spend reading, your thoughts and reflections, whether you share them with me or others, or keep them to yourself.

I am grateful to Mel Mathews and Patty Cabanas of Fisher King Press, who with the generosity of their hearts and with professional skillfulness have brought this treatise into its own life.

A primary tenet of my perspective on the journey through life is the confluence of fate and destiny, how conscious choice and the unexpected turns of the tide flow together. Little did I anticipate that this would become apparent in my search for a cover image, the face of the book. I traveled along rivers of time and traversed cultural continents, ending up, so it seemed, with a coverless book in my hands. Then, in a sudden bliss, I remembered a painter whose name was at the tip of my tongue. As I extracted his name, Benjamin Shiff, from the layers of my memory, I was reminded of the balance between lyric harmony and pensive concern, which characterized the painting I recalled.

As I traced the pictures on Shiff's canvas, my eyes fell for the first time upon his painting, 'Life' (1990). Undoubtedly, I had found the grail. The candles' soft light of life is poised against the painful inevitability of burning out. Yet, as long as they burn, there are shades and colors; there are the distinct faces of transient existence, and there are those of obscurity, hidden in distant nature; there is a lyrical melancholy, as well as a tense harmony.

The pain of death and extinction reflects the subtle strength and beauty of life. Only an unlit candle will never burn out. A fully lived life extracts the awareness of its finality. Mortality as the ultimate boundary of physical existence, serves as the container of human life.

I came across Benjamin Shiff's painting 'Life' in May 2011, only to learn that he died in March. As it turned out, not only did we live but half an hour apart, but his daughter, Orit Yaar, is also a Jungian analyst. I knew Orit, but had no idea that she was Benjamin Shiff's daughter.

With the sadness of having lost the possibility of meeting Benjamin Shiff in life, I hope that his painting 'Life' which provides *The Cycle of Life* with a face, will serve as a candle honoring and reflecting upon his life and work.

I wish to thank Shosh Shiff, who granted permission to feature this profound painting on the cover of *The Cycle of Life*.

# PREFACE

The Grimm Brothers tell the story of how God decided about the duration of life, and the dire consequences of man's demands:

When God created the world and was about to determine the duration of life for all the creatures, the donkey came and asked, "Lord, how long am I to live?"

"Thirty years," replied God. "Does that content you?"

"Ah! Lord," answered the ass, "that is a long time. Think of my painful existence! To carry heavy burdens from morning until night, to drag bags of corn to the mill so that others might eat bread, only to be cheered along and refreshed with nothing but kicks and blows! Spare me a portion of this long time."

So God had mercy and gave him eighteen years. The donkey went away satisfied, and the dog made his appearance.

"How long would you want to live?" said God to him; "thirty years are too many for the donkey, but you will be satisfied with that long."

"Lord," answered the dog, "is that thy will? Just think how I shall have to run. My feet will never hold out so long. And what can I do but growl and run from one corner to another after I have lost my voice for barking and my teeth for biting?"

God saw that he was right, and settled for twelve years.

Then came the monkey. "You will certainly like to live thirty years," said the Lord to him; "you need not work like the donkey and the dog, and will always enjoy yourself."

"Ah! Lord," he answered, "it may seem as if that were the case, but it is quite different. When it rains porridge, I have no spoon. I am always to play merry tricks and make faces for people to laugh, but when they give me an apple and I bite into it, why, it is sour! How often is sorrow hidden behind a joke. I shall never be able to hold out with all that for thirty years!"

God had mercy and gave him ten years.

At last man appeared, joyous, healthy, and vigorous, and begged God to determine the duration of his life.

"Thirty years you shall live," spoke the Lord. "Is that enough for you?"

"What a short time!" cried man, "when I have built my house and my fire burns on my own hearth; when I have planted trees that blossom and bear fruit, and am just beginning to enjoy my life, then I am to die! Oh, Lord, lengthen my time."

"I will add to it the ass's eighteen years," said God.

"That is not enough," replied man.

"You shall also have the dog's twelve years."

"Still too little!"

"Well, then," said God, "I will give you the monkey's ten years as well, but you shall have no more."

Man went away, but was not satisfied.

Thus man lives for seventy years. The first thirty are his human years, which are soon gone; that is when he is healthy and happy; works with pleasure, and is glad of his life. Then follow the donkey's eighteen years, when one burden after another is laid on him; he carries the corn that feeds others, and kicks and blows are the reward of his faithful services. Then come the dog's twelve years, when he lies in the corner growling, and has no longer any teeth with which to bite. And when this time is past, the monkey's ten years bring man to the end. Now man is weak headed and foolish, does silly things and becomes the laughingstock for children.[1]

This grim(m) story tells a fundamental, though not absolute truth of life. It provides a healthy and bittersweet compensation for our common belief in and virtual worship of seemingly eternal, or at least life-long youth, with the concomitant repression of life's darker sides and the denial of death. In fact, Ernest Becker claimed that man's hope and belief is that the things created in society shall be "of lasting worth and meaning, that they outlive or outshine death and decay." That is, Becker considers the very basis of civilization to be a defense against human mortality.[2]

When cosmetics and plastic surgery mold a stiff and unyielding mask of youth, or rather of fictitious youthful *appearance*, old age cannot wear its true face of wisdom. By flattening out the valleys of our wrinkles, we erase the imprints of our character. Fixation in a narcissistic condition of an outworn mask silences the inner voice of meaning in our life.

Jung defines life as the "story of the self-realization of the unconscious. Everything in the unconscious seeks outward manifestation, and the personality too desires to evolve out of its unconscious conditions to experience itself as a whole."[3] The purpose of this book is to describe some of the principal archetypal images at play as we navigate our journey through the cycle of life. In each stage of life, there is an image, or rather a cluster of psychological themes that pertain to that particular

1  Grimm Brothers, *The Complete Grimm's Fairy Tales*, pp. 716-718.
2  Ernest Becker, *The Denial of Death*, p. 5.
3  Carl Gustav Jung, *Memories, Dreams, Reflections*, p. 3.

period, such as the divine child and the orphan child. Usually, these themes and images do not correspond to actual events or traumata, but reflect internal, archetypal experiences. The feelings related to being an orphan are universal, and a vital facet of growing out of certain states of childhood; sometimes, however, the *archetypal image* of the orphan may devastatingly strike a child by the *traumatic loss* of a parent. Traumatic experiences often cause fixation; the archetypal image becomes frozen in the psyche of the traumatized person, rather than serving as a transitory psychic constellation, eventually integrating into the fullness of the personality.

Furthermore, sometimes we are struck by the disparity between a predominant archetypal image and the prevailing developmental stage, as for instance when we see a *senex-child*, that is, a child who seems to speak the old person's tongue, rather than to be dwelling in the world of childhood play. Or, for example, a mother of four teenage children, all of whom thought of her as a 'child-mother,' immature and childish. Even when they were small, they felt that she wanted them to be parental children taking care of her.

The archetypal idea of *a journey through life* is outlined in chapter I, in which Jung's theory of the stages of life, as well as other perspectives, will be reviewed.

A focus on the river of life as an image of the journey will help illustrate the process of transformation from predetermined fate to individual destiny. Hermes, god of thieves and merchants, souls and roads, will guide us toward the Hermetic aspect of life's journey, infusing the experience of life with meaning, when graced with those soulful gifts that alter life's course.

The first actual stage we encounter on the journey is unavoidably *The Child*, whom we tenderly receive in chapter II. Archetypally, childhood is the *idea* and the *image* of the child rather than the concrete experience. The *divine child*, such as the child-god Eros, dwells in the vicinity of the gods, while ego-reality still seems far away, in a future that shall all too soon whirl up at the horizon. The ego germ dwells as but a prospective seed in *the waters* of the self. However, even at the archetypal level childhood is not pure splendor; behind existence in paradisiacal divinity lies the deep, dark and threatening abyss of *chaos*, of *tohu-va-vohu*, as it is called in the Bible.[4] Moreover, after reclining on the blissful couch of paradisiacal innocence, the necessary feelings of

---

4  The term 'tohu-va-vohu' can be understood as 'waste and wild, wonder and
   bewilderment.'

*abandonment* creep up upon us, as the fleeting moments of divine existence escape us, finding ourselves in the misery of life's orphanage.

In this chapter, as in those that follow, dreams and tales will illustrate the archetypal images of life's stages, considering as well the pathology of the cycle of life, and the meaning that abides in it.

The *Puer* and the *Puella*, the young man and the maiden, rush into the pages of the book in chapter III. They hold *the fire* and *the spirit* of the gods, trying like Prometheus to bring it to the use of *man*—man, sometimes being the threatened father who tries to wrestle the fire out of his son's hand, extinguishing the flame and strangling the spirit, and sometimes in the image of the protective mother, carefully harnessing it by keeping the hearth's fire burning.

As *hero*, the young person brings the fire of the self to the use and benefit of the ego, and exposes in the light of consciousness that which lingers in the dark. The task of the *puer* is to bring the Promethean fire and the spirit to combine with *earth*. However, the young ones are always in danger of tripping off into unfocused associations, or falling recklessly to the ground, onto the harsh earth, drunk by the wine, burned by passion or overtaken by the spirit.

In chapter IV, we shall stand on the firm ground of *The Adult*. The King in the fairytales is the ruler on *earth*, the dominant principle of collective consciousness, powerful in a man-made world. While ours is a world of limits and limitations, borders and boundaries, kings tend to get inflated with their hubris, disregarding the fact of their supposed appointment by divine decree. Kings often forget that they merely represent the unfolding of an archetypal image in the human realm. In the fairy tales of our psyche, the king is the ruler of ego and consciousness, of the self's constellation in the ego, in the adult world of science, cities and organizations. The ego's rule on earth may be a mirror image of the self, the terrestrial replication of the celestial city, and of nature's order and organization, as we find it in a multitude of wonders, e.g. the beehive or the planets' course in the universe. However, inflation is often the insignia of royal rule, whereby the spirit is lost, the earth dries up, and hunger and starvation transpire, since the softness and transparency of the soul are not nourished by material wealth. When inflation possesses power over the king, the feminine soul leaves his fairy tale, escaping like a grasshopper to avoid being squeezed between the pages, as the angry king slams shut the annals of his royal book. But alas the king himself dies—the ink of his pen has dried, the remainder of his page in history remains unwritten. When the waters of childhood are

dry, and the fiery spirit of youth is obsolete, the collective consciousness of norms and rules often becomes repressive and oppressive.

In chapter V. i, we shall look for, and hopefully catch sight of the
*Senex*, the old man or woman,[5] who moves toward corporal invisibility,
who leaves ego behind to melt into that greater Self, the world soul,
that we can only intuit in the *wind*. He or she stands at the ultimate
crossroads of corporal dis-integration and meaninglessness on the one
hand, and a sense of humble participation in the unfolding of a greater
scheme that relies on the way man shapes his consciousness and carries
his destiny, on the other.

In chapter V. ii, we pay homage to Sophocles and his masterful play
*Oedipus at Colonus*. We shall ponder upon the perhaps never fully resolved or resolvable conflict between meaninglessness, stagnation and
disintegration versus a sense of purpose, meaning and transcendent
connection.

We need to balance all these ages of individual development along
the life cycle. The proportions change, however, and for instance a too
earth-bound young person may set too severe limitations on his spirit,
too soon. In the concluding chapter V. iii, we shall see how the puzzle
may come together in a meaningful way, as the ego turns toward the
Self.

As concerns psychology, we find that Freudian psychology is based primarily on the child archetype, as unfolding in childhood, in spite of,
or perhaps because of the fact that Freud himself was quite a neurotic
adult. The Jungian approach is more of a senex-psychology, in the sense
that central importance is placed on the quest for meaning. While Jung
remained quite a playful child throughout his entire life, building towers and castles at the shores of the lake, he plunged into his introverted
mind in search for meaning.

In so far as there is a nucleus of archetypal images at the center of
each stage of life, the archetypal *essence* of each age is present in us all,
throughout life, even if in various proportions and changing manifestations.

Jung spoke about the need for a modern myth based not only on
ego-consciousness but individuation, which we may define as a vital,

---

5  While *senex* principally is the old, not necessarily wise man, it is here applied
   regardless of gender, just as senior, seniority and senility pertain to and affect
   men as well as women.

dynamic and meaningful relationship between ego and self (or Self[6]),
an ever-changing relationship through life, which we shall explore as it
unfolds through the seasons of our life. As Thomas Mann says, "Myth is
the foundation of life; it is the timeless schema, the pious formula into
which life flows when it reproduces its traits out of the unconscious."[7]

---

6  Jung did not capitalize the Self as archetype. It is, however, useful to capitalize the Self as archetype of wholeness and center, in distinction from the self
   as representation in the ego.
7  Thomas Mann, 'Freud and the Future,' *Daedalus*, p. 374.

I

# THE JOURNEY

As you set out for Ithaka
hope the voyage is a long one,
full of adventure, full of discovery.
Laistrygonians and Cyclops,
angry Poseidon—don't be afraid of them:
you'll never find things like that on your way
as long as you keep your thoughts raised high,
as long as a rare excitement
stirs your spirit and your body.
Laistrygonians and Cyclops,
wild Poseidon—you won't encounter them
unless you bring them along inside your soul,
unless your soul sets them up in front of you.

Hope the voyage is a long one.
May there be many a summer morning when,
with what pleasure, what joy,
you come into harbors seen for the first time;
may you stop at Phoenician trading stations
to buy fine things,
mother of pearl and coral, amber and ebony,
sensual perfume of every kind—
as many sensual perfumes as you can;
and may you visit many Egyptian cities
to gather stores of knowledge from their scholars.

Keep Ithaka always in your mind.
Arriving there is what you are destined for.
But do not hurry the journey at all.
Better if it lasts for years,

so you are old by the time you reach the island,
wealthy with all you have gained on the way,
not expecting Ithaka to make you rich.

Ithaka gave you the marvelous journey.
Without her you would not have set out.
She has nothing left to give you now.

And if you find her poor, Ithaka won't have fooled you.
Wise as you will have become, so full of experience,
you will have understood by then what these Ithakas mean.
                    —Constantine Petrou Cavafy, Ithaka[8]


## Stages and Seasons

Freud defined and described the stages of psychosexual development
in childhood, while Jung brought to light human development during
the second half of life. Daniel Levinson, a portal figure in modern life
cycle research, who outlined the *Seasons of a Man's Life*, says, "Freud was
inclined to regard adulthood primarily as a scene in which the early
unconscious conflicts were re-enacted, rather than as a time of further
development."[9]

Psychoanalysis outlines what are presumed to be universal, archetypal patterns of development. It is the task of every individual to navigate safely between the stages of development, and to face the challenges that confront the child at each stage. Failing to do so, pathology
ensues. In *Three Essays on Sexuality* (1915) and 'The infantile genital
organization' (1923), Freud outlined the oral, anal, phallic, (period of)
latency and genital stages of development in childhood and puberty.[10]
The individual is expected to reach psychosexual maturity by successfully resolving the conflicts and challenges of each particular stage,
while unresolved conflicts will cause fixation. For instance, because of
too harsh, demanding and controlling parenting during the anal stage,
an anal-retentive personality may develop, characterized by obsession
and compulsion, orderliness and suspicion.

---

8  Constantine Petrou Cavafy, 'Ithaka,' in *Collected Poems*, p. 36f.
9  Daniel Levinson, *The Seasons of a Man's Life*, p. 4.
10  Sigmund Freud, *Three Essays on Sexuality*, in *Standard Edition of the Complete
    Psychological Works* (hereafter SE) 7, pp. 125-172; 'The infantile genital orga-
    nization: An interpolation into the theory of sexuality,' SE 19, pp. 141-148.

Later, Erik Erikson expanded this basic pattern. In *Childhood and Society*, he outlined eight stages, or *ages*, as the title of his chapter pertinently indicates,[11] of man. From crib to old age, the human child and adult are confronted with a series of polarities, which he or she must negotiate.

The unfolding of the successive stages follows an innate pattern, according to which each stage presents the individual with a crisis, based on physiological development as well as environmental conditions and requirements. In infancy, the child grapples with the polarity of *basic trust* versus *mistrust* of the oral sensory stage, while the adolescent asks, "Who am I?" That is, the central question that he or she has to deal with concerns *identity* versus *role confusion*. Then, in the final stage of maturity, the old person faces *ego integrity* versus *despair*. Integrity is found "in him who in some way has taken care of things and people and has adapted himself to the triumphs and disappointments adherent to being," while *despair* is the fate of someone who, when facing him or herself in the mirror of death feels that "the time is . . . too short for the attempt to start another life."[12]

In *The Life Cycle Completed*, Erikson and his wife Joan added a ninth stage, where "the dystonic element [is placed] first in order to underscore its prominence and potency." Thus, as the truly old looks back on the road taken, and gathers the polarities of his or her ages, mistrust may paradoxically prevail over trust as a basis for hope, when the elder "rejoice[s] to see [the sun] rise brightly every morning."[13]

In *The Seasons of a Man's Life*, Daniel Levinson divided the life cycle into four partly overlapping eras of roughly twenty to twenty-five years each, defining them as childhood and adolescence, followed by early, middle and late adulthood. From his perspective, Levinson emphasized that each era has its own "distinctive and unifying qualities, which have to do with the character of living."[14] These qualities account for biological, psychological as well as social factors.

The stage of pre-adulthood, i.e., childhood, adolescence and transition into early adulthood, is considered a prelude to adult living. In our present era, however, when the world allegedly belongs to the young

---

11 Erik H. Erikson, *Childhood and Society*, Ch. 7: Eight Ages Of Man. As I see it, a *stage* would limit the discussion to a linear, developmental perspective, while *age* enables us to look at the archetypal kernel these stages, or ages, embrace.

12 *Childhood and Society*, pp. 241-2.

13 Joan M. Erikson, in Erik H. Erikson, *The Life Cycle Completed*, pp. 106-7.

14 *The Seasons of a Man's Life*, p. 18.

(increasingly paid for by the no-longer-so-young), the stages of adulthood may rather be termed post-youth (at least for the supposedly unfortunate with whom Botox, peeling or lifting have not successfully obliterated the traces of age and aging).

Early adulthood presents young men and women with a series of major choices and decisions, such as occupation and life style. This is also, generally, an age of energy and potential, as well as social pressure.

In the stage Levinson terms 'Middle adulthood,' approximately from age forty to sixty-five, the qualities of strength and productivity may ripen into judiciousness and breadth of perspective. However, it also entails the midlife transition from youthful narcissism to awareness of one's mortality.

A primary task of late adulthood, says Levinson, resonating the voices of Erikson and Jung, is "to find a new balance of involvement with society and with the self."[15] Furthermore, by finding meaning and value in one's life, the old person may be better equipped to face up to death and dying.

Following Edinger and Neumann, we may say that the journey through our life develops along the ego-Self axis, in four prominent stages: *ego thriving in self; ego-self separation; ego-affirmation; ego-self reunion*, in a continuous process of alternating ego-self *union* and ego-self *separation.*[16]

In the first of these stages, the infant's ego dwells as a germ in the unconscious habitat of the primary Self. The early sense of being and playing enables life to rise from the divine waters, and for the ego to emerge from its dwelling in the objective psyche, and the depths of the collective unconscious.

Later, it becomes the task of the puer and the puella to light the torch with the fire of the gods, so that the flame and the spirit can be brought to human ground, where the adult stands, works, disciplines and delineates the boundaries required for the regulation and fulfillment of the individual and human society.

The ego assumes social roles and obligations, fulfilling superego demands, and becomes the core of the law-abiding, committed and contributing citizen. The essence of individuation in the first half of life,

---

15  *The Seasons of a Man's Life*, p. 36.
16  Edward Edinger, *Ego and Archetype,* Erich Neumann, *The Origins and History of Consciousness.*

according to Jung and Neumann, is the establishment of a conscious identity and a well-functioning and well-adapted ego.

In the *second half of life*, the ego needs to realize that it is not the owner of the house, but a temporary tenant in the dwelling of this life. The ego is required to turn toward and reunite with the Self—the Self, which provides the ground-plan, the blueprint of the house, of the personality we inhabit through life, and which is the invisible, gravitational force that enables the ego to keep the house erect. In the senex-part of our life, the ego must approach the deeper, inner layers of existence, the invisible and transparent dimensions of soul, in which the sense of meaning in one's life can crystallize.

These stages are not merely linear, but alternate constantly through life. As we go to sleep at night, the ego resigns its control and lets the Self preside, and when we rise in the morning, the ego turns on the light and dresses anew to meet the tasks of every day.

## Jung's Stages of Life

Jung introduced the idea of studying and defining the goals of the second half of life. Daniel Levinson thus considered him "the father of the modern study of adult development."[17]

Jung originally published his essay 'The Stages of Life' in 1930,[18] about twenty years before Erikson drew his epigenetic chart of psychosocial development. Jung emphasized the contrary directions of man's focus during the first and second halves of life. Whereas in the first part of life, the development of a firm ego that takes its foothold in the world predominates, in the second part of life, the individual must turn toward Self and spirit.

'The Stages of Life' appeared in 1933 in Jung's book *Modern Man in Search of a Soul*. It had initially been published as 'Die seelische Probleme der menschlichen Altersstufen' in *Neue Zürcher Zeitung* in 1930, but was later revised. His ideas regarding the stages of life will be our point of departure and guiding light throughout our discourse.

When Jung set out to "discuss the problems connected with the stages of life," he devoted several pages of this brief essay to discuss the notion of *problem*. He claims that *problem* is the kernel of culture and

---

17  *The Seasons of a Man's Life*, p. 4.
18  Carl Gustav Jung, *The Collected Works of C. G. Jung*, vol. 8, par. 749-795.
    NOTE: CW refers throughout to *The Collected Works of C. G. Jung*.

consciousness. "There are no problems without consciousness," says Jung. Confronting a problem instigates toward consciousness, and due to the development of consciousness, problems come into existence.[19] Furthermore, Jung emphasizes the psychological truth that serious problems can never be fully resolved—if they appear to be, then "something has been lost." The meaning as well as the purpose of problems lie not in their solution but, rather, in being constantly worked on.[20] Similarly, happiness and welfare do not lie in wait to be found at the end of the rainbow, but are aspects of the process and of our attitude, with sadness and misery appropriate company at times of pain, difficulty and loss. The journey entails both the road we take and *how* we take that road, our conscious *attitude*.

Unmistakably, Jung's conceptualization of the stages of life pertains to living the *conscious life*.

The first stage of life concerns the child's evolving consciousness, which is based on perceiving the connection between different psychic contents. However, lacking a continuous memory in early childhood, consciousness is sporadic, rather like "single lamps or lighted objects in the far-flung darkness."[21] Only when there is continuity of ego-memories does the ego-complex constellate, with a budding sense of subjective identity, whereby the child comes to speak of itself in first person.

*Problems* arise, says Jung, with the psychic birth and "conscious differentiation from the parents" in puberty.[22] This is not only an external process. By internalization, the external limitations become internal divisions, for instance, between opposing impulses. That is, the rise of consciousness both creates and is the result of an inner division between the ego and the perceived *other*—whether that other is an internal instinct or an external object, an autonomous complex detracting energy from the ego, or a split-off shadow.

The period of youth entails the transition from what Jung considers to be the dream of an essentially problem-free childhood to the harsh demands of life. The problem may be external, due, for instance, to "exaggerated expectations, underestimation of difficulties, unjustified optimism, or a negative attitude." Nevertheless, problems unmistakably may arise, as well, from internal conflicts and disturbances in the

---

19  CW 8, par. 750, 754.
20  CW 8, par. 770.
21  CW 8, par. 755.
22  CW 8, par. 756.

psychic equilibrium; Jung mentions the sexual instinct and feelings of inferiority.[23]

It is in youth, says Jung, that the individual needs to recognize and accept "what is different and strange as a part of his own life," in spite of the desire to cling "to the childhood level of consciousness,"[24] that is, a wish to avoid unpleasure, and to regress into a conflict-free existence.[25]

Achievement and usefulness, says Jung, "are the lodestars that guide us ... to strike our roots in the world," to find a place in society, which is essential in the first half of life. Development of a wider consciousness, "which we give the name of culture,"[26] is left, however, for a later stage in life. Therefore, while the child struggles to shape its individual ego, the aim in youth—or young adulthood—is to gain a place in society.

Jung's main concern as expressed in this essay is the arrival at midlife. "The social goal," he says, "is attained only at the cost of a diminution of personality. Many—far too many—aspects of life which should also have been experienced lie in the lumber-room among dusty memories; but sometimes, too, they are glowing coals under grey ashes."[27]

Jung notes that around the age of forty, a slow process of character-change takes place. Interests and inclinations alter. Simultaneously, however, moral principles tend to harden and grow rigid, "as if the existence of these principles were endangered and it were therefore necessary to emphasize them all the more."[28]

Jung ascribed the neurotic disturbances of adults to the common desire to prolong youth, and a reticence to crossing the threshold into maturity. The neurotic is someone "who can never have things as he would like them in the present."[29] Typically, the neurotic person projects the cause of his suffering onto the past or the future, and we often hear him or her say, "if only this or that would/would not have happened," or "if only ... then ..." The cult of youth and the widespread difficulty of accepting old age, typify the pathology of our era.

23  CW 8, par. 761, 762.
24  CW 8, par. 764.
25  Cf. Sigmund Freud, *Beyond the Pleasure Principle*, SE 18. The word *unpleasure* is "used to translate the German '*Unlust*,' the pain or discomfort of instinctual tension, as opposed to '*Schmertz*,' the sensation of pain. The pleasure principle is correctly the pleasure-unpleasure principle." (Charles Rycroft, *A Critical Dictionary of Psychoanalysis*, p. 174).
26  CW 8, par. 769.
27  CW 8, par. 772.
28  CW 8, par. 773.
29  CW 8, par. 776.

The fear of midlife is not of death, claims Jung, but of the sun's descent, which means "the reversal of all the ideals and values that were cherished in the morning. ... The sun ... draw[s] in its rays instead of emitting them. Light and warmth decline and are at last extinguished."[30]

However, it seems to me that ultimately the fishing rod of midlife fears does indeed dip into the lake of death, when light and warmth are extinguished. This, then, may be compensated by, for instance, what for many may be a reassuring faith and belief in existence after death, or, alternatively, the ambition to live a meaningful life. In his essay 'The Soul and Death,' published in 1934, Jung does state that,

> From the middle of life onward, only he remains vitally alive who is ready to *die with life*. For in the secret hour of life's midday the parabola is reversed, death is born. The second half of life does not signify ascent, unfolding, increase, exuberance, but death, since the end is its goal.[31]

The challenge in midlife is to come to terms with hitherto neglected features, sometimes conflicting with one's conscious attitude and recognized values. Jung mentions, as well, how bodily characteristics of the opposite sex can be discerned in the older person.

The psychological and biological changes that a person undergoes in the second half of life may thus blur the distinction between male and female traits, though this may be a far cry from the erotic character of juvenile androgyny. Consequently, the man must now put his feminine substance to use, and, says Jung, the woman "her hitherto unused supply of masculinity."[32] According to Jung's Weltanschauung, certainly influenced by the Zeitgeist, the spirit of his time, he associated the masculine with logos and the feminine with Eros.

Thus, in midlife it may happen that "the husband discovers his tender feelings and the wife her sharpness of mind."[33] These changes are dramatic and, says Jung, may lead to marital catastrophe. If so, I suppose that the wife's sharpness of mind may be more threatening to the man, than showing his tender feelings would pose a danger to his wife.[34]

---

30  CW 8, par. 778.
31  CW 8, par. 800.
32  CW 8, par. 782.
33  CW 8, par. 783.
34  As in some other instances, Jung's formulation here is quite archaic. Sharpness of mind is not egodystonic to women, whether young or old. Also, many a young man today need not wait till midlife to expose his tender feelings.

Jung expressed the essence of midlife transition beautifully when he says that, "what was great in the morning will be little at evening, and what in the morning was true will at evening have become a lie."[35]

In the second half of life, man must withdraw from external preoccupations, and seriously prepare for old age, death and eternity—which amounts to a (not necessarily formal) religious attitude. "An old man who cannot bid farewell to life appears as feeble and sickly as a young man who is unable to embrace it," says Jung sharply and poetically.[36] Rhetorically he wonders if not culture, beyond the nature to which family and children pertain, is the "meaning and purpose of the second half of life."[37]

To sum up, Jung's ideas on the stages of life pertain to the development of consciousness as it manifests in the life cycle. The essence lies in the *problem* that faces the individual at each stage; a problem less to be resolved, but rather to be confronted and challenged. Jung thus emphasizes life as a process of becoming conscious, which transforms the experience of life into a living experience.

As the individual traverses the arc of life, he or she may be resistant to the problems posed by each transition, such as an expanding ego consciousness; striking roots in society; confronting the decline and integrating the opposites, including those of gender; and then death and eternity. Jung says that, "the art of life is the most distinguished and rarest of all the arts."[38] For some travelers along the journey of life, the art of life becomes increasingly conceptual, for others more and more esthetic; for some minimalistic, for others increasingly abstract.

The second half of life should not merely be a repetition of one's youth and young adulthood, but rather a period that enables integration by accentuating those matters of one's psyche that have not been taken care of well enough.

Jung divides life into four parts. We shall elaborate here on the respective stages less from a developmental perspective, but rather as an effort to extract the archetypal images at the core of each age.

---

35  CW 8, par. 784.
36  CW 8, par. 792.
37  CW 8, par. 787.
38  CW 8, par. 789.

## All the World's a Stage, and a Stage of Life

There is an archetypal idea of the journey through life, unfolding in successive stages from a point of origin, across the summit, to a point of conclusion. Daniel Levinson says, "to speak of a general, human life cycle is to propose that the journey from birth to old age follows an underlying, universal pattern on which there are endless cultural and individual variations."[39]

It is an ancient idea that the human goes through universal stages of life, wherein he or she has to remove the garment of the previous stage, wear a new mantle and face new challenges. We find a wealth of descriptions of life's stages and its seasons in different cultures. It was a common theme in poems and profane iconography during the Middle Ages.[40] Has anyone described it more succinctly than Shakespeare, with his bittersweet British irony?

> All the world's a stage,
> And all the men and women merely players.
> They have their exits and their entrances,
> And one man in his time plays many parts,
> His acts being seven ages. At first the infant,
> Mewling and puking in the nurse's arms.
> Then the whining school-boy, with his satchel
> And shining morning face, creeping like snail
> Unwillingly to school. And then the lover,
> Sighing like furnace, with a woeful ballad
> Made to his mistress' eyebrow. Then, a soldier,
> Full of strange oaths, and bearded like the pard,
> Jealous in honor, sudden, and quick in quarrel,
> Seeking the bubble reputation
> Even in the cannon's mouth. And then the justice,
> In fair round belly with good capon lined,
> With eyes severe and beard of formal cut,
> Full of wise saws and modern instances;
> And so he plays his part. The sixth age shifts
> Into the lean and slippered pantaloon,
> With spectacles on nose and pouch on side,
> His youthful hose, well saved, a world too wide
> For his shrunk shank, and his big, manly voice,

---

39  *The Seasons of a Man's Life*, p. 6.
40  Cf. Philippe Ariès, *Centuries of Childhood: A Social History of Family Life*, p. 21ff.

Turning again toward childish treble, pipes
And whistles in his sound. Last scene of all,
That ends this strange, eventful history,
Is second childishness and mere oblivion,
Sans teeth, sans eyes, sans taste, sans everything.[41]

In the world of ancient Greece, the fate of one's life was spun at birth by the three Moirai, or Parcae, in Roman mythology. The three goddesses, as Hesiod describes in his *Theogony*, allotted mortals their share of good and evil.[42] According to Hesiod, they were the daughters of Zeus and Themis, goddess of divine order and law. However, they have also been ascribed daughterhood of Nyx, goddess of the Night. Furthermore, Ananke, goddess of Necessity, has likewise been said to be their mother.

Hillman, following Plato, outlines the relation between Necessity and the human condition, and sees Ananke as the mother of the Fates.[43] Sanford, who also calls attention to how closely Ananke is related to the three Fates, says she lays upon us "the necessity to create in whatever way is appropriate for us, for when creative energy is not expressed, then it turns against us."[44] Ananke demands of us not to deviate from necessary fate, be it the inborn gifts we have received, the limitations imposed upon us, or the call of our destiny.

Every individual carries personal responsibility to let the gifts one has been given unfold. At the beginning of our journey, we have been given a talent, a gift has been handed over to us, and it is our obligation to enable its materialization, to the extent that circumstances permit.

At birth, the predetermined *fate* of a person's soul was spun, but not one's personal *destiny*. Clotho was the spinner, Lachesis allocated one's lot in life, the "unalterable events and circumstances" one encounters, and Atropos represented the inevitable end to life. Described differently, the Fates held the thread of life allotted to each human soul. Clotho chose the thread, Lachesis measured it, and Atropos cut the thread, marking the end of a person's existence, at his or her "predetermined time of death."[45]

---

41  William Shakespeare, *As You Like It* (act 2, scene 7), in *The Oxford Shakespeare: The Complete Works*, p. 666.

42  Hesiod, *Theogony*, in Richard S. Caldwell, *Hesiod's Theogony*, p. 41.

43  James Hillman, 'On the Necessity of Abnormal Psychology: Ananke and Athene,' in James Hillman (Ed.), *Facing the Gods*, p. 15.

44  John A. Sanford, *Fate, Love, and Ecstasy*, p. 22.

45  *Fate, Love, and Ecstasy*, p. 70.

From this perspective, Fate overrides free will. Not even the hero, who stands up against the gods, escapes predetermined fate. His task is to break away, to wrestle himself out from the archetypal bonds that restrain the human ego. Yet, however strong his will and determination, his strength is limited by the boundless power of Fate. However, when Fate is reined in by Necessity and by the urge to follow one's path, individual destiny may take precedence over god-determined fate.

Prometheus, to whom we shall return later, tells the chorus, who claim he is neglectful of his own misfortunes,

> Not so nor yet hath all-determining Fate
> Ordained the end, but, when ten thousand pains
> Have crushed my body, from bonds shall I escape.
> For Art is weaker than Necessity.

He then tells the chorus that Zeus is less powerful than Fate and Necessity, unable to "alter that which is ordained."[46]

On our journey through life, an incessant tension prevails between predetermined fate and free will, between archetypal patterns as opposed to individual distinctiveness. For example, at the end of his journey, Oedipus claims innocence of his horrendous deeds, because he was "still unborn when that decree was spoken."[47] We shall later return to Oedipus at Colonus, and ponder upon such questions—are we guilty of our fore-doomed fate? Are we responsible for the genes we inherit?

Parents are to some extent transitional figures between the fate of the ancestors and the individual's free will. In modern psychology, the parents often carry the blame for the child's difficulty in resolving its complexes. From the child's point of view, the parents are the representatives of the rule and laws of the ancestors and what came before. They thus carry the chains of predetermined fate from which the child eventually needs to break away. We might say that the parents are representatives of the past who the child needs to oppose in order to establish his or her independence. While individuals differ in the quality of their parenting, *parents* constitute a target for the negative projections that are necessary, in order to express the sense of abandonment and neglect that necessarily accompany the growth toward independence.

Existentially oriented psychoanalysis tends, however, to emphasise the person's own freedom to decide, to find meaning, and responsibil-

---

46  Aeschylus, *Prometheus Bound*, p. 22.
47  Sophocles, *Oedipus at Colonus*, in *The Theban Plays* p. 101.

ity in formulating his or her destiny, with the concomitant anxiety this freedom causes.

Martin Buber tells the tale about the tzaddik, a righteous man, who while in his cell awaiting trial, converses with the chief of the gendarmes about God, man and the Scriptures. At one point he tells his warden, "In every era, God calls to every man: 'Where are you in your world? So many years and days of those allotted to you have passed, and how far have you gotten in your world?'"[48] This reflects the Talmudic saying that everything is foreseen, and everything is laid bare, yet everything is in accordance with the will of man. It concerns, as well, the saying, ascribed to Akaviya Ben Mahalalel, a contemporary of the sage Hillel the Elder (beginning of the contemporary era),

> Know where you came from, where you are going, and before whom you will in the future have to give account and reckoning. Where you came from—from a fetid drop; where you are going—to a place of dust, worms and maggots; and before whom you will in the future have to give account and reckoning—before God, the King of kings.[49]

Whether viewed in religious terms of a transcendent God, or psychologically, as an internalized God-image, the unaccounted-for life lacks the feeling of being rooted in a sense of meaning.

In Judaism we find two accounts, which seem to mirror each other of man's progression through life. In *Pirkei Avot*, we find the following highly ethical outline, man arriving at the end of life at a surprisingly advanced age:

> Yehuda ben Tema used to say: At the age of five, one is fit for the study of the Scriptures; at ten, for the Mishnah [the Jewish law, first part of the Talmud]; at thirteen, for fulfilling the commandments; at fifteen, for the study of Gemara [commentaries on the Mishnah, second part of the Talmud]; at eighteen, for the bridal chamber; at twenty to pursue a calling; at thirty, for the peak of strength; at forty, for understanding; at fifty, for counsel; at sixty, for mature

---

48  Martin Buber, *The Way of Man: According to the Teaching of Hasidism*, p. 5f.

49  From *Pirkei Avot*, Sayings (literally 'chapters') or *Ethics of the Fathers*, a Mishnaic tractate; notice that 'Fathers' here means fundamental principles rather than persons. Akaviya Ben Mahalalel seems to have been a lousy politician; after the death of Shammai, Hillel's eminent opponent yet his vice-president of the Sanhedrin, the ancient Jewish Council, Akaviya was offered the position on condition he retracts some of the opinions he had expressed, for which he refused. He declared, "Let it not be said that, for the sake of office, I changed my views" (Avrohom Davis, *Pirkei Avos*, p. 79).

age; at seventy, for the fullness of years; at eighty, for spiritual strength; at ninety—bent beneath the weight of years; at a hundred—as one that is already dead, who has passed away and ceased to be in this world.[50]

However, in the beginning of Ecclesiastes,[51] Kohelet (that is, Solomon), proclaims, "Vanity of vanities, vanity of vanities; all is vanity." He wonders,

> What gains a man from all his labor at which he labors under the sun? One generation passes away, and another generation comes; but the earth abides for ever. The sun also rises, and the sun goes down, and hastens to its place where it rises again. All the rivers run into the sea; yet the sea is not full; to the place from where the rivers come, there they return again. That which has been, is what shall be; and that which has been done is what shall be done; and there is nothing new under the sun.[52]

Despairingly he argues, "That which is crooked cannot be made straight; and that which is wanting cannot be numbered." With sorrow, he acknowledges that there is much grief in wisdom, and "he that increases knowledge increases sorrow."[53]

In the exegetic text 'Kohelet (Ecclesiastes) Rabbah,' we find an interpretation of King Solomon's reflections and exclamations about the vanity of life,

> R. Samuel bar Isaac said in the name of R. Simon ben Eliezer: The seven times Kohelet mentioned 'vanity' correspond to the seven worlds a man beholds. At the age of one, he is like a king lounging in a canopied litter, being hugged and kissed by everyone. At two and three, he is like a pig, sticking his hands into the gutters and putting whatever he finds into his mouth. At ten, he leaps about like a kid. At twenty, he is like a neighing horse, making himself attractive as he goes looking for a wife. Once wed, he has a saddle put upon him, and he works like an ass. After he brings children into the world, he has to brazen his face

---

50  Adapted from Hayim Nahman Bialik and Yehoshua Hana Ravnitzky, *The Book of Legends*, p. 578. The Mishnah is a compilation by Judah haNasi of Jewish Oral Tradition, c. 200 CE. Whereas the Mishnah is the first part of the Talmud, Gemara comprises the second part, a commentary on the Mishnah.
51  Greek, translated from Hebrew *Kohelet*, 'addressing an assembly,' referring to King Solomon.
52  Ecclesiastes 1:2-9.
53  Ecclesiastes 1:15, 18.

like a dog in order to provide food for himself and his children. When grown old, he is [bent] like an ape.[54]

The experience of human life as an animal, in pleasure as well as hardship, and certainly in its downward fall, seems to be universal, stretching beyond both the wise teachings of the Talmud, and the astute lessons of the Grimm Brothers.

The outline of the four stages of life, the Ashramas in Hinduism, however, leads toward a different perspective on the (ideal) path of the second half of life.

The first formative, student stage is one of practical and spiritual education. It is followed by the Householder stage, in which family and professional life dominate. Ideally, when the obligations as householder come to an end, the age of the Hermit follows. As described in the Laws of Manu, "when a householder sees his skin wrinkled, and his hair white, and the sons of his sons, then he may ... go forth from the village into the forest and reside there."[55] While this is usually not entirely practical for most modern men or women, the essence of withdrawal, of bringing the sacred fire "from village to forest," and carrying out the sacrifices that may add sacredness to one's life, may be psychologically valid in our era as well.

In the fourth Ashrama, the person renounces home and attachment, desires and responsibilities, and becomes a wandering beggar. Thus, with worldly ties broken, the sanyasi, devoid of attachment, devotes himself entirely to spiritual concerns. Again, while most of us whose existence is too worldly to allow us to come anywhere near the fulfillment of such ideals, we may reflect upon them as archetypal essences of the ages, or stages, of life. It is therefore important to let these core elements endow us with the soulfulness and spirit that they hold, so that they can accompany us, rather than be deleted from the chronicles of our journey.

## The Journey through Life

Willingly or not, everyone has to make the journey. The neurotic, however, is a reluctant traveler, who, as Otto Rank said, refrains from taking the loan, that is, the load of life, because one day he will have to pay

54 *The Book of Legends*, p. 577f.
55 *The Laws of Manu*, c. 1500 BCE, translated by George Buhler; http://www. fordham.edu/halsall/india/manu-full.html.

it back. The way through life is to some extent a given, following constitutional imprints and genetic tracks. Sometimes fortune as well as misfortune are determined by fate, while at other times we may claim the credit for our achievements. And sometimes, we must personally carry the burden of guilt for our wrongdoings. As we shall see toward the end of our journey, upon arriving at Colonus the old, blind and dying Oedipus, former King of Thebes, confronts the question of guilt, the debt we need to pay in our life. And now and then, we need to be grateful to another person for the happy turn of events, while at times we want to blame that other, whether human or transcendent, whether rightly or wrongly, for the calamities that have befallen us.

The perspective of life as a cycle lived through its stages enables us to bring the archetypal and the personal dimensions together. Heraclitus stated, as did Plato, that you cannot step into the same river twice,

> The river
> where you set
> your foot just now
> is gone—
> those waters
> giving way to this,
> now this.[56]

Man cannot step into the same river twice, says Bachelard, because, "in his inmost recesses, the human being shares the destiny of flowing water."[57] However, the neurotic person refrains from stepping into the river even once. He, or she, prefers to watch it from a far, or suffers from the absence of a river streaming through his body and soul. The absence of living his life *consciously* is not the neurotic's problem, but rather *living* his life.

While the river preserves its identity, it is incessantly moving and changing, simultaneously being and becoming.[58]

The journey of life's river flows along relatively stable riverbeds, such as genetic traits, that hardly or only very slowly change their route. Within these tracks, however, the character of the river may vary: in one, the bubbling water gushes forth, the beds splash with sparkling water at the slightest turn of the river, while along the route of another one's river, the water seems to have dried up, the weak stream more

---

56  Heraclitus, *Fragments*, translation by Brooks Haxton, fragment 41, p. 27.
57  Gaston Bachelard, *Water and Dreams*, p. 6.
58  Plato, *Symposium and the Death of Socrates* (Phaedo 71), p. 151ff.

reminiscent of an old man's urination than the river's joyous scream at springtime's new beginning. Moreover, in the span of a lifetime we might encounter stormy weather and upheaval, during which "[t]he waves of dark and bright rivers rush together, crashing over one another."[59] Dramatic, and sometimes traumatic turns and tides, may cause us to doubt the value of our journey, or even the possibility of ever realizing it.

If we consider the allegorical journey along the river of life, what relationship do we find between the universal, archetypal route, and one's individual course? In a small Swedish book from 1941 called *The Four Ages of Man*, which I found in a second hand bookstore in the Old City of Stockholm, the author, a wise doctor by the name of Jacob Billström, asks if a person changes during life. His answer is, "yes and no," and he continues,

> In a way, the personality is unchangeable and identifiable all through life. One can always hear if a violin, a flute, a French horn or a piano is being played, even if at one time it is a lullaby, another time a march, then a symphony, and at last "Silent Shadows."[60]

In myth and lore, as well as in the development of human civilization, life is often pictured as a journey, and many are the images that portray the journey through life. Sometimes we are summoned to endure the hero's challenges, to wander a sacred path in awe, or to bravely traverse the narrow bridge of hope that has been delicately stretched over the abyss of despair. For some, life's journey is like the seafarer who navigates across the great sea.

The essence is that the journey is not merely an instinctual and heedless passage through time, but the quest for an interrelated and meaningful life. Consequently, the pilgrimage to the center, or the way out of the labyrinth, serve as archetypal images of the journey.[61] "Only in him who in some way has taken care of things and people," says Erik Erikson, may the fruit gradually ripen, referring to the soulful journey through life.[62]

In the first half of life, the task of the young traveler is to depart from home, to step out into the world in search for his or her adventure, to

---

59  C. G. Jung, *The Red Book: Liber Novus*, p. 317.
60  Jacob Billström, *Människans Fyra Åldrar*, p. 6. *Silent Shadows* is a poem by the Swedish poet Erik Gustav Geijer, sung by choirs at funerals.
61  Cf. J. E. Cirlot, *A Dictionary of Symbols*, p. 165.
62  *Childhood and Society*, p. 268.

find his or her own individual path. However, in the second half, we find ourselves on what often amounts to a very long journey in search of Home. In many a tale, the hero, for instance Gilgamesh, sets off to find life's elixir, while other stories, such as the Odyssey, revolve around the hero's long and arduous journey home.

This archetypal journey of life is constantly repeated throughout the never-ending process of individuation. We find ourselves returning to this venture repeatedly, every night, as we set out on our nightly voyage into the landscape of our unconscious. Many dreams begin by being on the way, for instance, "I am on my way to ...," I am driving on a road that leads into the desert ...," I am walking through one room after the other in a long corridor-like building ...," "I am walking towards my office, but it looks different than in reality," "I walk on the pavement and on the opposite side of the street someone seems to follow me ...," "I go down into an underground parking...," "I am in my car, but someone I don't know is driving," or, "I have to go to the place from where I came ..."

Prominently, we are familiar with the journey of Dante, who at the very beginning of his *Divine Comedy* finds himself "midway along the journey of our life." Dante writes about *our* life, seemingly indicating that this is not an entirely personal venture, but a path toward a higher goal. Having "wandered off from the straight path," he finds himself in the dark, savage, bitter wood of midlife, which we often, just like Dante, enter without knowing how we got there, suddenly waking up from unconsciousness; "I had become so sleepy at the moment when I first strayed," reflects the poet, acknowledging his lack of consciousness.[63]

The following dream reflects how Danit, a woman midway through her life but seven hundred years after the *Divina Comedia*, finds herself in a similar awakening, in a dark cellar not very different from Dante's "wood of wilderness,"

> I am in a lit-up house. It's a conventional small-town or suburban house. I start walking around the house, as if I am somnambulistic, as if I am walking while sleeping in my own dream. I get down into the cellar, without knowing how I got there. The cellar is dark, frightening, cold and dirty, with dead animals and perhaps dead people there as well. I don't know how to find my way out.

---

63  Dante Alighieri, *The Divine Comedy*, p. 67.

Similar to the poet, this dream triggered the process to search for her soul, which seemed to have been lost in the little boxes of life's routines and obligations.

The core of many a fairy tale is the search for the missing *anima*, the elusive essence of soul and life. The king's stiffened heart, or the barrenness of the country, reflect a lack of vitality, a need for soul and renewal. The crucial and painful battle ensues between the cruelty of an empty, unrelated and meaningless existence, and the depth and full-ness of a soulful life. For the lucky few, individuation and tending to the archetypal, divine core comes naturally, while the rest of us need to consciously embrace the Self to create an animated life.

Consequently, the cycle of life pertains not only to man's inevitable development along the stages of life, but to the archetypal essence of *meaning* around which each age constellates.[64] As Jung says,

> There is a thinking in primordial images, in symbols which are older than the historical man, which are inborn in him from the earliest times, and, eternally living, outlasting all generations, still make up the groundwork of the human psyche. It is only possible to live the fullest life when we are in harmony with these symbols; wisdom is a return to them.[65]

Thus, wisdom according to Jung, is the return to eternal symbols, so that life can be fully lived. The following is a dream of Oshra, a forty-four-year-old woman, who felt depressed and estranged from herself,[66]

> I am on my way home, but on an unknown road, which seems not to be fully ready yet. I arrive at a grove, and find myself walking on a narrow path, in between trees. Then suddenly the path comes to an end, at the edge of a steep mountain. A short black man, not a dwarf though, helps me very carefully to descend the mountain. Then, it is like a valley or a canyon, and I set my foot on the banks of a broad river with streaming water. A group of black men

---

64 In so far as we assume that every phenomenon, including ego and com-plex, has an archetypal nucleus that defines its meaning, and to the extent that we consider the Self as the central archetype of meaning, the Self induces each age with its particular nucleus of meaning. The fully lived, conscious and experienced life is thus rooted in the Self.

65 'The Stages of Life,' CW 8, par. 794.

66 This name, like all others, has been altered to preserve anonymity. Names have often been chosen to express a characteristic trait of the person or a phenomenon relevant to the subject under discussion. 'Oshra,' for instance, means happiness, felicity.

> and women of all ages do things—they sing, wash clothes,
> etc. I cross the river, and walk along its other bank. I come
> to a place where an African woman sits. She sits on an old
> almost broken plastic chair with a small old plastic table in
> front of her. She hands me a key with a big ring, and tells
> me I am heading for a wedding. I continue on my way, but
> can't remember if I still have the key in my hand.

This woman's road home to herself has yet to be paved in order to become known to her—and no less, the road needs to become known, to become conscious, in order to materialize. On her way, the dreamer needs to walk through the grove, to dwell in the vicinity of Ashera, goddess of the grove, in order to restore her feminine self.

In the Bible, the male, patriarchal and monotheistic One God, fought relentlessly against the Goddess of the Grove. For example, in Judges 6:26, Gideon is told to "offer a burnt sacrifice with the wood of the Ashera which you shall cut down." *Ashera*, goddess of the grove, poses an immediate threat to Yahweh, whose name has been understood as 'ehyeh *asher* ehyeh,' in a splendid combination of multiple meanings, wherein the repressed and battled goddess remains, uncannily but naturally, positioned at the very center of the victorious God.[67] As regards man's psyche, Jung says, "Our true religion is a monotheism of consciousness, a possession by it, coupled with a fanatical denial of the existence of fragmentary autonomous systems."[68]

But the dreamer goes further into her internal depths. She is carefully led into the depths by an unknown animus, the short black man. Her life energy is rejuvenated by the stream of the river. To hear the singing and to feel the music, even in everyday tasks such as washing dirty laundry, of purifying the garment so that it can be worn in pleasure and delight, is healing to her depression.

In her dream, this woman performs the important task of crossing the river into a yet deeper, more alien realm of her journey, receiving a key on her way to the wedding, aiming at an internal integration of aspects that until now she had neglected. But the value of the gift may lie not so much in receiving the key, but to hold on to the awareness that it may be lost to consciousness, slipping into oblivion, the way we often all too easily forget the gods' most precious gifts. We often receive these gifts of Hermes when we least expect them, by unimposing people (or for instance by animals or trees or unexpected little creatures), so that we easily may neglect them, or even take notice. For Oshra, the

67  See below, p. 164.
68  CW 13, par. 51.

African woman's old and simple chair and table held a message—to see and respect what is so easily passed-by, arrogantly ignored. On the road to one's Self, to the experience of a meaningful life, the key needs to be constantly cared for. This is only possible by appreciating its value.

## The River of Life

The river receives its energy from the water with which Father Sky impregnates Mother Earth, who provides the material container, which shapes the water into its particular character, for instance as river. "River is vital fluidity," moving through the upper as well as the lower world. There are rivers of "fertility and prosperity, rivers of forgetting, rivers of binding oath, ... rivers of rebirth, rivers of death, rivers of sorrow, all presided over in our mythic history by beneficent deities, dreadful nixies or changeable river spirits."[69]

Rivers are holy and worshipped in many cultures. They are often the source of civilization, and have played a central role in the development and formation of human culture. Jawaharlal Nehru, India's first Prime Minister wrote,

> The Ganges, above all is the river of India, which has held India's heart captive and drawn uncounted millions to her banks since the dawn of history. The story of the Ganges, from her source to the sea, from old times to new, is the story of India's civilization and culture, of the rise and fall of empires, of great and proud cities, ... ever changing, ever flowing, and yet ever the same Ganga.[70]

The basins at the rivers of Euphrates and Tigris in Mesopotamia, today's Iraq, provided the cradle of civilization of the ancient world, around three thousand BCE. Not only does the river reflect the life of man, but life and humankind have developed along the rivers. Those were the first highroads, notes Mumford, enabling transportation and exchange of goods.[71] Cultures could connect with each other by sailing the rivers. Hence, control of the waterways became essential. Obstruction of the flow of merchandise could be a cause for warfare between cities.

---

69  The Archive for Research in Archetypal Symbolism, *The Book of Symbols*, p. 40.
70  Jawaharlal Nehru, *The Discovery of India*, p. 51.
71  Lewis Mumford, *The City in History*, p. 71f.

## The River—Source, Course and Dissolution

From their source, rivers flow along relatively stable beds, until they empty their life into the great waters, the sea or the ocean. According to their characteristics, rather than their actual age, rivers are classified as youthful, mature or old, emphasizing the river as an apt archetypal image of the journey through life. As human beings, we are able to hold and contain only a small and limited portion of the waters of life. Like the maiden *Psyche*, who brings an urn to fetch water from the river of life, also man's psyche can hold only as much of life's water as our human limitations permit.[72] As individuals, we are able to draw from the sources of archetypal potential, but not exhaust them entirely. In psychotic conditions and in narcissistic inflation, identification with archetypal forces leads to dire consequences.

The Jordan River is merely a tenth of the Ganges, but likewise one of the world's sacred rivers.[73] The Jordan is born out of the rivers of Syria, Lebanon and northern Israel, at the heights near Mount Hermon. It then descends[74] southward through the Sea of Galilee, pouring its water into the Dead Sea, at the lowest point on earth, 422 meters (1,385 feet) below sea level. It is interesting to note that in the Babylonian Talmud, it says that "the Jordan issues from the cavern of Paneas," eventually rolling on until it "rushes into the mouth of the Leviathan."[75] Paneas (today usually pronounced Banias) refers to the area and sacred site, temenos, of the Greek nature god Pan, in northeastern Israel. When we get lost in the savage areas of Pan, outside of civilization and conscious-ness, panic often ensues. Pan personifies nature by "metaphor and not mere geography," says James Hillman. "The 'caves obscure' where he could be encountered" is where "impulse resides, the dark holes of the psyche whence desire and panic arises." Thus, his habitat "was always dells, grotos, water, eoods, and wilds—never villages, never the tilled

---

72  Apuleius, *The Golden Ass*, p. 91f.; see also Erel Shalit, *Enemy, Cripple & Beggar: Shadows in the Hero's Path*, p. 191.
73  While 250 kilometers long, due to its winding course, its length from North to South is only half of that.
74  'Jordan' (Heb. Yarden) means *descend*; it may possibly be a combination of yeor (river), yored (descend) and Dan, i.e., the river that descends from Dan, Israel's northernmost area (as well as a river of that same name), allocated to the Tribe of Dan (Talmud, Ber. 55a).
75  Babylonian Talmud, Tractate Bava Bathra 74b.

and walled settlements of the civilized; cavern sanctuaries, not constructed temples."[76]

Pan is the god who watches over shepherds and their flocks. He has
the rear legs and horns of a goat, like a satyr. In some legends, he is the
son of Zeus and in some, he is the son of Hermes. His mother is said
to have been a nymph. The Homeric hymn to Pan describes him as
delight to all the gods, and thus his name Pan—all. Pan is famous for
his sexual prowess, and is often depicted with an erect phallus. He gave
Artemis her hunting dogs and taught the secret of prophecy to Apollo,
but he also induced sudden fear in lonely places.

The nymph Echo, by the way, was a great singer and dancer, and
while Narcissus resisted her calls, she ridiculed the love of any man.
This angered Pan, and he had his followers kill her. Echo was torn to
pieces and disseminated. The goddess of the earth, Gaia, received the
pieces of Echo, whose voice is no longer her own, but compulsively re-
iterates the words spoken by others. A fragmented self, like Echo, lacks
integrity—which etymologically means it can easily be touched by different forces. Such a self is not an *in*dividum but a dividum, divisible
and fragmented, an echo of others without an inner voice of its own.
This is a reflection of the seemingly well-adjusted as-if personality (see
'the empty shell,' p. 136ff.), without a firm core of individuality, characterized by transience and identification.

The Greek historian Plutarch (ca. 46-120 C.E.) reported in his treatise "On the failure of the Oracles," that a cry went through the an-
tique world that "The Great God Pan is dead!" His death seems to have
announced, or at least coincided with the shift from nature as a creative force to the beginning of Judeo-Christian morals, wherein nature
and instinct became repressed. And so Pan returns, as Hillman says,
"in the psychopathologies of instinct which assert themselves ... primarily in the nightmare and its associated erotic, demonic, and panic
qualities."[77]

In the *Song of Songs* we find God's blessing to life as emerging from
Mount Hermon, "Like the dew of Hermon descending upon the mountains of Zion; for there the Lord has commanded the blessing, life for
evermore."[78] Several decisive Biblical events took place along the Jordan
River: John baptized Jesus in the Jordan, and this is where Jacob strug-

---

76  James Hillman, *Pan and the Nightmare*, p. 17. "Caves obscure" is from *Orphic
    Hymn 11 to Pan*: "All-fertile Paian, heavenly splendour pure, in fruits rejoic-
    ing, and in caves obscure."
77  *Pan and the Nightmare*, p. 27.
78  Song of Songs, 133:3.

gled with the angel, thus receiving the name Israel, "because you have struggled with God and with human beings and have prevailed."[79]

The Jordan River comes to its end in the Sea of Death, where the water of life evaporates, only leaving the mineral remains, so that organisms cannot live in the saline water.

## The Source

Rivers are conceived by the primary act of fertilization between the World Parents. The source of the river in the highlands is often considered to be divine. It has come into being, become impregnated, by Father Sky pouring his water, which then gathers in the womb of Mother Earth. There the water incubates until the necessary libido has been mustered to spring forth through her vagina, forced out into the ever newborn river, crying its sometimes jubilant scream of the birth of life, however small the stream initially might be.

The source of the river was often believed to be beyond the realm of human nature, the dwelling place of gods and goddesses, nymphs, spirits and oracles, a source of healing and rejuvenation. Kerényi compares the goddess Mnemosyne to the source, "She is memory as the cosmic ground of self-recalling which, like an eternal spring, never ceases flowing."[80]

The Ganges had its transcendent source on the world-mountain Meru,[81] rushing forth from the Cow's Mouth. The Nile, the world's longest river, starts rolling from the cave of Hapi, androgynous god of the Nile River and source of life. As the deified river, Hapi was vigorous but fat, a man with a woman's breasts. He is dressed like the boatmen and the fishermen, with a narrow belt to sustain his massive belly. As the Nile of Upper Egypt he wears a crown of lotus, and as the river of Lower Egypt a crown of papyrus.[82]

---

79  Genesis 32:28 (RSV, TNIV). While Israel means struggling with God, it can also be read as "straight to God." The psychological essence may be understood that the path to the transcendent aspects in our soul is one of strife, the road to the Self passes through the battles that take place in our shadow.

80  Karl Kerényi, *Hermes: Guide of Souls*, p. 31. Kerényi's first name is variously given as Carl or Karl. The spelling appears as it does on each of his respective publications.

81  Hans Biedermann, *Dictionary of Symbolism: Cultural Icons and the Meanings Behind Them*, p. 285.

82  From Larousse, *New Larousse Encyclopedia of Mythology*, p. 38.

In the Bible, as well, we find that "a river went out from Eden to water the garden; and from there it was divided, and became four rivers."[83] Highlighting the river's metaphorical life energy, legend says that the source of the rivers of Paradise is a spring at the roots of the Tree of Life.[84] In the book of Ezekiel, we are told about the transcendent origin of the river of life, the healing water streaming forth from its source in the sanctuary,

> And by the stream, upon its bank, on this side and on that side, shall grow all trees for food, whose leaf shall not wither, nor shall its fruit fail; it shall bring forth fresh fruit every month, because the waters for them flow from the sanctuary; and their fruit shall be for food, and their leaves for healing.[85]

In Revelation, the river of the water of life, bright as crystal, flows from the throne of God and of the Lamb.[86]

The source of the river of life, the beginning of life's journey is in the dwellings of the divine, descending from the heights of mountains, finding the openings through which the libido of life spurts forth. Bachelard mentions that, "In popular legends, there are innumerable rivers which have come into being through the urination of a giant."[87]


## The Course

The river is born by divine grace and nature's delight, as divinity and nature reach out toward each other, often in mountainous springs. Having come into being, spurting forth from its source, the river takes on a life of its own. The course of each river is laid out by its beds, which have received their contours in the course of slow historical, temporal and geographical, spatial changes, thus outlining the river's character. Each river is different from every other, just like the course of every human being is individual.

Along the relatively stable beds designed by the history of nature along the earth's surface, the river runs its course—sometimes along changing landscapes, influenced by time and season, climate and terrain. Not only objective circumstances have an impact on the river and its course, but the river and how we relate to it influence the environ-

---

83  Genesis 2:10.
84  Cf. J. C. Cooper, *An Illustrated Encyclopedia of Traditional Symbols*, p. 139.
85  Ezekiel 47:12.
86  Revelation 22:1.
87  *Water and Dreams*, p. 9.

ment as well. The seemingly same river may for one person be an en-ergizing challenge, while for another individual it implies the terror of navigating between Scylla and Charybdis. Relating in a meaningful way to the energies and forces that the river of life provides us will influence our intra-psychic, interpersonal and ecological landscape.

Some rivers run deep, some are mighty and voluptuous, carrying an abundance of water like luscious fruit at the bosom, vigorously bub-bling along the riverbeds, full of life. Others, weak, asthenic rivers, may barely manage to trickle along their course, with only a tiny stream of water weakly crawling along, trying to slip through between the stones at its bare bottom, hardly managing its languid way through to the end. Yet, if the river is too pure, as the Zen says, it may yield no fish.

As one moves through life, along riverbeds that may only slowly change their course over generations, a characteristic energy level as well as temperament may be predetermined already at the source, yet influenced by the climate, the seasons and the obstacles along the jour-ney. Sometimes the river gathers strength and momentum as it flows on; sometimes it loses its energy and dries up towards the end.

The riverbeds hold the water of life, and within their confines, the water brings life. From the stream and the flow of the watercourse, elec-tricity may be generated. Unless too polluted by man, the river's fish may provide nourishment. Rivers have served as vital means of trans-portation for goods and merchandize.

The river is characterized simultaneously by permanence and tran-siency, stability and change. Furthermore, the river embodies matter and spirit, both nature and the "irreversible passage of time."[88] As Heraclitus stated, the river expresses the duality of life; while the river's identity remains stable, it remains alive by constant change and movement. For some, the river is a calm and constantly forward flowing motion, for others it provides an ever-changing journey of ups and downs, twists and turns. For some, the river has "a fearful look, so overcast and secret, creeping away so fast between the low flat lines of shore: so heavy with indistinct and awful shapes, both of substance and shadow: so death-like and mysterious," as in Dickens' description of the Thames.[89]

In the river, we see the flow of libido, the manifestation of life's energy. Primary narcissistic energy is necessary to make the journey through life—this is the narcissistic energy that flows freely, enabling a person to feel confident and sure of himself, and to meet life's obsta-

88  *A Dictionary of Symbols*, p. 274.
89  Charles Dickens, *Bleak House*, p. 653.

cles with a sense of competence and hope, rather than excessive doubt, negativism and anticipation of failure. Narcissus is the son of the river god Cephissus. Standing at the banks of the river, Leiriope, pregnant with Narcissus, that is, pregnant with incubating narcissism, asks the seer Tiresias a surprising question, "Will my son live a long life?" Tiresias answers affirmatively, but "on condition that he does not know himself."[90] Narcissistic energy, essential to the sense of spark and delight in one's life, is generated by the river, born out of the force of the river-god, and when fully alive, does not know itself.

The free flow of life, without an inhibitory consciousness, is characteristic of youth. Later, we may sense the burning desire to return to a sense of the natural flow of life's energy in puberty, often forgetting the pains and the scars that accompany the fire of passion and the heights of spirit. But conscious life requires that we know ourselves, which we come to do by recognizing our shortcomings and limitations. In his speech of defense, Socrates succinctly states that "the unexamined life is not worth living."[91] An abundance of narcissistic energy will make the riverbeds overflow, and may destroy the crop in the surrounding fields, the healthy growth of those nearby. An overly narcissistic river does not know its limits, its boundaries and its self-definition. Paradoxically, if narcissism is personalized, if we identify with it, we fail to know our limitations and to know who we are, and the life-inducing energy withdraws, leaving us alone in lifeless emptiness.

The natural decrease in narcissistic energy as we age, hampers the free flow of life, yet becomes necessary in order to enable its very continuation.

## Crossing the River

In the Bible, rivers may run their course as tears of pain and sorrow, "By the rivers of Babylon, there we sat down, we also wept, when we remembered Zion," but may also be the wellsprings of joy and glory.[92] The very name of the ancient Hebrews, which the Canaanites had given to Abraham, means "those who have come from across the river,"

---

90  I have elaborated on this in *Enemy, Cripple & Beggar*, pp. 28ff.
91  *Symposium and the Death of Socrates* (Apology 38), p. 109.
92  Psalms 137: 1; see also for instance Isaiah 66:12, "For thus says the Lord, Behold, I will extend peace to her like a river, and the glory of the nations like a flowing stream; then shall you suck, you shall be carried upon her sides, and be dandled upon her knees." See also Psalms 36:9, 46:5, and Lamentations 2:18.

thus defining the origin and the historical connotations of the Jewish people.[93] Moses received his name from Pharaoh's daughter, who had come down to wash herself in the river where she "drew him out of the water,"[94] which is the meaning of his name. He was thus born into the hero's task of leading his people across the desert and bringing them the Ten Commandments. However, Moses himself was not allowed to cross the river. He died at Mount Nebo, from where he could only see the land he was not to enter.

Rivers serve as natural boundaries and division between their respective banks, between tribes, cultures and peoples. They separate, as well, between the realms and the worlds, between hell and holy, between this life and the afterlife. In Greek mythology the river Styx, the river of hate separates the world of the living from the dead. Charon, the old ferryman, brought the dead into the underworld by crossing the river. Whenever a god would "swear a solemn oath, Iris fetched a jug of water from the Styx and the god poured it out while taking the oath."[95] However, a god who broke his oath would have to drink the water, which was so foul that he would lose his voice. That is, he would be ostracized, he would have no say, the archetypal energies represented by the particular god would not find vocal expression. Even the waters of the tiny stream Styx, near the village of Nonacris, were said to be not only fatal, but would "[break] all vessels that tried to contain it and corroded all materials except the hooves of horses."[96]

Besides the river of hate, the rivers of pain, lamentation, fire and forgetfulness separate between the realms of the netherworld and the living. As a personified deity, Styx was sister of the river god Cephissus, father of Narcissus, thus signifying how intimately the energies of life are related to the boundary between death and life.[97]

Crossing a river may entail passing between realms of the worlds, between the known and the unknown, the everyday and the holy, such as crossing beyond the mythological Sabbath River, the Sambation, beyond which the lost tribes lived a paradisiacal life of eternal Sabbath. In Greek mythology we find, for instance, how Jason lost one of his sandals when carrying Hera on his shoulders across the river. That is, crossing the river from one realm to the other at the beginning of his hero

---

93   Cf. Joshua 24:2-3.
94   Exodus 2:10.
95   Edward Tripp, *The Meridian Handbook of Classical Mythology*, p. 539.
96   *The Meridian Handbook of Classical Mythology*, p. 539.
97   Both Freud and Jung elaborate this subject; see also Erel Shalit, *The Complex: Path of Transformation from Archetype to Ego*, p. 30f, 48f.

journey, he steps into the world of humans with his one foot, while the other foot remains bare before the gods.

## The River and the Sea

The river's flow of energy finally runs into the sea. The individual life energy no longer remains separate, but converges into the grand basin, the mixing bowl for the growth of new life. "To disappear into deep water ... to become a part of depth or infinity, such is the destiny of man that finds its image in the destiny of water," says Bachelard.[98] The water of the river's soul joins the ocean, and the river's individual life ends, yet, perpetually renewed by the flow of newborn life in an eternal cycle. This cyclic nature of the rivers of life is expressed in Ecclesiastes 1:7, which says, "All the rivers run into the sea; yet the sea is not full; to the place from where the rivers come, there they return again."

While the river is individually identifiable, with its particular characteristics as long as it runs its course, it is also part of the globe's ecological (water) system. It partakes in that greater whole wherein its life force, its libido, eventually joins the indistinguishable world libido. For a while, for a defined distance and a limited length of time, between its birth in the mountains and its death in the ocean, the river has its particular features, evokes feelings and sentiments, facilitating transportation and providing lushness of life, or of contemplation and tranquility under the willow tree at its banks. However, as the river dies into a lake or the sea, it finally surrenders its individual character, and visibly partakes in the greater collective of psyche and matter.

A legend tells about Adam's expulsion from the Garden of Eden. God, however, was reluctant to drive him out and asked Adam if he did not want to explore the world outside the garden. Adam enjoyed life in the garden, and did not want to leave, but having sinned, he had no choice. God offered him to choose any of the treasures of Paradise to take with him on his journey. Among all the orchards and animals, the gold and the silver, Adam chose a diamond of exceptional beauty, shining as bright as the sun. Accompanied by an angel with the diamond in his hand, Adam left through the gates of Eden, knowing he could not return, and walked until he arrived at a river. While standing there, looking out over the river, the angel pushed him from behind, and the diamond fell from his hand into the river. Adam cried out to the angel,

---

98 *Water and Dreams*, p. 12.

"Why did you do that?" whereby the angel told him, "Go down to the river and find your diamond."

So Adam went down to the river to search. There he saw thousands and thousands of diamonds reflected in the water, and he could not recognize which one was his. Perplexed, he looked at the angel, who told him, "Do you think you were the first to be expelled from the Garden of Eden who took a diamond? Thousands did as you did, and their diamonds fill the river."[99]

The purpose of the river's journey is to recognize which diamond among the many is one's own, to find one's own unique Self, given to us while still in the Garden of Eden, thus creating a sense of living a meaningful life.

Lack of primary narcissism, of a basic sense of confidence in the flow of one's river, or a lack of desire for life, to sail along the river's course, reluctance to search for oneself, for one's diamond, indicates a pathology of the river's libido. That is, one's attitude to life is not only the vessel in which one travels, but an important aspect of the river itself. As shall be described in the following chapters, different pathologies can be associated with the journey itself, with one's attitude to life, as well as with the different stages of life.

# Being on the Way—A Way of Being

## Hermes and the Journey: Being on the Way

Socrates emphasizes the significance of living the *examined* life, and Jung refers to the *conscious* life. As an archetypal image, the god Hermes, or Mercurius in Rome, amplifies our journey through life. When we have a sense of meaning in life and are able to understand it to some extent by means of examining our personal journey, life becomes soulful. Being the trickster that he is, Hermes has a multifaceted personality, representing change and transformation. As Mercury, quicksilver, the elements are transformed and spirit is concealed in matter.

---

99  Adapted from Howard Schwartz, *Tree of Souls: The Mythology of Judaism*, p. 436.

The Journey                                                    37

Hermes has been called *the rescuer of the divine child*. As puer, he is a *messenger of the gods*, and in the world of adults, he is *protector of travelers, thieves and businesspersons*. To the senex within us, he is *guide of the souls*. That is, he travels swiftly across the life cycle and puts his mark on every one of man's ages. "For all to whom life is an adventure," says Kerényi, "whether an adventure of love or of spirit," Hermes is the common guide.[100]

The name Hermes derives from the word *hermaion*, a pile of stones marking boundaries; landmarks along the roads to which each traveler added a stone. Hermes is, as Kerényi says, an idea and a "way of being." The Hermetic *way* of being is, in fact *being* on the way. Kerényi says,

> The journeyer is at home while underway, at home on the road itself, the road being understood not as a connection between two definite points on the earth's surface, but as a particular world. It is the ancient world of the path, also of the "wet paths" (the *hygra keleutha*) of the sea, which are above all, the genuine roads of the earth. For, unlike the Roman highways which cut unmercifully straight through the countryside, they run snakelike, shaped like irrationally waved lines, conforming to the contours of the land, winding, yet leading everywhere. Being open to everywhere is part of their nature. Nevertheless, they form a world in its own right, a middle-domain, where a person in that volatized condition has access to everything.[101]

In the transformative condition in which *being* and *way* unite, the traveler has "access to everything," which includes *the secret regions*—from which we have the term *hermeneutics*, the science of the interpretation of the texts, of extracting the hidden meaning and the meaning of life, just like Hermes interpreted the messages of the gods. Moreover, Hermes is possessed by memory, carrying it "as inherited knowledge of all primordial sources of being. In this his consciousness reveals itself more exactly as spiritual-psychological," says Kerényi.[102]

While the so-called Transient Personality is constantly on the move, both in psyche and space, due to his lack of sincere affect, he is never fully present. Characterized by a lack of genuine being, he is not 'being on the way,' but merely a traveler in an associative web of replica-

---

100  *Hermes: Guide of Souls*, p. 91.
101  *Hermes: Guide of Souls*, p. 14f.
102  *Hermes: Guide of Souls*, p. 32.

tions.[103] Italo Calvino describes this lack of being while on the way, in the best of ways, when he arrives at the 'city of Trude':

> If on arriving at Trude I had not read the city's name written in big letters, I would have thought I was landing at the same airport from which I had taken off. The suburbs they drove me through were no different from the others, with the same little greenish and yellow houses. Following the same signs we swung around the same flower beds in the same squares. The downtown streets displayed goods, packages, signs that had not changed at all. This was the first time I had come to Trude, but I already knew the hotel where I happened to be lodged; I had already heard and spoken my dialogues with the buyers and sellers of hardware; I had ended other days identically, looking through the same goblets at the same swaying navels.
>
> Why come to Trude? I asked myself. And I already wanted to leave.
>
> "You can resume your flight whenever you like," they said to me, "but you will arrive at another Trude, absolutely the same, detail by detail. The world is covered by a sole Trude which does not begin and does not end. Only the name of the airport changes."[104]

Hermes is often portrayed as a young boy or man, wearing a broad-brimmed two-winged hat, winged sandals and the snake-coiled caduceus, the magic wand, as he travels along the road of life. He comes to the rescue of the divine child, be it the infant Dionysus or young Ares, and, as Bolen says, he "rescues the child in the depressed adult."[105] As youthful messenger, he makes certain man remains in touch with the spirit of the gods. He protects the adult in the realm of concrete reality as thief or as businessman, and in the sphere of the ego's rule on earth, he serves as ascribed inventor of language. He enables man to gain meaning and attain integration by bringing the ego in contact with the otherworld, the netherworld, the collective unconscious, the land of invisibility, the souls. Hermes has the sole privilege of entering and exiting Hades freely.

Hermes is, thus, the traveler and the intermediary, that inner function of the invisible wanderer that ensures that we go through life awake, aware and related. As Heraclitus says,

---

103  See Erel Shalit, 'Destruction of the Image and the Worship of Transiency,' *Jung Journal*, Vol. 4, number 1, Feb. 2010, pp. 94-108.
104  Italo Calvino, *Invisible Cities*, p. 116.
105  Jean Shinoda Bolen, *Gods in Everyman*, p. 171.

Men forget where the way leads....
And what they meet with every day
Seems strange to them....
We should not act and speak
Like men asleep.[106]

Hermes may serve us as a mythological image of the dynamic relationship between the realms, of being attached to the archetypal core, to the essence and meaning of one's journey through life, while freely walking the realms of common folks.

We may discern three major aspects of Hermes, which may add to our thinking and understanding of transition and transformation:

Firstly, Hermes moves backward and forwards, when he steals Apollo's cows; secondly, there is both movement and permanence (roads and stones), transition and boundary;[107] and his movement is horizontal (along the roads) as well as vertical (entering and exiting Hades).

## Backward and Forwards

The day that crafty and deceitful Hermes was born, he stole his brother Apollo's cows. By walking backward when leading the stolen cattle, he fooled his brother, god of light and reason, creating the impression he had walked in the opposite direction.

We count our life in progressive years from birth onwards. We move through life, often having faith in linear progress, accumulating experience as we go along. We believe in the strength of the Fates, whether we call the predetermined fate the will of God, or genes and constitution. Sometimes we may credit a sense of vocation for the direction of our path, as for instance Hillman outlines in his *acorn theory*. From this perspective, life unfolds according to our vocation (though parents sometimes distort this by overloading their children before they are even born with their own unfulfilled expectations).[108]

But that very first day, also a reversed time-line is set off. As Jung says, "life, like any process, has a beginning and an end and every beginning is also the beginning of the end."[109]

---

106  Heraclitus, fragment V, from Jacques Lacarrière, *The Wisdom of Ancient Greece*, n. pag.
107  *Ego and Archetype*, p. 30.
108  James, Hillman, *The Soul's Code*, pp. 3-40.
109  Jung, *Two Essays on Analytical Psychology*, CW 7 (2nd ed.), par. 34.

Time moves forward through life, from birth and growth to death as decay and termination. However, as Hermes shows us, time also moves backwards through life, with the same exactitude, beginning at the boundary of death, toward the point of our departure, thus requiring a sense of meaning, in contrast to the paradisiacal and boundless image of immortality, which in the long run turns into hell. Reluctant to count backwards, only as we die can we know the exact account, and only then do we know when for instance midlife actually took place. In fact, "How we approach the meaning of our journey is closely tied to how mindful we are of our mortality."[110]

That is, just as we progress through growth and growing up, we regress and diminish, grow down. Just as we have a birthday, we have a death-day, which is more of a possible but invisible awareness, creating a perspective on life and living.

## Permanence and Transiency, Roads and Stones

There is a static and a dynamic dimension to life—change and permanency, determinism and free choice, genetic codes and anxiety-provoking situations, archetypal structures and complexes, personal and collective. James Hillman speaks about two perspectives of personality; the *saturnine* view, as expressed for instance in astrology with its birth charts or in endogenic psychiatry, where personality traits are inherent and pre-determined, versus the *mercurial* (or Hermetian) view of psychodynamics in which ultimately "nothing is given and everything can be transformed."[111]

These contrasting perspectives appear in a dream of Rebecca, a twenty-eight-year-old woman, who sought treatment because of severe anxiety attacks. In the dream, she stands in front of two elevators,

> One of the elevators is very big, with lots of people entering. It stops at every floor, no matter which floor you're going to. The other one is tiny, and seems to be very shaky, one can see the rope it is attached to. I am the only one who has a choice which elevator to take, and I would like to go with the crowd, but in the 'one-person-lift' I can choose which floor to go to.

---

110  James Hollis, *On This Journey We Call Our Life*, p. 104.
111  James Hillman (Ed.), *Puer Papers*, p. 16.

This woman had to make the choice between the collective and her individual way. She had experienced the conflict between the strict norms of the small religious community in which she had been raised, versus her individual path, which left her alone, without the comfort and support of her family and childhood friends. Consciously, she wanted to continue on the clearly demarcated and mapped out road of her family and community. However, this collided with her individual path, provoking anxiety attacks and choking. The anxiety served as a call from her inner voice to make the choice of necessity, to choose the seemingly more dangerous "one person" lift, rather than the way of the collective. Only by making this choice, at the beginning of her adult life, would she be able to actively decide where to go, rather than to make the standardized stops of the collective crowd.

The *hermaion*, the piles of stones along the road, may less mark permanency and maybe rather the archetypal transitions of life, like teenage- or mid-life states of transition. In our age, we no longer make much out of those rites of initiation and passage, but the marks and the stones, the rites, are there, even if we do not pay attention to them.

The present-day paradox may be that while we seem to require the freedom of change and transformation, the compensatory search for permanency is expressed by finding the genes that supposedly determine our feelings and behavior.

Ultimately, Hermes is not only the traveler, but substantial transformation takes place in the Vas Hermeticum, the hermetically sealed confines of the vessel, such as the analytic enclosure. Keeping that in mind, we understand why travelling in soul-land demands that we sit still, quietly and patiently.

## Ascending the Olympus, Descending into Hades

Hermes traveled with hat and wand along the roads, but he also mounted the Olympus and descended into Hades. If we move along the road of life flatly on the earth's surface, without stepping down into Hades or ascending the Olympus, we come to live the dull and well-adjusted, even and horizontal life. If, on the other hand, we move up and down, manically and/or depressively, vertically without horizontal movement, we drop out of reality, like the puer straying into manic flight or trapped in depressive pain.

Hermes shows us the need to travel both along the road of reality, as well as along the vertical axis of soul and spirit. He serves as the psychopomp that guides us along our journey; often invisible, hard to notice, appearing in places and shapes we least would expect. For instance, in the many variations of the tale about 'the ruined man who became rich through a dream,' a person who has lost his fortune, follows a dream in which he is told to go to a foreign city, where a great treasure will be found. There, for instance the Chief of Police, who laughs at the man's foolishness to follow the divination of a dream, guides him—he himself has likewise dreamed he will find a treasure in a foreign place. In Pinhas Sadeh's rendering, the tale goes like this,

> Once a Jew dreamed that a treasure was buried beneath a bridge in Vienna. He traveled there, went to the bridge, and stood there at a loss, because he was afraid to start looking in the middle of the day with so many people around. Just then a soldier passed by and asked, "What are you standing there for?"
>
> The Jew thought it best to tell the truth, find the treasure together with the soldier, and go halves with him, and so he related his dream.
>
> "You foolish dreamer of a Jew!" exclaimed the soldier. "Why, I also dreamed that in a certain house in a certain town there was a treasure—do you think I was crazy enough to go all the way there to look for it?"
>
> The town the soldier named was the one the Jew lived in and the house was the Jew's own house. And so he went straight home, dug, and discovered a huge treasure. "A man," he said, "can have a treasure at home, yet unless he looks for it in Vienna, he'll never know it's there!"[112]

The man understands that the soldier (or the Chief of Police), representatives of collective consciousness, unawares tell him to return to himself, to his own garden. To find our way Home, requires making the journey. Usually we expect the guide of souls to impress us as such, but the art of living may rather be to detect the unexpectedly ordinary shape of our daemons. Likewise, in a dream I have recounted elsewhere, it is the unimposing post office clerk who tells the dreamer that he can find help in Jerusalem, at the symbolic cost of thirty-six, rather than "a

---

112  Pinhas Sadeh, 'The Treasure Beneath the Bridge,' in *Jewish Folktales*, p. 383. See also for instance 'Here Where One Stands,' in *The Way of Man: According to the Teaching of Hasidism*, p. 33f.; and Anonymous and John Payne, *The Book of the Thousand Nights and One Night*, tale 22.

thousand," on condition that the man looks *for himself,* that is, for his own self, individually, by himself.[113]

Besides the various meanings of thirty-six in Jewish tradition, such as two times eighteen (the Hebrew letters corresponding to the number eighteen make up the word 'life'), and the legend of the thirty-six righteous, unknown to all yet appearing in every generation, in this man's dream it may have indicated his midlife turn, from a material approach to life to a more soulful and symbolical one.

Since Jerusalem serves as a central symbol of wholeness, it often appears in people's dreams, just as people would bring dreams to Jerusalem, as the Talmudic legend tells us. Sometimes a person might dream that he or she takes the road to Jerusalem to bring a dream there. One woman wakes up, in her dream, realizing that she 'walks up' to Jerusalem, making a pilgrimage to her Self.[114]

The conscious search along the painful road of individuation, rather than the delusion of grand, absolute fulfillment—of peace or wholeness, the messianic age or paradise—is the crucial concern. As Jung says, "The goal is important only as an idea; the essential thing is the opus which leads to the goal; that is the goal of a lifetime."[115] That is, it is the *journey* along the river of life that counts. That journey takes place both forwards and in reverse, as progressive movement and reflective transformation, both horizontally and along the vertical axis of soul and spirit.

We profoundly recognize the significance of the journey, as well as the possible union of opposites, in the following dream. Hannah,[116] a psychologically mature woman in her mid-fifties, dreamed,

> I was walking along a road dragging a large and heavy black suitcase on wheels. The road proceeded across a lake or river but was no longer a hard surface, it actually now was just the water itself I was on. I moved along quickly so I didn't sink. Just to my right I saw that the water fell off into a steep waterfall. I couldn't believe I was okay crossing on the water at the top of a waterfall. I came to the other side and stopped on a large flat rock to rest. From here I

---

113  See Erel Shalit, *The Hero and His Shadow: Psychopolitical Aspects of Myth and Reality in Israel*, p. 34, and Erel Shalit, 'Jerusalem: Human Ground, Archetypal Spirit,' in Thomas Singer (Ed.), *Psyche and the City: A Soul's Guide to the Modern Metropolis*, p. 295.

114  In Hebrew, 'walking up' means to make a pilgrimage.

115  CW 16, par. 400.

116  Hannah, which means 'grace,' was the mother of the prophet Samuel, as well as mother (Anne) of Mary, mother of Jesus.

had to make a choice to go left or right down tributaries. The one on the left was steeper and faster while the one on the right was a more gentle slope. I was deciding which would be better especially with the big suitcase—wondering if I would need speed to keep the bag afloat or if the many small rocks in both that the water flowed over would hold it up. On both, it was no longer deep water. I would be fine either way. Each way led into the forest and came together at some point.

Hannah, who had already competently dealt with major childhood trauma, was able to carry, or drag the heavy black suitcase of her shadow along the roads and the rivers of her life. While she was surprised she did not sink, walking on the water confirmed her sense of having a protective daemon. Her decision regarding which tributary to take was based on caring for the shadow rather than advancing the ego, in lieu of an inner sense of being "off the dangerous part of the journey and on to safety in the forest, my introverted safe place—the place where I come home in me." At this point, the question is no longer which direction to take, but allowing for the different attitudes and qualities, such as steep and fast versus gentle and slow, to come together in the complexity of one's soul and personality, that is, coming home.

## The Crossroads

Perhaps we should not forget to take notice of a major element that the traveler encounters along the road of life—the crossroads.

It is here that Hecate, goddess of the crossroads, representing the darkness of the night and its terrors, who on moonless nights would roam the earth with a pack of ghostly, howling dogs, holds the key to the underworld (which also Hades does). Hecate haunts at three-way crossroad, each of her three heads turning in a different direction. It is here, at the crossroads of life, that we sometimes have to make the most difficult decisions that may determine the course of our life.

"Hecate is a real spook-goddess of night and phantoms, a nightmare," says Jung,

> Her symbols are the key, the whip, the dagger, and the torch. As the deadly mother, her attributes are dogs . . . As the "spirit-mother" she sends madness, the moonsickness. . . . Where the roads branch off or meet, dog-sacrifices were

offered to her, and there too were thrown the bodies of the executed: the sacrifice occurs at the point of union.[117]

In Roman mythology, Trivia,[118] Hecate's equivalent, is the personified deity of crossroads. That is, if one does not sincerely and seriously contemplate one's way, choose one's direction, decide on one's options, determine one's destiny, then one may bow in defeat to the triviality of one's predetermined fate. As Kerényi says about Oedipus the Crossroader, "The crossroads themselves were the fate."[119]

Zeruiah,[120] a woman in her early forties, opens the session by saying that for once, she did not get upset when waiting for the green light at the crossroads, on her way to therapy. What did she mean? Was she finally overcoming her resistance? We should perhaps not interpret every obstacle en route to therapy or analysis as aspects of the transference or as symbolic adversaries on the way to consciousness, and not every intersection is an opportunity to find the direction of one's life, as if it were the Trivium, the three way crossroads of ancient Rome. While we should not turn every crossroad into a quest for meaning, we might still ask our patient what she was contemplating as she patiently waited to cross over, especially since she said this was different from her usual experience.

Zeruiah felt that she had made several important decisions during the last couple of years. She and her family had left the village in which she had grown up and moved to the city. She had changed her place of work and even her field of specialization. However, she now felt the emptiness after having completed these important and desired changes.

She felt her new home lacked soul, and she felt that she herself was unable to bring soul into their home. She longed for nature, which she had felt so close to, and which had surrounded her in the village. City life had seemed attractive from afar, but suddenly now seemed to have lost its excitement. The lively sounds had become intrusive, empty, and disturbing noise. She realized that the decision to move had been im-

117  CW 5, par. 577.
118  Trivia is derived from the Latin *trivium*, which means '[the meeting of] the three roads.' In medieval universities, the trivium comprised the three subjects grammar, logic, and rhetoric.
119  Karl Kerényi, 'Oedipus: Two Essays,' in Karl Kerényi & James Hillman, *Oedipus Variations*, p. 11.
120  Zeruiah, 'guarded,' was a sister of King David.

portant, but not accompanied by any depth of reflection. Neither she, nor her husband, and probably not their teenage children, had given a thought to what they would lose and be missing, which would require a process of mourning.

Asking her what she had been thinking about as she waited at the crossroads, Zeruiah responded that she did not really remember what she had been thinking about… But then, as she thought of it, and contemplated how she patiently waited at the crossroads, she recalled having had a dream that morning. In the dream, she is looking for her car in an underground parking. She cannot find it, feels lost. She said she really does not like those big underground parking lots; they are cold, frightening, unfriendly and alienated, lifeless. In the dream, a man approaches her. Initially she can only see his shadow, and is afraid that he will attack her. However, as he comes closer, as if out of his own shadow, he in fact shows her the way to find her car. He then points at her open suitcase in the backseat, and tells her, 'you need to bring with you what is really important, both nature and noise, and then close the suitcase very carefully, so that you know it is yours, and then you can go.'

The Writer of Dreams had sent this soul-guide, or animus, to enable her to bring together the two aspects, village and city, nature and noise, rather than split them on the two respective sides of the crossroads. She awoke from her reverie by noticing the change of behavior at the crossroads. Thus, they could serve as that particular transitional space in which we briefly reside, in which we make a right turn or a wrong turn, leave something behind and cross into the new, where doors open up or close, where we make fateful decisions or miss the opportunity. Zeruiah needed to pre-consciously recognize and sense the soft touch of the soul-guide at the crossroads, and then, as if by chance, turn it into a seemingly minor therapeutic issue, recognizing the loosening-up of the transference resistance, in order to retrace its origin in the dream, reflect upon it and understand its meaning.

## Pathology of the Path

Following Hillman, we may say that psychopathology pertains to the meaning of the soul's suffering, or, the soul's suffering of meaning.[121] Angerona, the protecting deity of ancient Rome, stands with bandaged mouth and a finger to her lips demanding silence. She is the goddess of

---

121  James Hillman, *Re-visioning Psychology*, p 71.

secrecy, silence and suffering, of fear and anguish—or, as Sardello says, goddess of silent suffering and the suffering of silence. She is sometimes thought of as goddess of death—but she is also goddess of the Winter Solstice (December 21), "the moment many ancient cultures celebrated as the opportunity for rebirth and renewal, a moment often reserved for the celebration of initiation rites, which marked the rebirth of the individual as well as the tribe and, by extension, the cosmos."[122]

Sophia, the Wisdom of the Soul, the Wisdom of the Self, springs from Silence and Depth, the Abyss. Silence is the mother of the Self. Silence and suffering, the soul's silent suffering, psyche-pathos, is the guardian not only of illness, but of renewal as well; at least when hard work and conscious efforts are combined to retrieve the soul from its silent suffering.

Pathology is likely to ensue, when the individual deviates from his or her path of individuation and the sense of meaning of one's life. "When you are not quite one with yourself," Jung warns, "you are approaching a neurotic condition."[123] James Hall asserts that the ego holding back or resisting the natural individuation process leads to neurotic symptoms, and depression indicates deviation from individuation.[124] Yet, depression may sometimes be an insurance that one resists external pressures and demands, and serves as a means to hold on to one's own 'secret way.' Jung makes an interesting observation when he says, that his mother thought he was depressed when he was occupied contemplating his secret.[125] Sometimes when we hold on to a secret—some that provide relief when shared, others that must be set apart and kept away from public eye in order not to lose their value—the introversion of energy may be or seem to be a depression.

In health, the ego-Self axis is open, not clogged. The individual is attentive to what lies beyond the ego, such as the complexes and their archetypal core of meaning.

In the modern world where rationality has replaced the gods, we refrain from hearing the voices of the archetypes. However, everything repressed has a tendency to reappear in unwanted form or under undesirable circumstances. Thus, in 'Commentary on "The Secret of the Golden Flower,"' Jung declared that, "The gods have become diseases; Zeus no longer rules Olympus but rather the solar plexus, and produces

---

122  Robert Sardello, 'Archetypal Silence,' *Oregon Friends of C. G. Jung Newsletter.*

123  CW 18, par. 383.

124  James A. Hall, *The Jungian Experience: Analysis and Individuation*, p. 48.

125  *Memories, Dreams, Reflections*, p. 42.

curious specimens for the doctor's consulting room, or disorders the brains of politicians and journalists who unwittingly let loose psychic epidemics on the world."[126]

In the same paragraph Jung says, "We are still as much possessed by autonomous psychic contents as if they were Olympians. Today they are called phobias, obsessions, and so forth; in a word, neurotic symptoms." It seems as if the gods and what their images represent cry out exactly where they can be heard and seen and felt—in the very defense against them, in the neurotic defenses against the archetypal world.

The Self, the archetype of meaning, comprises the symbol-forming capacity of the psyche. Edward Edinger considers the symbolic life as "a prerequisite for psychic health." Symptoms, he says, "are degraded symbols, degraded by the reductive fallacy of the ego." They are,

> disturbing states of mind which we are unable to control and which are essentially meaningless—that is, contain no value or significance ... Symptoms are intolerable precisely because they are meaningless. Almost any difficulty can be borne if we can discern its meaning. It is meaninglessness which is the greatest threat to humanity.[127]

The meaninglessness of the symptom is a symptom of the failing connection with the archetype of meaning, the Self. Struggling with a problem creates significance. Jung stressed the importance of *problem* as regards life's stages, and Rilke expresses the crucial importance of problems for the sake of recognizing oneself, that is, one's sense of identity,

> Ever since I was a child I believe I have prayed for *my* problem alone, that I might be granted mine and not by mistake that of the carpenter, or the coachman, or the soldier, because I want to be able to recognize myself in my problem.[128]

It is in *my* problem, and in my *problem* that I recognize myself. If a person turns away from the suffering that a psychological conflict entails, he or she will, instead, suffer from a neurosis.[129] Pathology ensues when there is an avoidance of problem, when everything is assumed to be without problems—which commonly leads to problems for others, prominently children who have to carry their parents' split-off shadows. Without problems I become flat, a flat surface without personality,

126  'Commentary on "The Secret of the Golden Flower,' CW 13, par. 54.
127  *Ego and Archetype*, p. 117.
128  Rainer Maria Rilke, *Letters to a Young Poet*, p. 77.
129  CW 18, par. 383.

without an inner voice—both the Voice of the Self and the voice of my-self, of whom I am and conceive myself to be. Without that voice, I be-come an impersonal mask, a faceless persona, an un-individuated part of the collective, unidentifiable, without individual colors and shapes and complexity. My problems make me into the unique individual that I am. While there is nothing romantic about pathology, crucial mean-ing can be found in suffering.

We also find pathology when someone does not merely *have* a prob-lem with which he or she struggles, suffers, tries to deal with, but when the problem becomes the captain of the ship, leading the journey away from one's path.

The neurotic is a reluctant traveller on life's river. He always arrives too late for the trip, or complains it is not safe enough, or that he first needs to read the instructions, or ... While the neurotic is a 'tragic man,' the psychotic is carried along recklessly by archetypal forces and the forces of nature, by water, wind and weather, by steep falls and sud-den obstructions—recklessly, because s/he is not equipped, does not have ores to row with, or a compass to navigate. S/he is not captain of the ship, and the ship sails without instruments for navigation or gyroscope for stability.

Pathology of one's path pertains to living a life outside of one's own story, without a sense of direction, meaning and narrative. This may be the imitated life, as for instance when living according to norms or expectations, rather than authenticity and loyalty to one's Self. There-fore, we obviously search for the meaning of disease. What meaning (logos) does the soul (psyche) try to express by means of pathos, suffer-ing? Analysis often means tracing, detecting, observing, and relating to one's own authentic story.

II

# The Child

## The Child in the Mirror

When we depart on life's journey, we first encounter *the child*. We are born a child, and we are born into our parents' fantasies about the child to be born. These fantasies are a mixture of personal desires and fears, hopes and expectations, as well as archetypal feelings and images.

It is essential that the *archetype* of the child constellates in the psychological space of the environment into which the child is born, and in which it will grow and develop. A father, in whom the archetype has not constellated, may prefer "soccer and sweeties to home and family," as one disgruntled wife stated her frustration. He might be present primarily by his absence, as expressed by his children's yearning for the missing father.

Similarly, a mother, who does not feel ready for the child she has given birth to, might suffer post-partum depression; while everyone around her relates to her as mother, she might feel it is all "a big mistake." The supposedly happy event seems to have nothing to do with her. It is as if she is an outsider in the drama in which she has been assigned the leading role. She may feel the horror of *not feeling*, unable to attach to the newborn, lacking any sense of joy and bliss, obsessed by the thought that "it really isn't my child."

When the Child archetype has constellated, the imagination and the feelings of the expecting parents constellate accordingly, and the child can be mirrored as a *Child*, as someone who at least in the beginning of life is archetypally connected with a sense of divinity, evoking our love and warmth, anxiety, pride and awe. When the child is only a few weeks old, it smiles at us, making the bells of grace ring aloud, and marvel pound in our hearts.

A child is always born into conscious or unconscious fantasies and expectations. However, if the child archetype has not constellated, or is too strongly interfered with because of trauma or early complexes, such as abusive or neglectful parenting, the touch of divinity, which pertains to the birthright of every child, is not properly personalized by the parents. The adequate mirroring of the child is then impaired. While sometimes this may cut the child off from its archetypal foundations, in other instances it may leave the child open to unmediated exposure to the archetypal parents. One woman, for instance, replaced her absent mother with a cherry tree, which served as a compensatory good mother.[130]

Batya, who gave birth to her first-born son at age thirty-three, suffered from a powerful father complex. While her mother had three children from a previous marriage, she was her father's only child, born when he was fifty-two and her mother thirty-five. Her father was himself an only child. He was a well-respected judge, with little experience of intimate relationships. Batya was convinced he loved her deeply, but completely unable to express his love in words or physical contact. She felt that his exaggerated expectations, his demands and scolding of her, were clumsy efforts at showing his love. In her several relationships with men prior to marrying Benjamin,[131] she had searched for men who would be able to express their feelings, only to reject them as effeminate, if they did. She believed that in Benjamin she had found "the right kind of man, both strong and manly and soft and loving." However, he increasingly focused on his career as a lawyer, often complaining about "the stupid judges—behind the façade of formal authority, behind their gown, they are often quite stupid." She understood her husband's contempt for judges as a weakly veiled attack on her

---

130  Nancy Furlotti has described this as regards similar cases; "The veil of the unconscious realm may open so that, on the one hand, it needs to be defended against but, on the other hand, it remains a place of safety. The protective daemons can aid the child in lieu of the parent. However, the child may live in this realm, with its powerful good and bad, rather than in reality, which has proven to the child to be all bad. Borderlines, for example, when healed, when the archetypal child is reunited with the adult, can have a particularly strong relationship to the divine" (personal communication).

131  Batya means 'daughter of the Lord.' Daughter to a pharaoh, she married Mered (which means uprising or revolt) of the tribe of Judah. Biblical Benjamin was Jacob's youngest son. His mother Rachel wanted to call him Benoni, 'son of my sorrow,' but his father renamed him Benjamin, 'son of the south.'

father. Since the issue obviously touched upon autonomous complexes of both partners, emotions ran high daily. Eventually she came to feel that her husband had emotionally abandoned her. She felt insecure, and wondered whether he returned home late every evening because of work, or if he dated other women. She turned away from Benjamin, and came to project her need of a loving male, fatherly figure upon her son, whose role already as an infant had been to mirror her, his mother. Projecting her father-complex on her infant son, she misinterpreted the requirement to fulfill his basic needs as commands to be obeyed, as if by crying he expressed *dissatisfaction* with her, rather than his *needs*.

As in the case of Batya, an autonomous complex may interfere with the appropriate constellation of an archetype and the feelings related to it. When the mother too strongly projects her own needs and complexes onto the child, the child cannot be mirrored well enough purely as a *child*. The developing child will then not be able to retain its natural divinity, i.e., the archetypal core of the child; the child will be mirrored not for whom it is, for itself, for its true self—as carried *naturally* by the divine child, who is divine because it is *itself*. Instead, it will carry the mother's projected complexes. The child may serve as the 'self-complex' of the mother, and be mirrored as such.[132] That is, a powerful complex may prevent the constellation of an archetype; in the above example, the unfolding of the archetypal mother-child relation is obstructed by the mother's interfering father-complex.

Furthermore, the traumas of one generation often become the complexes of the next. For example, the mother of Dinah[133] had managed to escape the Nazis in Hungary because of her blond hair, fair skin and blue eyes. When she was born, her mother was obsessed with Dinah's appearance, constantly checking if she was blond enough, which she was not. This triggered the mother's post-traumatic anxiety; she became severely over-protective, predicting the child's future misfortune. The actual trauma was projected onto the future as a huge dark shadow, constantly in fear of personal and collective catastrophe. Dinah felt her appearance was never pleasing to her mother, and she naturally internalized the anxiety that accompanied her since birth. Till late in life she had near-psychotic fantasies about various kinds of unheard-of

132  Cf. Erel Shalit & James Hall, 'The Complex and the Object: Common Ground, Different Paths,' *Quadrant* 36:2, pp. 27-42.
133  Dinah, 'the judged,' was the daughter of Jacob and his wife Leah. Shechem, son of Hamor, had fallen in love with her. Hamor suggested that his and Jacob's clans intermarry, but Dinah's brothers Simon and Levy killed all the males, including Hamor and Schechem.

plastic surgery, which she believed would alter her sense of present and future misfortune.

It is important to note that a good enough environment provides for the adequate conjunction of the personal and the archetypal dimension, whereby the personal, human child encounters and can internalize the archetypal *Child* to a satisfying degree, even if never completely. The absence of archetypal mirroring may cause a sense of emptiness and a constant search for narcissistic gratification.

Prolonged identification with an archetype may likewise be disastrous, leading for instance to narcissistic inflation. The human hands that serve as the midwife for the psychological birth of the human infant, constitute a crucial aspect of Mother. They make the transition into the complexity of human life bearable. In the absence of adequate mothering, the complexes may fail in their task of transforming archetypes into living reality. The complex, as link between archetypal nucleus and personal experience, may then become dysfunctional. One possible result is an unintegrated assimilation of objects—the person may speak the words of the father, or make the gestures of the personal mother, but seems not to be genuine, merely wearing a mask, identifying with different personae.[134]

While the British psychoanalyst and pediatrician Donald Winnicott may object, I see him as the brilliant exponent of Jung's ideas in the sphere of personal psychology: the Mother archetype may be split into the *Good Mother*, as in the image of the good fairy, vs. the *Terrible Mother*, such as the cruel stepmother who forces the poor child out of the house. In real life, however, Winnicott's *good enough* mother, who manages to hold a constructive balance between the nurturing aspect of motherhood, and the necessary but inevitably unpleasant aspects of life, suffices more than well. The good enough mother is human, and conducive to the child and its development, whereas prolonged identification with the Mother archetype, as when the personal mother tries to be entirely good, will likely impair growth.


## The Child in the Vicinity of the Unconscious

Many images and associations center on the child and childhood. Some embrace joy and playing, others bring forth fear and loneliness.

---

134  This is the case, for instance, with the Transient Personality, see 'Destruction of the Image and the Worship of Transiency.'

In Peter Bruegel's *Children's Games*, the children have taken over the street from the adults. The games of childhood seem in many ways to replicate the affairs of adults. As French historian Philippe Ariès observes, there was no childhood culture before the 17th century.[135] Children were actually small adults. However, while there may not have been a childhood in today's sense, we may discern the divine child, such as Moses, orphaned and saved by being pulled out of the water, the miraculous birth of the Jesus child, or little Horus riding on the back of a crocodile. We also find the orphan child, who in its human aspect embodies the premature abandonment of childhood. In its archetypal kernel, orphanhood "expresses the *primal solitude*…, delivered up to every force of destruction and exposed to all the elements."[136]

## Psychotherapy and Childhood

In psychotherapy, when we set out to explore the narrative of a person's life, we naturally begin with the image of the child. We do so by returning to the person's childhood. We approach the past from a position of consciousness: we write up an anamnesis, review critical events as well as the nature of childhood relationships, and we inquire about early memories and childhood dreams. When we ask the person to expand on biographical details from childhood onwards, we proceed spirally from historical marker events to the person's increasingly subjective narrative. We take note of critical and traumatic events in the patient's childhood, and of key episodes. We are told about significant objects and object-relations, parents, siblings and teachers. As we in therapy or analysis approach the patient's inner world, a picture eventually crystallizes, in which internalized events and significant others, initially one's parents, converge with an archetypal core of meaning, taking shape as internal images.

Jung calls these internal images *imagos*, to emphasize that the internal picture is not merely a photographic representation of the other person, but is derived, as well, from unconscious fantasies and archetypal nuclei, blending into our internal, subjective painting of the external object. Jung says,

---

135  *Centuries of Childhood: A Social History of Family Life*, p. 46.
136  Carl Kerényi, in Carl Gustav Jung & Carl Kerényi, *Essays on a Science of Mythology: The Myth of the Divine Child and the Mysteries of Eleusis*, p. 36f.

> The *imago* is frequently more an image of a subjective functional complex than of the object itself. In the analytical treatment of unconscious products it is essential that the *imago* should not be assumed to be identical with the object; it is better to regard it as an image of the subjective relation to the object.[137]

A person's father imago, for example, manifests in his or her father complex.[138] If the person who fulfills the role of father has carried the archetypal energies and qualities that we associate with fatherhood well-enough, and if no severe trauma has impeded the development, then the complex is likely to become integrated well enough into one's conscious identity. However, in the absence of an adult, who has taken upon him (or her) self to transmit the archetypal qualities of father to the child, the father complex might likely take on an autonomous life, a life of its own outside of conscious identity, detracting energy that should be available to consciousness.

*Childhood*, which is brought up so prominently for examination in the consulting room, is a narrative related to objects, relations and events of the past. It is the narrative that crystallizes in the looking glass of retrospection. In the same mirror of our psyche, this narrative of childhood will reflect back upon us, painting the colors of our present experiences and sense of identity. That is, child and childhood reflect a *"vision of oneself,"* as Jung has said.[139]

As we search for the unconscious, we soon arrive at the world of the child, as did Freud, because the child is a prime *representative* of the unconscious. 'Child' means *being* in pleasure (and in unpleasure as well) rather than *doing* in reality, dwelling in id rather than its replacement by the ego. It means functioning according to primary processes, rather than the secondary processes of rational thinking and reality testing. We search for our way back from the reality principle to what was disrupted in the pleasure principle, in our efforts to avoid unpleasure, and in the development towards the demands of ego-reality.

Freud certainly struggled with his child. He was unable to experience the child's oceanic feelings, the sense of eternal oneness and belongingness with the world, which his friend Romain Rolland described to him. "I cannot discover this 'oceanic' feeling in myself," Freud wrote in *Civilization and its Discontents*. Freud's skill and experience was, rather,

---

137  CW 6, par. 812.
138  CW 6, par. 812; see also Andrew Samuels et. al., *A Critical Dictionary of Jungian Analysis*, p. 73f.; *The Complex*, pp. 36-37.
139  CW 9i., par. 274.

one of intellectual insights. "It is not easy to deal scientifically with feelings," he writes, and continues, "nothing remains but to fall back on the ideational content which is most readily associated with the feeling. ... It is a feeling of an indissoluble bond." While Freud spent most of his adult life exploring the child, he "could not convince [him] self of the primary nature of such a feeling."[140]

In Freud's psychology, the developing child—possibly emerging out of the oceanic feelings that Freud so much longed for but could not experience—becomes the focus of serious adult scrutiny. What Freud found, however, might perhaps have been more a small adult than a little child.

In psychotherapy, we search for the child we once were, and for the wounds and the neglect that the child within us has to carry. However, while the child embodies the past, as well as our memories and ideas of our past, it also embraces our hopes for the future. The child holds the key to our potential and development. The child, says Jung, "paves the way for a future change of personality. In the individuation process, it anticipates the figure that comes from the synthesis of conscious and unconscious elements in the personality."[141]

## Archetypal Child and Personal Shadow

We tend to think in a linear perspective, and thus follow the track back to our actual childhood. From an archetypal perspective, however, *the idea precedes empirical experience*. Thus, we do not crystallize the concept of *child* solely from the actual experience of our childhood, but, as Jung says, "The child motif represents the preconscious, childhood aspect of the collective psyche."[142] This is the *archetypal motif* of the child, not one's personal childhood. Thus, the child carries the image of living in "the mysterious world of mythical images and magical relatedness," as Gerhard Adler says, "indeed it is immersed in the world of the images of the collective unconscious, of the mythological past of mankind which is as yet undimmed by the concrete realities of the present."[143]

Childhood is the age of man most directly exposed to the collected wisdom, as well as the folly of past generations. In so far as youth remains an age of learning, and the young are willing to listen, and

140 *Civilization and its Discontents*, SE 21, p. 65.
141 CW 9i., par. 278.
142 CW 9i., par. 273.
143 Gerhard Adler, *Studies in Analytical Psychology*, p. 122.

the old have not become obsolete, childhood is the age of unmediated exposure to the insights, the wrongdoings and the traumata of past generations. In certain ways, the dead are resurrected in the child. Jung says, "Not only are ancestral spirits supposed to be reincarnated in children, but an attempt is made to implant them into the child by naming him after an ancestor."[144] In the aftermath of the Shoah, this has carried arduous implications, particularly when children who came to bear the names of murdered relatives were turned into petrified monuments of memorial, and called upon to bear the heavy burden of living the un-lived lives of the dead.

When we recall, remember, and have recollections from our child-hood, we look at that which lies behind us. We try to call it forth, to gather and collect it into a sense of unified identity. As adults, it is child-hood that most prominently lies behind us—and developmentally, it is the formative years and the experiences of childhood that linger in our past. Archetypally, childhood is an earlier layer of humankind's psyche, located behind us, in our past. The childhood psyche precedes the de-veloped consciousness of the adult. Our individual as well as ancestral collective past is what lies behind us—and what lies behind us, what we carry on our back, is our shadow. Our childhood visibly and tangibly carries and encompasses our shadow. It is the satchel that holds the wonderful sentiments, as well as the ills and the wounds, which we carry on our shoulders. It holds the secrets and the charms, the burden of complexes as well as the weight of what has been forgotten. Behind us lies the shadow of oblivion.

The child is the set of archetypal ideas and images that pertain to a 'pre-ego state of mind,' a condition contrasting that of the adult ego. Living in pleasure and avoidance of unpleasure, wish fulfillment and instinctual satisfaction, *being* rather than *doing, playing* rather than *real-ity, paradise* rather than *knowledge,* the ocean and the oceanic feeling rather than the harsh ground, all refer to the *divinity* of the child.

The child represents participation mystique, the mythical layer, the world of magic, play and fantasy. This is the child's experience "of be-ing one with the external world as a whole," as Freud knew,[145] far away from the adult ego's emphasis on consciousness, reality and rational-ity.

---

144  CW 9i., par. 224.
145  *Civilization and its Discontents,* SE 21, p. 65.

## The Divine Child—Dwelling in the Oceanic Waters

The *divine child* represents a paradisiacal aspect of harmonious creation, of something new, whole and holy being born, reclining in divine nature and natural divinity. This is the miraculous birth of the divine child, who later is often to become the hero in mythology. Perseus, for example, is born to an archetypal father, Zeus, who transforms himself into gold, raining into imprisoned Danae, thus making the virgin pregnant. The sense of the child's holiness is brought forth by the *coniunctio*, the union of transparent spirituality and untouched, unhampered nature.[146] We find this, for instance, in a Jewish legend about the *Angel of Conception*:

> When the time has come for a couple to conceive a child, God directs Lailah, the midwife of souls, to find a soul hidden in the Garden of Eden. She instructs the soul to enter a drop of semen. Usually, the soul refuses, for it desires to remain pure, and still remembers the pain of being born— and possibly how the reality of human life has a tendency to neglect the soul. Nonetheless, Lailah compels the soul to obey. When she succeeds, God pronounces the fate of that particular sperm, whether it will be male or female, strong or weak, rich or poor, of bad fortune or good.
>
> The angel then turns around, and places the soul in the womb of the mother. While the infant grows in the womb, Lailah lights a candle and places it at the head of the unborn infant, so that it can see from one end of the world to the other, as it is said, 'His lamp shone above my head, and by His light I walked through darkness.'[147]
>
> For nine months, Lailah watches over the unborn, teaching it the entire Torah, as well as the history of its soul. Before the child is born, it is given an oath to keep its soul pure. Lailah then accompanies the child into the Garden of Eden, and shows it the righteous ones. She then leads the child to the netherworld, and shows it the punishments of Gehenna.[148]
>
> When the time has come to be born, the angel extinguishes the lamp, and brings forth the child into the world. The instant the child emerges, Lailah lightly strikes the newborn above the lip, causing it to cry out. At that very moment, the infant forgets all it has learned. This is

146  For an analysis of the Perseus myth, see *Enemy, Cripple & Beggar*, pp. 47-78.

147  Job 29:3.

148  Gehenna, that is Hell, derived from 'the valley of the son of Hinnom,' the dumping place of the wicked in ancient Jerusalem.

the origin of the mark on the upper lip, which everyone
bears.

Indeed, Lailah, the Angel of Conception, is a guardian
angel, who watches over the child all of his days. When
the time has come to take leave of this world, she reap-
pears and says, "Do you not recognize me? The time of
your departure has come. I have come to take you from
this world." Lailah leads the person to the World to Come,
where he or she gives an account before God, and is accordingly judged.[149]

This legend distinctly reflects the idea of the transition, separation
and *coniunctio* between the divine and the human. The process and
conception of life is guided by Lailah, whose name means Night, who
at the end of one's days guides the soul from this world to the next.
Lailah and Lilith, whose name also means Night, are opposite aspects
of the Great Mother archetype—the creative life-giving matrix vs. her
destructive and terrible side, both of whom essentially walk side-by-
side and hand-in-hand. Even when good fortune gives Lailah the upper
hand, it seems to be the obligation of man to remain aware of Lilith,
lingering in the dark corners of the night.

Perinatally, the child dwells in the oceanic waters. Water is the substance of the primordial sea of the unconscious, from which life springs
forth.[150] For Thales, father of philosophy, water, or moisture, was the
*arche*, the original substance, thus considering "the unconscious psyche
[to be] equivalent to water."[151] In "pre-human" symbols, says Neumann,
"the Mother is the sea ... and the child a fish swimming in the envelop-
ing waters."[152] The primal waters are "the arena of becoming."[153] Water
is the birth-giving source of life, and it serves the purposes of healing
and purification in sacred rituals. The initiation and salvation through
Baptism is prominent in Western culture. Purification through immersion in water is found as well in the Jewish custom of ritual cleansing
baths, the mikvah. It is the "immersion in the bath," that enables the

---

149  *Midrash Tanhuma-Yelammedenu, Pekudei* 3; adapted from *Tree of Souls: The
      Mythology of Judaism*, pp. 199-200.
150  Erel Shalit, *Will Fishes Fly in Aquarius – Or Will They Drown in the Bucket?*,
      p. 5.
151  Edward Edinger, *The Psyche in Antiquity, Book One: Early Greek Philosophy*,
      p. 17f.
152  *The Origins and History of Consciousness*, p. 43.
153  *Hermes: Guide of Souls*, p. 64.

bond of love that makes the soul come into being, the *vinculum*, the ligament or bond between spirit and body.[154]

The child to-be-born is given life in the waters of the womb, in the womb of the unconscious. After birth, the protective womb is re-created in the cradle, as the newborn continues its perinatal movement back and forth between slumber and emerging wakefulness. The feeling of *Home* enables the baby to incubate in the cradle, which is saturated with the oceanic feeling of, as Freud says, "an indissoluble bond, of being one with the external world as a whole."[155] Parental care and nurturing enable the child to swim in its own divinity, to remain in undifferentiated unity with the mother.

When parents create an environment of warmth, love and protection for their newborn child, it is an attempt at creating the condition in which the divine child can be brought into this world without exposing it too soon to the cold and to the inevitable demands of life, that it will have to meet in due time. When unfortunate conditions do not provide this loving bridge into extra-uterine existence, the spark of life may fade away all too soon.

The divine child carries the magic of childhood, the natural libido prior to expulsion from paradise. This is the innocent and purposeless (yet of greatest importance) play of the child, rather than the educational play and games of trying out adult roles and tasks; it is a non-competitive ball game rather than playing doctor and nurse, firefighter or bank manager.

The divine child is close to the gods, that is, to the archetypal structures and energies. In fact, the divine child is sometimes that vital core of inner life, which survives even under horrendous circumstances. The divine child does not pertain to literal childhood, but holds the daemon and the kernel of divinity. It appears frequently in "the maturation process of personality induced by analysis of the unconscious," that is, the process of individuation.[156] As Jung says, "If you marry the ordered to the chaos you produce the divine child, the supreme meaning beyond meaning and meaninglessness."[157]

Chaya,[158] for example, was a forty-six-year-old woman, who had suffered years of abuse during her childhood. Ever since, she had had a recurrent dream in which she watches a little girl from afar. The little

---

154  CW 16, par. 454.
155  *Civilization and its Discontents*, SE 21, p. 65.
156  'The psychology of the child archetype,' CW 9.i., par. 270.
157  *The Red Book: Liber Novus*, p. 235.
158  The meaning of the name Chaya is 'to be alive.'

girl looks very much like herself, but "more beautiful." In the dreams, Chaya's father often beats the little girl badly. He spanks her back and slaps her face. As Chaya fearfully watches, she wonders if the little girl in the dream will survive. She recalls that around the age of ten, the dream changed; she now began to pick up the little girl, who remains the same age, from the floor and holds her in her arms. Later, she would add a fantasy that she gently rocks the girl in a washtub. She notices that the beatings have left no signs or scars, and the little girl rests calmly in her arms and smiles back at her.

This dream, simultaneously disturbing and comforting, accompanied Chaya from early childhood into midlife. It served as an inner daemon, as her guarding spirit. As post-traumatic dreams often do, it seemed to have portrayed the ongoing trauma quite literally. However, in the dream, the trauma was both split-off, the little girl being beaten and not Chaya herself, and at the same time striking right at her inner core, at the small, innocent and beautiful child that resided deeply within her. As Chaya gained increasing ego strengths, she was able to rely on herself to care for this inner child. She was able to take her in her arms, to protect herself and thus alleviate her suffering.

While her self-embrace slightly eased the pain of her wounds, and the dream reflects the soul's capacity to protect her inner kernel, the abuse had left her wounded, with recognizable signs and indelible scars.


## Eros—The Divine Child


### From Divine to Human

The divine child is barely born into human life, still angelic, dwelling in the paradisiacal phase, or segment, of the archetypal unconscious. Only a moment ago has it been born out of the primordial *golden egg*, the Original Self. The vivacious god *Eros*, who for Freud represented the principle of life,[159] epitomizes the divine child.

Eros, the god of love, was the youngest and yet the first-born god. In the world of interpersonal and family relations, the parents are there

---

159  Cf. Sigmund Freud, *An Outline of Psychoanalysis*, SE 23, p. 148.

to give birth to the child. However, in one's individual development, and in the development of consciousness, the child precedes the adult; many adults will testify they have not reached their present age yet. The child is born, and comes to life before the adult personality takes shape. In this sense, the child is not born *from* the adult, but *gives birth* to the adult, just as we may claim that psychologically, the Self as an original unity precedes the ego. In the Divine Child, the umbilical cord to the transcendent has not yet been cut off. The sparks of divinity have not yet gone into hiding, withdrawing from the growing ego's perhaps necessary onslaughts, but may still glow like the aura in for instance many paintings of the nativity scene. The sense of original wholeness has not yet shattered, but is present together with the instincts that ignite life, evoking the love that affects all beholders.

Eros was a child-god born out of the *World Egg*. From the seed in the Egg, the world will manifest. In the Homeric and Orphic creation myths, as Robert Graves tells us, the "black-winged Night, a goddess of whom even Zeus stands in awe, was courted by the wind and laid a silver egg in the womb of Darkness."[160] Double-sexed and golden-winged, Eros was hatched from this egg and set the Universe in motion, creating earth, sky and moon.

Marie-Louise von Franz points out that "[t]he egg is sometimes identified with the whole universe and sometimes more especially with the rising sun." She quotes the *Chandogya Upanishad* 3.19,

> In the beginning this was non-existent. It became existent, it grew. It turned into an egg. The egg lay for the time of a year. The egg broke open. The two halves were one of silver, the other of gold. The silver one became this earth, the golden one the sky, the thick membrane [of the white] the mountains, the thin membrane [of the yolk], the mist with the clouds, the small veins the rivers, the fluid the sea.

"Thus," says von Franz, "the sun is born,"[161] enabling life.

As von Franz goes on to say, in the golden germ, or the egg, we find "the motif of the preconscious totality. It is psychic wholeness conceived as the thing which came before the rise of ego consciousness, or any kind of dividing consciousness."[162] Similarly, we find in Egyptian mythology that the sun god Ra sprang from an egg. He then became the cause and the creator of life on earth.

---

160  Robert Graves, *Greek Myths*, p. 10.
161  Marie-Louise von Franz, *Creation Myths*, p. 225.
162  *Creation Myths*, p. 229.

In the comment to his image of the divine child, Jung writes that in Orphic cosmogony, "Aither and Chaos are born from Chronos. Chronos makes an egg in Aither. The egg splits into two, and Phanes, the first of the Gods, appears."[163] Phanes, generator of life and father of the Night, was hatched from the primordial egg, which was split by Chronos and Ananke, by Time and Necessity.

Eros, born out of the World Egg, signifies the birth of the human, in its very first, primary state. This original birth is not an outgrowth of human love and desire, by instinct and lovemaking. Rather, the birth out of the cosmic egg relies on the willingness of the divine, or the transpersonal, to let man come alive. However, at this mythological stage, the child still dwells in the vicinity and under the rule of the gods.

The egg from which Eros springs, was laid by the nocturnal abyss, the primordial womb of darkness, *Chaos*, similar to the Bible's tohu-va-vohu. Chaos is eventually replaced by *Paradise*, the playground of Eros, the beautiful, naked, angelic child who shoots his golden arrows. Alternatively, we find Eros represented as little erotes. Androgynous and represented not as one but as many, are signs that at this stage, Eros does not yet pertain fully to individual, differentiated relatedness. Eros does not yet concern conscious love and love-making. However, when touched by Eros's golden arrows, even the most cold-hearted adult may lose his (or her) discriminating consciousness, and fall right into the snares of love.

In Apuleius's story *Amor and Psyche*, Eros lives in Paradise, and the young maiden *Psyche*, i.e. the human soul, lives a peaceful paradisiacal existence, before she, the germinating human psyche, slowly comes alive by her very sleep in Paradise,

> Thus fair Psyche being sweetly couched amongst the soft and tender herbs, as in a bed of dewy grass and fragrant flowers, ... she fell softly asleep... and when she had refreshed herself sufficiently with sleep, she rose... In the very heart of the grove beside the gliding stream there stood a palace, built by no human hands but by the cunning of a god. ... Truly it must be some demi-god, or rather in very truth a god, ... that put all these beasts into silver.[164]

The palace in the grove beside the gliding stream of Paradise is built by a god or a demi-god. That is, existence wavers back and forth. It is

---

163  *The Red Book*, p. 301.
164  From *The Golden Ass*, p. 68; also Erich Neumann, *Amor and Psyche*, p. 9f.

not yet fully human, but on the verge of becoming. Apuleius continues to tell us, "It seemed a heavenly palace built by great Jove [Jupiter, Heavenly Father] that he might dwell with mortal men."[165] That is, we hear of paradisiacal existence as an initial act of the gods to set foothold in the human world. Or, we may look at it the other way around: the paradisiacal condition is the human reconstruction of the womb, which enables the divinity of the child to unfold in the realm of the living.

The story continues, "But wondrous as was the sight of such vast wealth, yet more marvelous was it that there was no chain nor bar nor sentinel to guard the treasure of all the world."[166] In this divine, paradisiacal existence there are no constricting chains, which otherwise characterize our human consciousness and the human condition. In the myth of Perseus, for example, his mother Danae's father, king Acrisius of Argos, representing the dominant ego-principle, puts his daughter behind bars, so that no son, no new element shall rise up against him. This is the typical fear of every despot. We might say that overly powerful habits and beliefs dominating our consciousness have a tendency to become like tyrants on the royal throne.

Divine existence is necessarily unconscious or pre-conscious; as we are told in Apuleius's tale, "First for a while she slept, then, waking, bathed to refresh her weariness."[167] This refreshing bath is neither the cold shower of early morning waking, nor the ritual bath of purification, such as the mikvah or baptism. Rather, it is the pleasurable and rather drowsy bath, which allows the preconscious to remain in a state of incubatory sleepiness.

We are then told,

> Forthwith she was served wine with nectar and many a delicious dish. Still no one waited on her, ... [n]either could she see any person, she only heard words that fell from the air, and none save voices were her servants. ... another struck the lyre, though never a lyre was to be seen. Then the harmony of a multitude of musicians was borne to her ears, ... though no one was visible.[168]

The human soul is not yet awake and conscious, but slumbers in the unconscious realm of invisibility. The elements are there, but not

---

165  *Amor and Psyche*, p. 10.
166  *Amor and Psyche*, p. 10.
167  *Amor and Psyche*, p. 11.
168  *Amor and Psyche*, p. 11.

*individuals.* Psyche could not see any person; so far, no one was visible. There are archetypal energies, but no conscious, human beings. There is self and divinity, but without ego and identity.

By shooting man with his golden, love-inducing arrows, Eros brings life to him or her. Eros penetrates and stirs the hearts of men and women, creating attraction and a reason for togetherness and relationships. Consequently, man can continue the divine task of enabling life, to re-create and pro-create. Without Eros, human life would cease, in spite of the fact that merely for the sake of procreation, we may already manage without the eroticism of Eros, whether in his divine or his instinctual manifestation, and rely entirely on the laboratory. However, assuming that human life is not only physical existence but also relationship, not merely producing offspring but love and sex as well, we might wonder what a world without Eros would look like. Even though it might sometimes seem as if in today's harsh world Eros has often been fired, stripped of its fiery nature, or is at least too frequently absent from the job, the calls and the yearning for his come-back, is a testimony of his presence, lurking in unexpected quarters.

## Eros, Psyche and Pleasure

Interestingly, Eros has a second birth. He is reborn, this time with Aphrodite as his mother. The goddess of love, nature and beauty, in her relationship with Ares (Mars), the god of warfare, gives birth to Eros, sibling of Fear, Panic and Harmony.

Eros, the creative principle of life and relatedness, is re-created by the principles of love and war, of harmony and conflict. Love now pertains to and depends upon union as well as separation, which means it has taken its place in the hearts of human beings. Eros is both a necessary pre-condition and a result of the combination of love and war, togetherness and strife, of Freud's instinct of life, as well as Winnicott's life-force, the latter ensuring "movement rather than stillness."[169] Ares and Aphrodite, with Eros as their progeny, are the instinctual dynamics that enable archetypal energies to transform into the sphere of the human. They form the essential union for creating a human, personal existence, as we find in the characteristics of Oedipus, as I have elaborated elsewhere.[170] The story tells us that as Aphrodite's son, Eros has to

169   Donald W. Winnicott, 'Aggression in Relation to Emotional Development,' *Collected Papers: Through Paediatrics to Psycho-Analysis*, p. 204.
170   *The Complex*, p. 48ff.

break away from his paradisiacal but invisible, unconscious existence and impregnate Psyche, the human soul. He impregnates her with himself, with Eros, that is, with love and relatedness, the principle of life. Without relatedness there is no life, and without a sense of divinity in the human, there is no soul. Eros and Psyche come together as soulful relatedness, inwardly as well as outwardly, vis-à-vis internal objects as well as external events, other humans and beings. We may understand relatedness as the human expression of divinity—between men, between man and God, and between mother and infant. In the absence of Eros, the human child will not grow and develop. Even in Apuleius's story, Eros is reborn in and by the young maiden *Psyche*, i.e., the still young soul of man, who "bears a child like to you. If you keep my secret in silence, he shall be a god; if you divulge it, a mortal."[171]

The child that Psyche bears resembles Eros. The life principle is reborn in the soul's womb. As the principle of life, Eros has both divine and mortal attributes. Like the newborn child, he might be a god or a mortal. The divine child wavers back and forth between divinity and the human. When our caring human hands stretch out silently, in awe of divine secrecy[172] and wisdom, we may to some extent preserve the godlike features at the core of human life. Simultaneously, we are mortal because of the very manifestation of the divine secret. Erich Neumann comments, "The eternal union of the goddess Psyche with the god Eros means that the human bond with the divine is not only eternal, but itself of a divine quality.[173]

If we desire further mythical evidence that divinity and the life principle crystallize initially along the lines of Freud's pleasure principle, we may notice that the name of the daughter born to Eros and Psyche is—*Pleasure*. Neumann says,

> [T]he maternal world is life and psyche in one; it gives nourishment and pleasure, protects and warms, comforts and forgives. It is the refuge for all suffering, the goal of all desire. ... All the positive maternal traits are in evidence at this stage, when the ego is still embryonic and has no activity of its own.[174]

---

171  *Amor and Psyche*, p. 18.
172  As I have mentioned in *Enemy, Cripple, Beggar* (p. 189), 'secrecy' (from the Latin) and 'holy' in Hebrew (kadosh), both mean 'to set apart.'
173  *Amor and Psyche*, p. 143.
174  *The Origins and History of Consciousness*, p. 15.

Images of peace and wholeness, incubation, the Uroboros, and the Good Fairy in the fairy tale pertain to the stage of dwelling in Paradise. It is a fairy tale world, pertaining to the prolonged Sleep of Beauty. The word fairy comes from 'fate.' It is a world more of fate than destiny, the latter having to do with finding the way to one's destination, whereunto one is destined. There are no roads in Paradise, just a peaceful rest, until one is inevitably expelled. Since there is not much will-power in paradise, one might easily be tempted to remain forever and ever.

By holding and caring, with love and nurturing, the child can cross the threatening primordial abyss. Dwelling in paradisiacal pleasure, enables the transition into human life. But in an excessive state of prolonged peaceful paradise, evil is projected onto the Other. The tale about Hansel and Gretel tells us that there is danger behind the sweet temptation of the little house, the garden, the womb. The witch in the fairy tale, the Terrible Mother, is necessary to chase one out of Paradise and ensure development.

The seeds of depression are already planted in the Garden of Eden. There is a pleasurable reclining in harmonious stillness, which becomes stagnant meaninglessness of passive death if one remains there too long. As introversion of libido, psychic energy, depression may be the shadow condition of reclining in paradisiacal harmony.[175]

## The Divine Child in Dreams

The child, not the least the divine child, is a frequent visitor in our dreams. Rona, a young, unmarried woman dreams,

> I have just given birth, in a natural pool at the slopes of a mountain. I pick up and hold the newborn baby in my arms. I walk along a path up around the mountain. Suddenly my child points his little finger and looks toward the sky, and says, "look, fishes fly in the sky!"[176]

This is the divine child speaking. He brings a message from within, from the Self. The rational mind immediately objects to the non-sense of this psychic event. Newborn children do not talk. The illogical and

---

175   As I see it, different kinds of depression may pertain to different stages in life; as regards youth, see 'tristia and hilaria' below. A sense of having lived a meaningless life that cannot be repaired, naturally pertains to old age.

176   *Will Fishes Fly in Aquarius – Or Will They Drown in the Bucket?*, p. 32-3. Rona means joy, singing.

paradoxical content reflect the absurdity of dreams and their ludicrous language, says rational man. However, if we are attentive to the symbolic spectrum, we shall gracefully wonder about the coniunctio of opposites that is given birth and shape in the dream. The newborn child in Rona's dream is itself a union of human and divine, expressing a symbolic union between fishes and flying, between the elements of water and air. The ascent along the mountainous path, from the birth-giving waters below toward the sky above, may pertain to her individual psyche and life situation, as well as to the transition of the times and the aeons, from Pisces to Aquarius.[177]

When we receive a message from the Self, brought to us by the divine child, we feel touched by numinosity, even though we may wonder why. When initially coming for analysis, Talia[178] brought a dream that she said "is too straightforward to bring to a psychoanalyst, but it keeps waking me up at least one night a week, and for the whole following day I just can't get it out of my system." In the dream, she says,

> I sit in my childhood room. I am telling a story to a two-and-a-half-year old girl. Suddenly, the little girl gets up, runs out and away from the house. I keep reading to her, as if nothing happened. I then understand she is going to fall into the lake, which is polluted. It is as if I wake up (sometimes in the dream, sometimes I am not sure if I really am awake). I run to the lake and manage to save the girl, who has nearly drowned. I clean her and clean her, but the skin does not get clean of the dirt.

After years of abuse as a child, and in her marriage to a much older man, she needed to protect and save the small child, her inner core. The turning point in analysis manifested itself by a sudden change in her repetitive dream. As always, Talia is telling the child a story,

> The story is about a little boy and a little girl. The girl [to whom I am telling the story] and I are invited to a wedding—I don't know whose wedding, even though these are people close to me, I don't know who they are. We have to get dressed, but I realize that I don't need to rush or force the little girl, I have to adapt to her needs and be patient with her—in fact, she can dress, if need be, when we get there, when we get to the wedding.

---

177  See *Aion: Contributions to the Symbolism of the Self,* CW 9ii.
178  In Greek, Talia means' to blossom,' in Hebrew, 'dew from God.'

The coming together, the wedding or the sense of internal unity, could take place when Talia adapted and tuned in to the needs of the little child, her inner self, who had suffered trauma at an early age. Only then could she move away from a constant sense of emergency, from the trauma threatening to psychologically drown her, requiring her readiness to save her.

Chronological age does not restrict the capabilities of the divine child. Even as an infant, the divine child talks and walks, performs miracles and guides us along our path, sometimes by performing miracles, at other times by theft—like newborn Hermes, who by trickery stole his brother Apollo's cows.

During a time of personal crisis, following her unexpected dismissal from a prominent academic position, Zemirah[179] dreamed that she was going up to the top of a hill to hang herself. Having arrived at the top [of the hill, and of her career as well], she sits in the shade of a big tree. She enters labor, and to her surprise gives birth to a small baby. Her breasts are full of milk, and she feels a great joy filling her entire body, as she feeds the baby. The newborn baby, of unknown gender, brought life to this depressed woman. She experienced the rebirth of an inner connection. As she could feel reconnected to her inner Self, a sense of meaning, value and understanding brought life back to her. She was eventually able to employ her skills and academic experience in a personally satisfying way.

In another case, Saul,[180] an ambitious and moderately successful entrepreneur, always on the outlook for bigger enterprises, dreamed that he was hitchhiking on a long, steep road. A huge semi-trailer stopped to give him a ride. As he entered, he was surprised to find the driver was an eight-year old boy with long, black hair. When Saul told the boy in the dream he was scared, the exceptionally young driver answered him authoritatively, "It is scarier the way you drive. Trust me, I know the way."

Saul, however, was reluctant to share the driving along his personal, seemingly smooth highway of his life, with a young child. He rejected the dream's message, which in its simplicity might have hit directly into his soul. Only much later, when his wife left him and he became aware how alienated he had become to his children, did he recall the dream.

179  Zemirah means 'song.'
180  Saul, 'loaned,' was the first of the Hebrew kings. He did not realize, until his bitter end, that whatever kingdom, external or internal, we are appointed to rule, it is merely a loan; even autocratic rulers, whether in society or in our psyche, do not remain forever in power.

He painfully realized that his relentless ambition and his business skills did not serve him well in family affairs. This realization was poignantly expressed in a dream, in which he lay in bed alongside the crib of his newborn grandson. The infant then stood on his knees, walked over to the other end of the crib, and as he lay down in the opposite direction, the infant looked fiercely at Saul. Already in the dream, Saul felt he understood the child's message: "Change direction, 180 degrees!"

The divine child, as a reflection of the life-igniting spark in our Self, can have a healing and anti-depressive effect. For example, at forty-two, Ma'ayan[181] dreamed that she points a gun at her solar plexus, an indication of her state of fatigue, depression and anger at herself. She fires right in the center, but does not die from the shot. Instead, to her great surprise, a baby is miraculously born. She holds the infant close to her breast. She feels the warmth of the child, and has an urge to feed the child. She is overtaken by a wave of love, and a sense of mutual understanding between her and the baby.

As reflected in these dreams, we understand that the divine child, as an image of the Self, may appear in times of crisis and transformation. In the dreams of Zemirah and Ma'ayan, the transition from psychological death and depression to the rebirth of warmth and liveliness is evident. When in need, the Self often constellates; it serves as the inner daemon that sometimes enables a person to be anchored within him or herself when passing through inhuman trauma.

It is often in periods of transition, when we suffer internally or when external upheaval seems to inundate us, that we unexpectedly open up to the transcendent. While there is always the danger of being led astray, in situations of crisis, we may be guided toward change and renewal by the divine child, or other manifestations of the Self. Jung writes,

> The self appears in dreams, myths, fairytales in the figure of the 'supraordinate personality,' such as king, hero, prophet, saviour, etc. or in the form of a totality symbol, such as the circle, square, *quadratura circuli* [the squaring of the circle], cross, etc. When it represents a *complexio oppositorum*, a union of opposites, it can also appear as a united duality, in the form, for instance, of *tao* as the interplay of *yang* and *yin*, or of the hostile brothers, or of the hero and his adversary (arch-enemy, dragon), Faust and Mephistopheles, etc. Empirically, therefore, the self appears as a

---

181  Ma'ayan means fountain, spring.

play of light and shadow, although conceived as a totality and unity in which the opposites are united.[182]

The Self being multifaceted and incomprehensible in its fullness, I believe that most anything can serve as a symbol of the Self, depending on how we relate to it, on condition that we discern the awe-inspiring quality of the "play of light and shadow." Although we fear and tremble when anxiety causes our defenses to crack in times of crisis, we are given the opportunity, as well, to expand the boundaries of the ego and our conscious identity.

The child is the product of *the coniunctio between the unconscious and consciousness*, of archetype and human. When Socrates and Diotima, a woman from Mantinea, discussed the nature of Eros, she proved to Socrates that neither is he a god, nor a mortal, but occupies a middle position between them, thus playing "a vital role in holding the world together."[183] For the divine child to become a living person, it has to be painfully labored into the human world, and carefully received and cared for by human hands. A fifty-year-old woman dreamed of a three-eyed baby being born out of the beautiful mosaic that was uncovered as she washed layers of dust from the floor. The soulful third eye was born out of a change in conscious attitude, from extremely rational to a more motherly one, both in relation to her children, the world and herself.[184]

In the absence of human intervention, the divine child soon becomes an orphan, deserted and left to its own fate. Many an orphan in the real living world does not survive. He or she may become psychologically crippled by childhood trauma, lacking the means of survival, sometimes condemned to physical or psychological death, as in anaclitic depression.[185] This is different from the kernel of orphanhood, which is an archetypal and necessary experience in the development of a child. This is reflected in many children's fantasy of being adopted, while his as if "true" or "real" parents, that is, *archetypal* parents, being either miserably poor or of royal wealth.[186] The necessary archetypal fantasy is obstructed when reality tragically causes a child to actually become an orphan.

---

182  CW 6, par. 790.
183  *Symposium and the Death of Socrates*, (Symposium 202), p. 36.
184  *The Complex*, p. 117.
185  Rene Spitz, Hospitalism: An Inquiry Into the Genesis of Psychiatric Conditions in Early Childhood, *Psychoanalytic Study of the Child*, 1, 53-74.
186  See p. 83f. below, as regards the fantasies of Jung and Erikson.

## Chaos and Annihilation

Eros in Paradise is the nucleus of the *child archetype*, the spark of life
that brings archetypal divinity into life. As such, Eros holds the key and
the ability to *relate* to one's essential core and to the inner daemon, to
one's sense of having a guardian spirit. This enables us to experience a
sense of meaning in our life, of walking a path of meaningful destiny.
In the absence of Eros, without a key to our inner core or Self, we suffer
from coldness and alienation, lack of meaning, senselessness and the
boredom of routine, a hellish waiting for something to happen. I cannot but refer to Jung's essay on Joyce's Ulysses:

> I had an uncle whose thinking was always direct and to
> the point. One day he stopped me on the street and de-
> manded: 'Do you know how the devil tortures the souls in
> hell' When I said no, he replied: 'He keeps them waiting.'
> And with that he walked away. This remark occurred to me
> when I was ploughing through *Ulysses* for the first time.
> Every sentence rouses an expectation that is not fulfilled;
> finally, out of sheer resignation, you come to expect noth-
> ing, and to your horror it gradually dawns on you that you
> have hit the mark. In actual fact, nothing happens, noth-
> ing comes of it all...[187]

However, beneath the bridge that leads from the beyond, over to the
beginning of life in paradise, stretches the threatening abyss of *chaos*,
the black hole, *abaddon*.[188] This is "the abyss, the inanity of eternal
chaos," which may rush "toward you as if carried by the roaring wings
of a storm, the hurtling waves of the sea."[189] Yet, even for the lucky
ones, who as vulnerable infants have safely been brought across the
abyss to dwell for a while in Paradise, pain and trouble do not end here.
The necessary and inevitable exit out of paradise is accompanied by the
painful experience of *abandonment*.

The *abyss* is located at the transition from not-being to coming-into-
being, and pertains to what Melanie Klein described as annihilation
anxiety.[190] Even the womb, in which the human fetus incubates, has itself a dark, engulfing aspect, closely connected to the coldness of death.

---

187  '"Ulysses": A Monologue,' CW 15, par. 165.
188  Abaddon (or, avaddon), the bottomless pit of Hell, the realm of the dead.
     From Hebrew, the place of destruction, the place where you perish (cf. Psalms
     88:12; Proverbs 27:20; Job 31:12, "For it is a fire that consumes to Avaddon,
     and would burn to the root all my produce").
189  *The Red Book*, p. 295.
190  Cf. Hannah Segal, *Introduction to the Work of Melanie Klein.*

As Neumann says, "The lower level of this belly zone is the underworld that is contained in the 'belly' or 'womb' of the earth. To this world belong ... the subterranean darkness as hell and night ..."[191] And prior to the womb there is an even more distant, cosmic sense of nothingness and annihilation. Ronald Laing has described the experience of engulfment and annihilation in psychosis, the absence of existence, of even a flicker of fire.[192]

The fear of annihilation is the fear of being devoured by the dark unconscious, by the Terrible Mother, that is, by the negative end of the Great Mother archetype. This is the dark and unknown, "the abyss, the world of the dead, anything that devours, seduces, and poisons, that is terrible and inescapable like fate," as Jung describes the negative facet of the mother archetype.[193] She is Kali, dark and all-devouring, simultaneously giver of life and devourer of her children; and she is the Gorgon, "the counterpart of the life-womb, ... the womb of death or the night sun" as Neumann says.[194]

The Terrible Mother is the dark and frightening aspect of the unconscious, from which the child can only be born heroically, and whom the hero later will have to return to in order to overcome, or at least to disempower. The Sphinx, who strangled the Thebans one by one until Oedipus resolved her riddle, is an image of the Terrible Mother, who has taken her place at the boundaries of the ego.[195]

In dreams, we frequently find the child who is threatened and endangered by dark forces. This may serve as a signal that the *child within* is in stress and possibly neglected. This is the case in the following dream of a thirty-eight-year-old woman, struggling with her individual expression of femininity,

> I am a baby girl, sleeping in my cradle. And while I am
> sleeping, a dead relative, a woman dressed completely in
> black, rises from her grave. She takes me, grabs me in her
> arms. I am very scared, but completely silent.

The silent suffering of fear, the catatonia of panic, is that of Angerona, goddess of silence and suffering. The dream brought the feeling of

---

191  Erich Neumann, *The Great Mother*, p. 44.
192  See Ronald Laing, *The Divided Self*.
193  *The Archetypes and the Collective Unconscious*, CW 9i., par. 158.
194  *The Great Mother*, p. 166; on the Gorgons, see *Enemy, Cripple, Beggar*, p. 49ff.
195  See *The Complex*, p. 45ff.

early suffering into consciousness, and by 'talking the memory' her suffering was shared and recognized, slowly relieved by careful holding.

Dahlia was forty when she turned to therapy, complaining about depression and anxiety. While her presenting symptoms had been present since she was a teenager, the termination of a long, non-sexual extramarital affair had been the trigger for seeking help.

She was a skilled social worker, high-functioning professionally, but felt unsatisfied both at work and in her marriage. While Moshe, her husband, provided her with a sense of basic security, she was unhappy. She complained about his rigidity, describing him as "a man whose heart was squeezed between [Moses's] Tablets of the Law."

Dahlia[196] was born 1953 in Denmark. Her parents had separately arrived there as refugees in the aftermath of the Second World War. Each had remained almost alone; their respective parents and several siblings had died in the ghettos or perished in the camps. Dahlia's mother had had several miscarriages, and immediately prior to becoming pregnant with Dahlia, a baby daughter had died. She had been bed-ridden during almost the entire pregnancy, but had told Dahlia that the birth had been "easy" compared to what preceded it, and what came after.

Her mother had unmistakably suffered much pain and anxiety before Dahlia was born, and during the pregnancy. She had likely been both physically and mentally exhausted, having suffered the loss of much of her family, as well as miscarriages and the death of her first infant daughter. She had probably been depressed after Dahlia's birth. Years later she was hospitalized following a suicide attempt.

Dahlia described her father as a 'luftmensch,' who each day would bring home a basket full of promises, but very little bread. He was talented in many fields, but unable to hold on to a job for any period of length.

She was not yet two-years-old, when the family decided to move to Israel. Her younger brother, who had suffered several psychotic episodes, was born in the new country. Dahlia characterized herself as 'the barely surviving survivor,' and cynically referred to her brother as 'The Great Zionist Hope,' who plunged ever so deep into the depths of disappointment.

Both her parents claimed, and Dahlia was sure that she herself recalled, how she constantly used to scream and cry as a baby. She thought of herself as someone "with the appearance of an adult, but

---

196   Dahlia is a flower, named after Swedish 18th century botanist Anders Dahl.

really a constantly hungry and craving infant." She would often imagine herself as a nearly dying baby in the arms of a mother whose arms would become thin, stiff and motionless, whereby she, little Dahlia, would come crashing down to the floor.

The following was a recurrent dream, similar to her fantasy of falling out of her mother's arms,

> I am in a small town in the desert, where I see a small child, a girl, drinking water from a polluted well. I [at this stage in the dream the dream-ego has merged with the little girl] fall into the water, and I just keep falling, down, down. I wake up feeling panic, and I don't know if I am still falling or if I have crashed and died.

Dahlia always felt as if at the edge of a void, often feeling that she would fall helplessly into an empty abyss. The dream expresses this fall into the annihilating, devouring abyss. Dahlia's parents had not had the strength to bring her safely across the abyss that constitutes the transition from not-being to coming-into-being.

In therapy, Dahlia needed perfect conditions in order to experience the temenos, the "sacred grove" of the therapy room, to feel the necessary holding, the holding hands, the human hands that receive the newborn baby, pulling it across the bridge from not-being into being. She would not be satisfied with a 'good enough' space, but her desperate quest was for the unattainable 'perfectly good' order.

When her analyst told her that she was going on vacation, Dahlia would have fits of rage lasting weeks. She was constantly attentive to her analyst's breathing behind the couch, needing it to be deep and calm. She experienced analysis as being in an incubator, which needed to be tuned exactly to her basic needs of emotional moisture and temperature, free of any harmful particles. If her need for perfect conditions was not met, therapy would transferentially recapitulate her sense of being like a premature baby who has to take care of herself—on the one hand unable to, on the other hand all too able to care for herself. She would be extremely sensitive to every change in her analyst's office, feeling that anything that had been moved, left behind it an empty space that could not be filled.

Dahlia said, sadly, that she had been given a life, but she did not know how to live it; or worse, she blamed herself for having stubbornly fought for a senseless life. She felt like a fetus in a constant state of emergency, prepared to be aborted. Her skin was an all too thin and unprotecting membrane, serving as an extremely sensitive monitor. Subjectively, she felt the presence of soul and life in every detail and every object—or, alternatively, a sense of deadness. When she felt the soul was absent, for instance from a piece of furniture at home, she would re-internalize the depression, which had been deposited in external objects, and experience it as even more devastating.

Some extent of healing of illness pertaining to the abyss can take place by incubating in a sacred place, a Temenos that provides the necessary tranquility and the healing wholeness. Dahlia needed to hold on to her early perinatal trauma, by means of memories, thoughts, feelings and images. Otherwise it would, as if, not have taken place, that is, it would have been denied. This is similar to the experience of many Holocaust survivors; it is painful but possible to live with the memories, but unbearable to encounter the denial.

Dahlia may never have been fully able to climb out of the abyss, or not feel the ground as stable under her feet, but she needed the memories of Mnemosyne repeatedly to replace the silence of Angerona. Eventually, when able to work with psychotic children, she came to experience a sense of meaning, by the very living "at the edge of the black hole."

## Out of the Abyss

At this very basic stage, before gaining a secure foothold in this world, the infant's small and germinating ego may be overwhelmed, threatened by the frightening danger of being drawn back into the devouring depths of the Great Mother. In this, her negative aspect, the unconscious constitutes the Terrible Mother, the abyss of chaos, of Kali, who destroys, annihilates the child. This stage entails the unmediated and dangerous exposure to archetypal forces and the forces of Mother Nature. This is where heroes find themselves soon after birth, for instance Oedipus when thrown out of Thebes.[197] However, more commonly in the real world, unmediated exposure like this causes severe damage rather than the birth of heroes.

The death instinct is partly deflected into aggression, which enables the infant to "pull away" from the threat. Melanie Klein describes the "original fear of the death instinct," which is transformed into the fear

---

197 *The Complex*, p. 44ff.

of a persecutor, and consequently the fear of annihilation is projected onto the external object.[198]

This is notable in the associations to the following dream by Deborah,[199] a thirty-year-old woman;

> I am sleeping in a big house, not mine, in a big strange bed. I feel very very small. The house belongs to a woman my real age, but she looks much older. She is big and fat, quite vivacious. It's noon, but I am resting, sleeping in this big bed. Suddenly, this woman, the owner of the house, wakes me up. She is dressed up as the Angel of Death, and I get very very scared. The woman tells me she has just dressed up and is only playing a trick, but it takes a long time for me to accept.

In her associations to the dream, Deborah said she had been a greatly desired child. However, since she was born prematurely, her parents had always been very anxious about her. Both of them compulsively emphasized issues of control, and she was toilet-trained before she was a year-and-a-half. It seems as if the annihilatory fear around the premature baby, the fear that she would not be able to pull away from the danger of death, had evoked a need for control. While defensive and exaggerated control aimed at protecting the child, it augmented the underlying anxiety. Over the years, the death anxiety had been deflected from the original annihilatory threat, and was projected onto her body. Consequently, she suffered from a variety of hypochondriac fears, and never-ending concern for people around her, fearing they might die prematurely.

The dream serves as an attempt to come to terms with Deborah's death anxiety; the house-owner merely *pretends* to be the angel of death, but she is not *really* death, a differentiation the dreamer had yet to internalize.

In the newborn, biological as well as psychological life functions have not yet stabilized; they are in the process of taking shape. Therefore, the infant experiences the ultimate anxiety inherent in being at the edge of existence. We may say that the neonate finds itself at the crossroads of not-being-into-being.[200] The very proximity to not-life constitutes a threat, with a consequent fear of annihilation. There is

---

198   See *Introduction to the Work of Melanie Klein*, p. 25.
199   Deborah means 'bee' in Hebrew. She was a 12th century BCE judge and prophetess.
200   *The Hero and His Shadow: Psychopolitical Aspects of Myth and Reality in Israel*, p. 84.

a *stillness* of not-life, and, as mentioned above, we may assume that the death instinct is partly deflected into aggression, which enables the child to 'pull away' from the threat. The basic aggression may be found in the child's very first movements; Winnicott sees the origin of aggressiveness as "almost synonymous with activity," as the life force that ensures "movement rather than stillness."[201] Only by attaining this initial movement, similar to the primary movement of the uroboros, the tail-eating serpent, does the child come into human hands, into the paradise at the interface between divine and human.

There is a need to gain control and tame the forces of the dark side of the universe or of God, of annihilation into the primordial womb-tomb, and we find it most strikingly in magical thinking and compulsive rites, in superstitions and the private rites of the obsessive-compulsive, and for instance in the need for amulets. Gerhard Adler writes:

> [N]early all children practice certain peculiar ceremonies, especially at bedtime, for the transition from waking to sleeping is of particular importance, representing as it does the mysterious moment of transition from light to darkness. ... These puerilities ... are, properly considered, survivals of magic apotropaic, that is protective ceremonies, customary in primitive races. Just because a child has an instinctive knowledge of the minuteness of its own small ego as opposed to the primeval force of the collective powers, it seeks by means of such ceremonies before going to sleep to ensure that its tiny ego will not be completely reabsorbed into the lap of the great primeval night.[202]

A common example of children's archaic fears of being drawn into the primordial darkness, is the fear to be swallowed by the 'dark vaginal mouth of the bathtub,' drawn into the water hole, into hell, or being eaten by the monster.

When the archetypal image of the Divine Child has constellated, Eros touches the parents' heart and soul with love and relatedness. This enables them to carefully carry the infant across the bridge over the abyss of annihilatory threat, and labor it into this world. The recreation of paradise by parental love, comfort and protection enables the child to be born out of the abyss, out of the chaos, out of the darkness, and also to gather enough connectedness with the self to survive and cope

---

201  Donald W. Winnicott, *Playing and Reality*, p. 108ff, and 'Aggression in relation to emotional development,' *Collected Papers: Through Paediatrics to Psycho-Analysis*.
202  *Studies in Analytical Psychology*, p. 122f.

when it later has to exit paradise, in the necessary stage of abandonment.

As an archetypal image, the pain and agony of dwelling in the void, at whatever age, gives birth to the images that emerge from the unconscious and compose the reality of the psyche. "The notion of abyss can inspire fear and terror, and equally ecstasy, allure, safety and haven."[203] Kathryn Madden says that for Jacob Boehme, the German mystic and theologian (1575-1624), the abyss, where one finds nothing and all things, is "a 'place' beyond time and space from which emanate all possibilities."[204] We must therefore recognize that the image of the abyss holds not only a frightening, annihilatory and negative aspect, but is archetypally bipolar. The abyss pertains to the original self no less than the sense of wholeness that the paradisiacal aspect provides, and from the abyss, wisdom is born. As wholeness, the Self entails its own partiality, as fullness, its own nothingness. In Kabbalistic terms, the Ein-sof designates "both the totality of being and the abyss of complete 'nothingness.' As such, it is the union of all things and their opposites."[205]

Biblical Joseph, who dreams and interprets the dreams that so often upset and bewilder, is thrown into an empty and waterless pit in the wilderness, into the shadow of oblivion and seeming death—his brothers bringing his blood-stained garment to their father as a sign of his death. It was, says the legend, "a well dug in a vain search of water, and was now the home of snakes and scorpions"[206]—truly not a place of light and compassion—even though, as we know, the snake is quite conducive to forward movement. Thus, while the danger is to be immovably trapped in the abyss, it is also from within the depths of the abyss's psyche that images are driven forth. Were it not for the void, the blissful rest in paradise could cause the child to avoid life.

## Abandonment

The paradisiacal condition of undifferentiated existence, must eventually—for many it seems too soon—be abandoned. Development of human consciousness begins when man is forced out of paradise. This marks the beginning separation of the ego from the undifferentiated and oceanic, paradisiacal aspect of the primary, or original self.

203  Kathryn Wood Madden, *Dark Light of the Soul*, p. 34.
204  *Dark Light of the Soul*, p. 60.
205  Sanford L. Drob, *Kabbalistic Visions*, p. 12.
206  Robert Graves with Raphael Patai, *Hebrew Myths*, p. 272.

We cannot rest eternally in Paradise—the *divine child* has to be abandoned. Jung has emphasized that, *"Child* means something evolving towards independence," which is possible only by "detaching itself from its origins," which inevitably creates a condition of abandonment.[207]

The divine child has to be left behind, which creates a feeling of 'paradise lost,' of "punitive expulsion from paradise."[208] This is the archetypal basis of longing for a golden age that no longer exists, the sometimes burning loss of a childhood that probably never was so wonderful, of a Golden Age, which seems to exist in the life of every individual as well as of all societies and thought traditions.[209]

Growing up requires that we cede the sense of wholeness and harmony of the divine child, a process which even when relatively smooth, is painful. The experience of abandonment, and the need to care for the abandoned, neglected or orphaned child, is a common experience, and a frequent motif in dreams.

Growing consciousness, doing instead of being, the ego-functions of control and judgment, require that we let go of the wholeness and the harmony of the divine child. What remains may be a stroke of sadness and longing, and often the projection onto a partner, whose task it then becomes to reflect the joy and the treasures of paradise. As Neumann says, "Ego consciousness not only brings a sense of loneliness; it also introduces suffering, toil, trouble, evil, sickness and death into man's life."[210]

Dreams may be compensatory to a life lived too long in Paradise. Ehud[211] was a middle-aged man, who in many ways remained a *Puer Aeternus*, a seemingly eternally young man. He was married to a young photo model, drove his sports car without considering the consequences of his sometimes reckless driving. Without hesitation, he told everyone willing to listen, that he desired a perfectly harmonious life, and believed this was possible "because to live right is my art." He had not read Jung's essay, in which he refers to the art of life as the most

---

207 CW, 9i., par. 287.
208 *The Origins and History of Consciousness*, p. 118.
209 See for instance Mario Jacoby's *Longing for Paradise*.
210 *Longing for Paradise*, p. 115.
211 Ehud, 'God of praise,' was a Benjaminite leader and judge, left-handed like many of his fellow tribesmen. When king Eglon was alone in his "cool upper chamber," Ehud thrust his dagger into the obese king's belly, "And the haft also went in after the blade; and the fat closed upon the blade, so that he could not draw the dagger from his belly; and the excrements came out (Judges 3:20-22).

distinguished of all arts, and Jung may have had something different in mind.

Ehud had a strong sense for aesthetics and perfection, and material well-being, which he had arrived at not only because of heritage, but also due to his talent. However, he resented hard work.

He was a single child. Following the death of both his parents, whom he loved and visited daily, anxiety began to creep in through the cracks. "I never really believed they would die, everything was good, we were all so happy," he said. He compensated this anxiety-threat by refurbishing his home and purchasing a new sports car. He soon felt that "everything was, again, in place," but was disturbed by the following dream,

> I drive my new car out into the country. I arrive at what seems to be a hospital, which makes me a bit scared; I wonder "why am I here?" I calm down as it turns out I have been put in charge of the internal ward, even though I don't know what I am supposed to do—but knowing myself, I'll find a way to manage. The place is crowded with patients of all ages, and I wonder, "what do all these young people do here?" The place is awful, it smells of feces and urine, and the worst is the smell of the hospital food—it stinks of old and sick bodies. The place is dirty, dark, ugly. There is an old dying woman that no one takes care of, and in the corridor, a retarded man with a distorted and oversized body stands right in front of me. I think to myself, "this is not my ward, I am leaving," but this retarded, grotesque man answers me, "You are one of us, one of the patients." I wake up, and think to myself that I am like those schizophrenics who think they are in charge of the ward.

While Ehud had no desire to plunge into the shadow, the shadow had here found a clever way to hold him in its grip. In the dream, Ehud exits the city, drives out into the country, into the woods, where Pan lurks, embracing the naïve and ignorant with panic. It does require of him to exit his conscious identity and enter the world of the retarded and the crazy, to relate to the old and sick, to smell not only the fragrance of youth but the stench of death, as well. Only when respectful to his shadow, will he humbly be in charge of his interior ward; on condition, he is aware that he is not director of the hospital.

The Terrible Mother, who lingers in the abyss and threatens to draw the child back into the bottomless pit of nothingness and non-existence, also instigates toward movement and development. If it were not for her and her emissaries, such as the serpent, many or most might chose to dwell in the eternal bliss of Paradise.

Some deserted, exposed orphans, such as for instance Asclepius, Oedipus and Moses, taken care of by animals or compassionate humans, grow up to become the heroes that bridge the divine and the human. In so doing, they fulfill the task of the *puer*, of the young person.

Concurrently with the child's development into a human being, it experiences the abandonment of archetypal fantasy. That is, the experience of abandonment is the psychological manifestation of departing from dwelling in the archetypal world, which is a necessary stage in the development of the ego. Many mythological heroes are abandoned orphans, because the hero's crucial struggle is to release the ego from being in the grips of the archetypal world of the Great Mother, who, in fact, *is* the archetypal world.

We only need to read Dickens to get the feeling tone of the orphaned, abandoned and maltreated child. His experience as a twelve-year-old boy working in the warehouse, and his father imprisoned because of debts, was the secret agony of his soul. He portrays the horrors of childhood in David Copperfield, who is persecuted by his stepfather and whose beloved mother dies in childbirth. In Oliver Twist we find the poor, good orphan child who has to deal with a corrupt and evil world. Andersen's *Little Match Girl*,[212] who freezes to death on New Year's Eve, whose only comfort is found as her grandmother embraces her in death, is no less of a heart-breaking picture of misery.

I think it is in lieu of the necessary abandonment that the archetypal fantasy of *The Good Parents* constellates, because abandonment pertains to the stage when the archetypal projection upon the personal parents is withdrawn. They are no longer seen as omnipotent. The archetype splits, which is necessary in personal development, and the parents become more human and complex. The archetype constellates as a fantasy, for instance of the royal couple, or the poor but truthfully good peasants, who are the child's, as it were, 'real' parents.

Jung held on to the fantasy of being a descendent of Goethe,[213] and Erik Erikson had a fantasy throughout his life that his father had be-

---

212  Hans Christian Andersen, *The Complete Illustrated Works*, pp. 357-359.

213  Barbara Hannah writes, "The rumor that the elder Carl Gustav Jung was a natural son of Goethe should be mentioned here. Jung spoke of this to me more than once, but I did not receive the impression that he took the rumor seriously. Rather, the existence of this singularly persistent idea—against all the external evidence—was exceedingly interesting to him in and for itself, taken in connection with the enormous impression that *Faust* had made

longed to the Danish royal family. As his daughter says, "my father found much comfort in the thought that his father might have been of noble birth; thus an abandoning parent was transformed into a source of pride."[214]

Abandonment distinctly reflects the difference between complex and trauma. As an actual event in childhood, being abandoned by a parent due to loss, abuse, violence or likewise, inflicts a catastrophic wound, even if there are victims that appear to, or actually do cope well. It will often lead to a compensatory search for protection. Not only physical, but emotional and psychological maltreatment imply, as well, parental abandonment. Yet, even the person who has not been exposed to the *trauma* of abandonment can usually with ease recognize *feelings* of abandonment, since abandonment is archetypal.

Avivit[215] had been divorced for six years when at the age of forty-six she came for therapy. Her husband, eight years her elder, had left her after she had found out that he had a long-term relationship with the principal of the school in which she worked as a teacher. All their four relatively grown-up children had sided with the father, accepting his need for a relationship with a more mature woman. They all considered Avivit to be a "child-mother." She herself was aware that her husband had been both father and mother, and in a resigned, childish voice she said she was "the smallest of all the children."

When Avivit was three, her parents had divorced, and within weeks, both moved in with new partners; "New?" she wondered, "Perhaps they both had had these relationships a long time? Just like my husband? Only that in their, my parents' case, both had betrayed each other." She was her parents' only child, but before she turned ten, she had six siblings, and felt mostly that she had to "get out of the way." She remained with her mother, her new husband, and eventually their four children, in the village where she was born, while her father had moved to a nearby town. He rarely came to visit, and she did not recall ever visiting him. Only when she served in the army, did she demand to meet him in cafés. She said,

---

upon him ..." (*Jung: His Life and Work*, p. 22). Aniela Jaffé points out that we "should not ascribe too much significance to this 'little great-grandfather' legend ... Jung's references to it are generally characterized by a playful tone. What was more important was Jung's sense of a spiritual affinity to Goethe" (*C. G. Jung: Word and Image*, p. 11). Henri F. Ellenberger does make a point out of the physical resemblance between Goethe and Carl Gustav Jung the elder (*The Discovery of the Unconscious*, p. 661).

214  Sue Erikson Bloland, *Fame: The Power and Cost of a Fantasy*.
215  Avivit, 'spring-like' in Hebrew.

> I don't think my mother's husband wanted me to see my father. I used to have a fantasy that he and my mother prevented my father to come and see me, and that he had to overcome all kinds of obstructions the few times he appeared. Only when I grew older did I painfully realize that he wasn't that keen to see me, busy with his new little family. Unlike my mother's husband, who insisted I call him 'dad,' but who had fits of rage and was violent, my real father was a very nice man, but perhaps weak, and perhaps couldn't really stand up against his wife. I feel sorry for him.

During her childhood, Avivit would have fantasies that her father would appear in the middle of the night and carry her away, holding her lovingly in his arms.

Avivit's feelings of abandonment were not only an internal manifestation of her psychological development, but echoed her actual childhood experience. She was very well-adapted, "I quickly learned that crying didn't get me anywhere but to punishment," and outwardly capable. She had been accepted for officers' training, but soon disqualified because she was unable to take the responsibility of a commander. At twenty she met her future husband, who was enchanted by her seeming joie-de-vivre. He probably became disillusioned when he discovered this was only an external façade, a vulnerable persona behind which Avivit's underlying depression lingered. When the children were born, her immaturity surfaced visibly. Avivit herself needed her husband more as a father than for them to be equal partner. He may have remained in the marriage out of a sense of responsibility, if it were not for Avivit, who demanded a divorce when she discovered his extra-marital relationship. She had obviously found it particularly humiliating that this had carried on for a long period of time with the principal of her school.

Many of Avivit's dreams centered on abandonment. She would dream that "I am walking barefoot in the street, but have lost my direction," or "I go and visit my aunt at the kibbutz, then I go to the dining hall, but as they hardly use it anymore, it is dark and I am all alone."

Her self-image as an abandoned child kept searching for conscious expression and manifestation, both in her dreams as well as in her somewhat promiscuous behavior. After her divorce, she would easily and indiscriminately fall in love "with nearly everyone I passed in the street." Within weeks she would want to move in with the man, any man, thus repeating her parents' act of divorce and quick remarriage.

However, this seemingly scared away every man she met. While she claimed she could understand them, she was unable to refrain from compulsively repeating this pattern. She thus remained fixated in her own trauma of abandonment, unable to wrestle herself out of the archetypal fantasy of dwelling in a unitary, symbiotic reality.

## Pathology

We can distinguish three categories of pathology pertaining to the *child* archetype. Connected to the archetypal dimension, these pathologies are not confined merely to the period of actual childhood, but may be present at various stages of life:

i. Remaining *too close to annihilation*, not having the aggressive life-force necessary to move away from the dark abyss of chaos, emptiness and nothingness. This is a, sometimes psychotic, condition of engulfment and destruction, a deep and terrifying experience that there are no human hands that hold and protect. There is no human harbor in which to put down anchor; there is not even an anchor to put down.

   We recognize this condition in images of annihilation, such as mass graves and the burning pit in Treblinka. We find it, as well, in dreams and anxieties of being thrown off the cliff, of falling into a black hole or total darkness, into nothingness, or losing the ground under one's feet. It may take the shape of being outside the boundaries, control and consciousness of one's ego, or invaded by dark, black, or monstrous forces, or suicidal fantasies of crashing into the abyss; or, a common theme in dreams, Satan's fall from the sky, now often in the image of airplane crashes.

   The archetypal nucleus here is the rupture at the very edge of coming-into-being. This archetypal idea resides in all of us. It may emerge as images in dreams and non-psychotic symptoms. However, when the archetypal idea has constellated prominently in real life, for instance because of a physical or psychological threat to the infant's life, such as the absence of human hands that hold and carry the infant away from the threat of falling back into the abyss, then the rupture in the individual's soul may actually take on psychotic dimensions.

ii. *The orphan child.* The divine child needs to be mothered, and to be "let be in being" but not abandoned, just held and related to, for the flame of divinity not to be extinguished. The orphan child has not been fully held by human hands, by personalized parenting. He or she has been abandoned prematurely and left to his fate and destiny. His *divine childhood* may have been too short or non-existent. This is prominently the case with children who have suffered abuse, neglect and rejection, but also those who very early were heavily burdened by parental expectations, often emanating from parental incapacity to carry their own shadow, thereby projecting unfulfilled or compensatory expectations onto their children. Such burdensome projections may extinguish the spark of life and hamper the sense of joy of life. Likewise, parental obsessions, such as premature concern with toilet training and cleanliness at the expense of Eros, may deepen the sense of abandonment.

While the phenomenological, though not necessarily clinical essence of the abyss is psychosis, this is not the case in abandonment (though clinically, it may, as well, trigger psychotic reactions). Too early or drastic abandonment of the paradisiacal and blissful aspects of childhood, entailing for instance separation of the World Parents, sometimes concretely taking place by early parental divorce, does not pertain to the dark side of the Self, but to the ego's sense of loneliness, abandonment and possible estrangement.

iii. The third pathological category would be the *failure to abandon paradise*. As a result, the ego's development is impaired. We find this in the *puer aeternus*, the eternal youth, often with a sociopathic stroke, immature and irresponsible. Longing back is natural, but remaining there becomes psychotic; identification with it characterizes the *puer aeternus*, the eternal youth, who is "all promises and no fulfillment."[216] The longing for paradise entails the desire to avoid life's necessary and unavoidable conflicts. The puer's identification with original wholeness disables him, in as much as actual work and accomplishments necessarily entail the giving up of other potential possibilities. Commonly, a puer will dream of being trapped or imprisoned, because adult reality, reality outside paradise, may be experienced as a prison.

A perhaps far-fetched example would be the aristocracy of olden times that dwelled in an eternal childhood paradise of castles, gardens, play and hunting—something that quickly smacks of corruption and ridicule. And in the post-modern era, when the boundaries between fantasy and reality, as well as play and work on the computer become blurred, the propensity for living in a never-ending wonderland increases.

One young man, a gifted musician, had been over-protected by his devoted and admiring parents. As he began to move out into the world of everyday reality, he started to have fainting spells. He had incubated far too long in the well-tended and protected garden of his mothering parents. As Adler says,

---

216 *Ego and Archetype*, p. 14.

> How seductive and enchanting is the prospect of remain-
> ing sheltered in this magic world—how cold and cruel ap-
> pear the hard, sharp contours of the conscious ego in com-
> parison.[217]

In summary, we discern three central images of the Child:

Firstly, the essence of the child archetype is *divinity*, the connection between the unconscious and consciousness, at the interface between the archetypal dimension and the realm of the human, which, how-ever, is not yet fully personalized. Here we find the archetypal image of the divine child, reclining, playing and finding pleasure in paradise, that is, in the realm of the Good Mother.

Secondly, the shadow aspect of divinity is the hell of nothingness, the anxiety of annihilation, the abyss of chaos and disintegration, which the ego often struggles with an entire lifetime to avoid, and that the senex within us will have to come to terms with, as he returns to face death and disintegration at the end of one's days. Yet, nothingness and the abyss pertain to the Self as much as wholeness and divinity. The abyss that threatens to annihilate the vulnerable new-born child is a manifestation of the Terrible Mother who constantly lurks in the dark, threatening to destroy and draw us back into non-existence.

The germinating ego's dwelling in these two realms entails the pri-mary manifestation of the Self in the human realm, and the beginning of its splitting into wholeness and nothingness. At this stage, the split is in the realm of the Mother, while later, as consciousness and the ego develop, the split is between Mother and Father.[218]

Thirdly, the ego's departure from dwelling in the realm of the pri-mary Self, crystallizes in the image of the orphaned child within us, the wounded child who has not been well-enough cared for, with con-comitant feelings of abandonment. This dramatic departure is inevita-bly accompanied by a sense of loneliness and abandonment, which is incongruous to the feeling of having been well-enough cared for. This is one of the common motivating forces that drive people to seek therapy. It is an intrinsic aspect of the child archetype to give up the divine child of paradise, with its unavoidable feelings of loss.

---

217  *Studies in Analytical Psychology*, p. 128..
218  See for instance *The Complex*, p. 81ff.

III

# The Puer and the Puella

## Between Shame and Fear

Who are they—the young man and the maiden—the *puer* and the *puella*?

We easily recognize them in everyday confrontations with moody teenagers, when sexual desire competes with dark rage, the one setting the house on fire, the other breaking up the walls. Alternatively, and even worse, inexplicable withdrawal makes the earth quake in deadening silence.

There is beauty struggling with acne, and tender sensuality trying to contain awkward clumsiness. Eros and desire break through the face of insecure constraint, mercilessly exposing their blushing flare. Hope for the future competes with anxiety of failure and apocalyptic fears.

Art and poetry, mythology, music and literature, abound with tales and pictures of the pain, suffering and sorrow of young Werthers, of hidden loneliness when the birds sing out of tune in a world without love, of trying to save the child in a world characterized by alienation and wicked adults, of the heights of falling in love, and then, perhaps of the inevitable and steep climb out of the abyss of opaque emptiness.

When young and unfortunate Actaeon, Cadmus's grandson, steals sight of the beautiful maiden goddess Diana, bathing undressed in the fountain, he becomes understandably speechless. Diana transforms him, as it were, from stag to stag, from having turned up unaccompanied at the party of the naked nymphs, to a stag with "antlers on his wet head." And as he flees in fear, he wonders, "what to do? go home? to royal palace? hide in woods? shame blocks one, fear the other ..."[219]

---

219  Charles Boer, *Ovid's Metamorphoses*, p. 54.

How painful is the conflict of youth, to be trapped between shame and fear! Shame blocks the regressive return to the safety of childhood's royal palace, while slinking into the woods, where secrets of desire and the treasures of passion lie hidden, may be all too frightening. Eventually, however clumsy, the lad will have to overcome his fears and venture into the virgin forest, and the maiden will turn the stones to find and anxiously open the moss-covered treasure shrine.

Serving as a narrow and dangerous bridge between childhood and the adult world, the puer functions not along the horizontal road of linear development, but attempts, rather, to unite what is above with what dwells below. "The horizontal world, the space-time continuum which we call 'reality,'" says Hillman, "is not its world." Furthermore, the puer is "weak on the earth, because it is not at home on earth. Its direction is vertical." The puer has a "propensity of flying and falling."[220]

In his playful puerility and poetic language, Hillman beautifully portrays the ups and downs of youth. Noticeably, he calls the puer *it*, presumably not as a sign of political correctness, but a manifestation of the puer's blurry gender boundaries and more fluid identity.

Hillman describes the temporality and verticality, the transiency and the loftiness of the puer, for whom "[t]he beginnings of things are *Einfalle*; they fall in on one from above as gifts .. or sprout up out of the ground as daktyls, as flowers." And he continues,

> Its wandering is as the spirit wanders, without attachment and not as an odyssey of experience. It wanders to spend or to capture, and to ignite, to try its luck, but not with the aim of going home. ... The puer ... understands little of what is gained by repetition and constancy, that is, by work, or of the moving back and forth, left and right, in and out, which makes for subtlety in proceeding step by step through the labyrinthine complexity of the horizontal world. These teachings but cripple its winged heels, ... [i]t is anyway not meant to walk, but to fly.
>
> But the direct connection to the spirit can be indirect or, rather, can be mis-directed through or by the Great Mother ... who is in love with [the puer figures] as carriers of the spirit; ... She feeds their fire with animal desire and fans their flame with promise of scope and conquest over the horizontal world, her world of matter.[221]

---

220  James Hillman, Senex and Puer, in *Puer Papers*, p. 24.
221  *Puer Papers*, pp. 24-25.

Even at the risk of death, the puer has to conquer, or at least resist as much as possible the dullness of the adult world, with its customs and suffocating stability. Mediocrity is a curse. There are no alternatives to complete success or death. The puer knows well that anger may serve as an antidote to boredom, and the angry young man may all too easily find himself tired and weary of this world.

Flora, a sixty-five-year-old woman, had always resisted settling down. She had lived the life of a *puella aeterna*, a youthful life of travel and adventure free of commitments. However, as Edinger says, "to be something in reality [the puer] must give up being everything *in potentia*."[222] Lately, she had developed symptoms of anxiety and depression. She shared the following dream,

> I live on the 15th floor. I am forcefully told to leave, and move into an apartment at ground floor. I don't like this apartment—*I really don't like it*! There are walls between the rooms, but doors have not been installed yet, and it is not clear which room is which. I am told I have to do my matriculation exam, but since I don't have a cognitive plan, or map yet of the apartment, I can't go for the exam.

The dreamer is compelled by an unknown force to leave the life she lives, high up on the 15th floor. She is required to mature,[223] to settle in close to the street and the earth at ground floor, but she does not have the plan. She has lived disconnected from grounded reality, without a map to guide her. Her maturational process entails gaining access to the map of the territory, to *under*stand the ground on which she stands.

She reluctantly finds herself in a place with differentiating walls, however without doors, yet to be installed. "[D]oors have soul," says Robert Sardello, "They are guardians of boundaries, they serve both to divide and to connect the psychic topography of the house, keeping its imagination multiple, and each part in direct or indirect relation with every other part."[224] Without doors there is separation without transition, preventing movement between the spheres. In this locked in condition the air is stale. This may reflect the common feeling of suffocation that many a teenager experiences at home. The need to breathe fresh air propels them out and away from the imprisoning walls of their parents' home.

---

222  *Ego and Archetype*, p. 14.
223  In Hebrew, maturation and matriculation stem from the same etymological root, b-g-r.
224  Robert Sardello, *Facing the World with Soul*, p. 36.

Flora was in the grips of her parental complexes. She felt devastated and furious whenever she sensed the tiniest trace of similarity with her mother, whom she thought of as "a stiff and old person, hardly a woman, no softness, probably from the day she was born." In contrast, she made conscious efforts to be like her "mad and always playful" father, and felt pleased when she managed to draw anger from the adults, which "always was the case with Dad—he always played with people, teasing them, managing to make them crazy."

While she did not feel that her life-style was morally or otherwise wrong, she felt an urge to settle down and accommodate for her aging process. However, reflecting this painful process, she brought the following dream a few weeks later,

> I am on a sailboat, it's wonderful! The waves, the seawater splashing my face, the fresh wind, what energy! Then, suddenly, the wind turns, it's in my back, threatens to push me overboard, the sea becomes frighteningly rough, I am at a loss. Then the scene changes, and I am lying flat on my back, under the ground as if in a grave, with a fifteen floors high structure on top of me. This entire structure is like thin, empty façades, just an empty space within. It is the emptiness that makes it heavy.

The sudden change of the wind indicates a cruel and relentless turn from youthful joy to a sense of being buried under the emptiness of her life. Just like the puer serves as transition between child and adult, the adult serves the same function between the puer and the senex. Thus, overly delayed transition into adulthood sometimes causes the puer to age prematurely, suffering the weight of the heavy burden that seems to have been placed so abruptly on his shoulders.

## Wine, Spirit and Fire

To the earth of horizontal reality, the linearity of the adult ego, the puer brings the vertical axis of wine and fire, soul and spirit. Diotima from Mantinea tells Socrates that, "Spirits are midway between what is divine and what is human," and thus act as "interpreter[s] and means of communication between gods and men."[225]

The puer is like Dionysus, god of wine and harvest of the grapes. He is like the grapes of the earth elevated to spirit. The 'grapes of wine' is

---

225  *Symposium and the Death of Socrates*, (Symposium 202), p. 36.

the spirit hidden in matter, the transformation from below upwards, the inspiration elevating from the ground. The puer refuses to take part in the flatness and grayness of the adult world; he needs to burn the matter into spirit and to fire the instincts into passion. The puer, as Peter Tatham says, "is not just to do with boys but is an image of the dynamics of change itself ... the very process itself by means of which the present transforms itself into something fresh."[226]

Like the child who is close to water—the Chinese say all life comes from the waters, phylogenetically life in water precedes life on land; and Freud says, "Birth is almost invariably represented by something which has a connection with water"[227]—the puer carries *the torch of fire*. There is fire of air, spirituality and consciousness, and there is fire of earth, of body and of passion, as well as Hestia, the hearth's fire of home. In adolescent rites of passage, the young initiate often has to pass through fire. Much adolescent activity involves and revolves around fire. Fire is played with, gathered around, experienced. Teenagers are often fascinated by fire, for instance playing with matches for hours, seemingly in a state of trance. When pathological, we have a mania of fire, pyromania.

Fire has to be confronted, experienced, dealt with, and controlled, so that it can be utilized constructively. If fire is left to nature alone, it becomes untamed and destructive. Fire may light up the Logos, igniting enlightenment and consciousness. The flames of Eros make our hearts burn of desire and passionately long for the heat and the touch of the other. The Martian fire of fury may leave bridges burned by hatred and revenge, the scorched earth of death and devastation.

Fire may be utilized for human creation, but as a natural transformative energy, it is inherently bipolar, and may be as destructive as it can be constructive. Fire-rites entail the acculturation of fire, a Promethean act of stealing from the gods and handing it over to man, to make purposeful use of it. These rites and activities constitute a transitional space, in which freedom from parental and social super-ego authority enables the young to experience their own feelings and their own fire. Consequently, it now comes under their control and responsibility.[228]

Rites of initiation and transition enable the termination and internalization of one stage of life, and the entrance into another, noticeably so in adolescence. We are less accustomed in today's world to rite

---

226  Peter Tatham, *The Makings of Maleness*, p. 25
227  Sigmund Freud, *Introductory Lectures on Psychoanalysis*, SE 15, p. 153.
228  *The Hero and His Shadow*, pp. 5-6.

and ritual than in the past. However, we sometimes see how they oc-
cur in dreams. One teenager, who had been required to see a therapist
after several incidents of participating in minor burglaries, brought a
dream to his therapist after approximately half a year of hard work—
more on behalf of the therapist than the young man. In the seemingly
simple, but, to the young man, very disturbing dream, he found himself confined to a small, approximately ten square meters playground,
surrounded by insurmountable walls. In the dream he then notices that
there is hole in one of the walls. It would not be difficult for him to
leave; all he would need to do is to *bend down low*. But even if the
pleasure of play turns into a prison when boundaries of morality and
maturity are ignored, the seemingly simple message of humbly bending low is not easily adhered to. As legend tells us, there seem to be no
miracles in the world today, because we do not bend down low enough
to notice.

## Hero and Torchbearer

The puer brings the divine fire from above down to earth, to human
use and conscious control. This is the fire of Prometheus, whose name
means *forethinker*. The Promethean fire is the capacity to *plan* the use of
that natural transformative energy, fire, for the benefit of humankind,
to create light, consciousness and acculturation, heating and cooking,
creating new materials and new ideas. However, just as it brings light
and progress, by its very nature, fire, if not handled skillfully and with
care, may well destroy whatever it has enabled us to construct. Persephone, the daughter of Demeter, whom Hades abducted into the netherworld, prominently represents the Kore, the maiden in Greek mythology. Her name means *she who destroys the light*—the fiery energies
of youth may bring light to humanity, or destroy it.

The puer brings the dawn of a new day in the evolution of human
consciousness. Thus the angel, the messenger of God, appears to Moses, whose task it is to bring the commandments to the awareness of
man, in a flame of fire, in the midst of the bush. The entire scene of
the burning bush is one of transition between the divine and the personal. Thus, the bush is not consumed by the fire. The fire is not left to
its unconscious destructive nature. Likewise, Moses takes off his shoes,
respectful of the holy ground on which he stands.[229]

---

229   Exodus 3: 2-5. Cf. Jason, whose one foot remains bare after carrying Hera
across the river; see above, p. 34f.

The puer abandons childhood but tries to retain divinity, struggling with a down-to-earth world of adult grayness. The puer is full of hilarious hopes and expectations—or in tristful lack thereof. He, or she, is full of passion—or suffers its painful absence and its hurting wounds.

## The Hero

The puer is the hero who steals, revolts and sets on fire. His heroic task is dual: firstly, his (and equally her) task is to personalize the archetypal, to wrestle himself out of the grip of the archetypal world. This is primarily done by means of the complexes. With the help of complexes, the archetypes are, as it were, sliced up, dismembered, so that they can be fed and internalized into the human ego. We see this process already in the infant and small child, for instance when it crawls around, taking hold of new objects, chewing them one by one in the process of incorporation. This is not merely a process of internalizing the external world, but making it comprehensible. The objects of the world become differentiated and identified by the process of chewing.

The hero's second task is to bring sparks of the divine, as represented by the Self in the human soul, into the life of the ego, of conscious identity, into the realm of reality and the boundaries and limitations of ego-reality. Thereby the ego will preserve its roots in the Self, and can adequately shine of splendor.

The *tragic hero* is caught, killed or imprisoned by the divine. If he goes too far, is too virtuous or makes an error in judgment, the gods are likely to take revenge. They may reverse his attempts at determining his destiny, and return him to the fold of misfortune and disastrous fate. Oedipus becomes the condemned, blind and sick wanderer, his sons killing each other, and Prometheus is nailed to the cliff, the eagle pecking out his liver every day.

Thus, the hero revolts against the gods, against the archetypes, by *theft*. However, his revolt is no less against the earthly kings. The young hero detests the earth-bound kingdom of materialism, as represented by his parents' generation, refusing to let his divine self and lofty ideals be smothered and crushed by the discipline and orderliness of the ego. At this stage in his or her life, he will accuse his poor parents, whom he often experiences as having fallen flat to the earth, shamefully subjugating to the falseness of this world, for lack of spirit and ideals.

The characteristic aggressiveness of adolescence is, as Adler says, an outward manifestation of the inner conflict inherent in the task of breaking away from identification with the archetypal, and "step[ping] into the world of the individual ego."[230]

No one seems better suited than Prometheus the forethinker, to steal the fire from the iron-fisted and punitive gods.


## Prometheus—the Thoughtful Thief

The Titans, enormous in strength and incredible in size, were god-like personifications of the forces of nature that preceded the younger Olympian gods. Cronus, youngest son of Gaia and Uranus, ruled over his sibling Titans, until his son Zeus behaved like many an oedipal son, dethroned him and seized power.

Prometheus was a son of the Titan Iapetus. His mother is likely to have been his father's sister Themis. Thus, he was born from an incestuous relationship—not an uncommon theme, those days. There are those that say that Themis, goddess of good counsel, was the mother, as well, of the Moirai. If so, Prometheus was half-brother of the three Fates. However, others claim his mother was Clymene, renowned goddess of fame and disgrace.

His brothers Atlas and Menoetius, the latter whose name means 'ruined strength,' bet on the wrong party and sided with their fellow Titans in the ten-year war with the gods, in which the Titans were defeated. The gods therefore punished them; Atlas was condemned to uphold the sky so that it would be separated from the earth. His enormous task was instrumental in the life of every human child—to keep his parents, Gaia and Uranus, Earth and Sky, apart, so that there will be enough space for an independent ego to develop.

Prometheus together with his brother Epimetheus, on the other hand, had joined the winning side of Zeus, thus betraying their own folks. Zeus, the upcoming god, should have perhaps learned his lesson, and been more aware of Prometheus' ability to think ahead independently, and betray.

When the gods decided to create man—certainly a questionable decision and a sensitive mission—they delegated the task to Prometheus and his brother. Epimetheus, however, had an impulsive, somewhat immature personality. Before giving shape to man, he did not heed the

---

230  *Studies in Analytical Psychology*, p. 128.

warning not to accept any gift from the gods. Thus, he gave all the best of the god-given gifts to the animals: strength and swiftness, courage and shrewd cunning, fur, feathers, wings and shells—until no good was left for man, no protective covering and no quality to make them a match for the beasts. Too late, as always, he felt regret, and had to ask for his thoughtful brother's help.

Prometheus, then, took over the task of creation and thought of a way to make humanity superior. He molded man out of clay and water, and formed him in a nobler shape than the animals, upright like the gods.

When the human race was later extinguished by a flood, the sole survivors were Deucalion, son of Prometheus, whose name may mean the new, sweet wine and the fisherman, and Pyrrha, the fiery one, the first mortal-born woman, daughter of Epimetheus and Pandora. Like Biblical Noah, Deucalion and Pyrrha survived the flood by sailing their ark until the water subsided. Consequently, humankind after the flood, after the waters, owes its existence to them; perhaps the flood and the river and the waters necessarily precede mankind, to be followed by Pyrrha, the fiery one, and the sweet wine that rises from the soil.[231] Perhaps they are the necessity, the Ananke that molds the contours of human fate, within which destiny can be shaped, so that life can be induced with spirit and a sense of meaningful passion.

The gods demanded constant sacrifice from man, who had a hard time finding food for himself. Prometheus persuaded Zeus to allow humans to sacrifice only a part of the slaughtered animal, not the whole beast. He then deceived the gods by wrapping up bones and skin for them in an enticing package, while he left the nourishing meat for mankind. Zeus became furious when he opened the package, taking the white fat, only to discover the bones. But having made his choice, he had to abide by it. Thereafter only fat and bones were burned to the gods upon their altars, while humans kept the good meat for themselves. Thus, the lot of man improved, but Zeus never forgave Prometheus for his rebellious trick.

However, humans were still unable to keep warm, cook their food, or make tools for farming, since fire was reserved for the gods. Prometheus was determined to help humankind. He went to heaven, to the sun, where he lit a torch and this way stole the fire from the gods. He hid it in a trunk, carrying it secretly down to earth. Fire was "a protection to

---

231  Noah, the tiller of the soil, was the first to plant a vineyard (Genesis 9:20).

men far better than anything else, whether fur or feathers or strength or swiftness."[232]

Zeus was enraged, and swore to take revenge, first on humankind and then on Prometheus, "the immortal prototype of man as the original rebel," as Kerényi defines Goethe's Prometheus.[233] Since only men were upon earth, the suitable punishment, Zeus thought, would be to create woman. With the help of Hephaestus, he made a sweet and lovely thing to look upon, a shy maiden. All the gods gave her gifts, silvery garments and an embroidered veil, a wonder to behold, and bright garlands of blooming flowers and a crown of gold, from which great beauty shined. Because of all that the gods gave her, they called her Pandora, the gift of all. Wonder took hold of gods and men when they beheld her. Vered Lev Kenaan writes that her "radiant appearance is, as the text tells us more than once, *thauma idesthai*, 'a wonder to see.'" Wonder, Plato observed, is the beginning of philosophy. "Wonder is the feeling, or the mood, or the kind of experience that presents the world to us in a manner calling for our reflection,"[234] the essence of lunar consciousness.

Yet, Hesiod also makes his view unmistakably clear when he says that from Pandora emanate "the deadly race and tribes of women, a great plague to mortals."[235]

The gods presented her with a box into which each had put something evil and harmful, and forbade her ever to open it. They then sent her to Epimetheus, who took her gladly, although Prometheus had warned him never to accept anything from Zeus. Pandora could not resist her curiosity. She needed to know what was in the box. She lifted the lid, and out flew innumerable plagues, sorrow and troubles, wickedness and deceit. In terror, Pandora closed the lid, but too late. Only the feather of hope, which was the only good the casket had held among

---

232  Edith Hamilton, *Mythology: Timeless Tales of Gods and Heroes*, p. 69.

233  Carl Kerényi, *Prometheus: Archetypal Image of Human Existence*, p. 17.

234  Vered Lev Kenaan, *Pandora's Senses*, p. 41.

235  *Theogony*, line 590-591, in *Hesiod's Theogony*, p. 62f. Hesiod's view of woman is, and was fortunately not shared by every man. However, "wherever the male's ego-development is disturbed and he has not attained independence … every demand to develop toward something unknown and away from whatever provides security, is answered with fear and defensiveness … Only when a man related to his Self can collaborate and conflict with the foreignness and otherness of another Self, or with a different facet of his Self represented by a woman, can a relationship bear the fruit of the authentic encounter of two individuals." (Erich Neumann, *The Fear of the Feminine*, p. 253f.).

the many evils, remained, and it remains to this day a comfort for humankind in misfortune.[236]

Zeus had his servants *Might* and *Violence* seize Prometheus and bring him to the Caucasus Mountains, "The tract of Scythia, waste untrod by man."[237] He then ordered Hephaestus, the smith-god, to nail Prometheus to a cliff, and sent an eagle each day to peck out his liver, which grew again each night.

As faithful servants to the god, Might and Violence told Prometheus,

> Forever shall the intolerable present grind you down.
> And he who will release you is not born.
> Such fruit you reap for your man-loving ways.
> A god yourself, you did not dread God's anger,
> But gave to mortals honor not their due.
> And therefore you must guard this joyless rock—
> No rest, no sleep, no moment's respite.
> Groans shall your speech be, lamentation your only words.

"But nothing, no threat, nor torture, could break Prometheus" for the thirty thousand years his torment persisted. "His body was bound but his spirit was free," says Hamilton. Is this not the duality of conscious human existence, to be eternally bound by limitations, yet with the possible and potential freedom of thought and spirit, for which we then might be punished by the pain and the torment that consciousness often brings?

Hermes asks Prometheus to surrender, but unrelentingly the latter tells him,

> There is no force which can compel my speech.
> So let Zeus hurl his blazing bolts,
> And with the white wings of the snow,
> With thunder and with earthquake,
> Confound the reeling world.
> None of all this will bend my will.[238]

---

236 However, there may, perhaps, be circumstances in which it seems that even the feather has lost its hope, and hope needs to find a different image, cf. Erel Shalit, *Requiem: A Tale of Exile and Return*, p. 3.
237 *Prometheus Bound*, p. 1.
238 *Mythology: Timeless Tales of Gods and Heroes*, pp. 72-73.

Nothing, says Prometheus, will bend his will. His will power is enormous, and forms the essence of the very ego consciousness that his fire engenders.

Eventually, Hercules slew the eagle and delivered Prometheus from his bonds. "The name of Prometheus," says Hamilton, "has stood through all the centuries, from Greek days to our own, as that of the great rebel against injustice and the authority of power."[239]

Prometheus represents the puer's task of bringing the divine into humankind. Like other sun-heroes, he has one foot in heaven, one on earth, one in the realm of the gods, and one in the sphere of man. He is half god, half man. This delicate balance is established by Prometheus' grand act of splitting the sacrifice between man and the gods, signifying, as Edinger says, "a separation of the ego from its archetypal origins."[240]

For ego and consciousness to be born and to develop, this separation of the ego from its origins is necessary. It is enabled by the hard work of Atlas, who carries the heavy burden of keeping the original opposites, the world parents, earth and sky, apart, so that man can walk upright; thus, the ego can grow.

The gods, the archetypal forces, do not willingly share the energy of their meat. There is a need to deceive them, to steal from them. Yet, the ego, humans on earth, must not take all. When they grab it all, they have dethroned the gods, the archetypes, and the spirit is lost. The ego is elevated to autocratic ruler. Nevertheless, by taking the meat for themselves, humans gains energy, whereby the ego no longer remains passively in the grip of archetypal forces.

The other great act of Prometheus is the theft of fire. Hereby humans gain control of that natural transformative energy, which when merely razing outside the realms of the ego may be the destructive fire of nature, of falling prey to uncontrollable passion or rage. In the hands of the Promethean capability of consciousness and 'thinking ahead,' fire may, as has been mentioned, serve acculturation, light, warmth and relatedness, conscious will, focus and intention. Hephaestus and Hestia each signify two important aspects of the civilized fire, the crafts and the home.

However, like everything archetypal, consciousness is bipolar. It entails Promethean forethought as well as the afterthought of Epimetheus. They coexist. Epimetheus, as desire and impulsiveness, when not bal-

---

239  *Mythology: Timeless Tales of Gods and Heroes,* p. 73.
240  Edward Edinger, *The Eternal Drama,* p. 12.

anced by forethought, is the adolescent's hurried action, his misguided or undirected libido. Even curiosity, like Pandora, so necessary for humankind's development, needs the balancing constraint of the adult, so as not to unleash all the evils that come with consciousness; something that scientific development and progress sometimes seem to be painfully unaware of. Do we reflect in a thoughtful manner, when headless frogs and flying fish, humans cloned with computers, and many other aspects of post-modern deconstruction and deconstructed hybridism is what we allow our frenzy for change and novelty lead us to create without restraint?

Not only was Prometheus punished by being bound to the cliff, but an eagle also pecked out his liver every night. Plato tells us, that God "placed in the liver the seat of divination," whose function it is to "reflect images from the ... soul above"—terrifying images by its bitterness, joyful ones by its sweetness. The liver produces gall, which according to the physicians of ancient Greece, emptied its bitter substance into the heart and the lungs, and was responsible for "the strong emotions of love and elation but especially the darker strains of hate, fear, grief and defiance."[241]

Jung refers to the liver, commenting on his dream about Liverpool, which he tells in *Memories, Dreams, Reflections,*

> I found myself in a dirty, sooty city. It was night, and winter, and dark, and raining. I was in Liverpool. With a number of Swiss ... I walked through the dark streets. It reminded me of Basel, where the market is down below and then you go up through the Totengässchen ("Alley of the Dead") ... When we reached the plateau, we found a broad square dimly illuminated by street lights, into which many streets converged. The various quarters of the city were arranged radially around the square. In the center was a round pool, and in the middle of it a small island. While everything round about was obscured by rain, fog, smoke, and dimly lit darkness, the little island blazed with sunlight. On it stood a single tree, a magnolia, in a shower of reddish blossoms. It was as though the tree stood in the sunlight and were at the same time the source of light.[242]

In his comment to the dream, Jung says,

---

241  George, R. Elder, *The Body: An Encyclopedia of Archetypal Symbolism, Vol. 2,* pp. 269-270.
242  *Memories, Dreams, Reflections,* p.197f.

> Everything was extremely unpleasant, black and opaque—
> just as I felt then. But I had had a vision of unearthly beau-
> ty, and that was why I was able to live at all. Liverpool is
> "the pool of life." The "liver," according to an old view, is
> the seat of life—that which "makes to live."[243]

Prometheus used the gall, the secretion of the "seat of the divine," that is, of the Self, to deflect the fire from the Self to the ego, from the divine into human consciousness. This act of defiance against the gods, essential to the process of separation-individuation, brings with it the "gnawing" sense of guilt, eternal picking on the seat of life, and the bonds of creative depression—remember, it is Hephaestus, the master craftsman, that chains Prometheus to the mountain, who feels pain and guilt for what he is doing to Prometheus. "O most abhorrent hand-icraft of mine!" he exclaims. Zeus' servant *Might*, however, urges him on, "Why do you hate it? In plain truth, your art is guiltless of the work that's now to do."[244]

The eagle of Zeus, the divine fatherly spirit, picks on Prometheus' vital energy, the life force that takes its vigor from the divine, yet turns against the gods. The struggle goes on incessantly, day and night, in-jury and recovery, between divine spirit and human consciousness.

Creativity is the energy that brings them together, and youthful de-fiance, the force that dares to extract, to steal, both the instinct and the spirit as well as the meat and the fire, that need to be deferred from the archetypal to the personal. The price to be paid is often the juvenile torments of being torn between sublime and elevated heights, and the earthly gloom of grown-ups.


## Puer Pathology

Several psychopathological categories are connected with the formative years of adolescence, tracing their archetypal roots in the image of the puer. Some diagnostic categories are specifically related to adolescence, such as juvenile delinquency and conduct disorder. Identity disorder and the "inability to reconcile aspects of the self into a relatively coher-ent and acceptable sense of self,"[245] naturally pertain to the young man or woman, whose very task it is to formulate and establish a separate

---

243  *Memories, Dreams, Reflections*, p. 198.
244  *Prometheus Bound*, p. 3.
245  American Psychiatric Association, *Diagnostic and Statistical Manual of Men-tal Disorders*, p. 65.

and coherent sense of whom he or she is. As Erik Erikson, says, youth may constructively *choose*, "playing at *making it happen*," rather than *suffer* from identity crisis.[246] While developmentally, identity confusion may be present at later stages in life (though then usually other diagnostic terms are appropriately applied), we may link the issue of identity to the archetypal stage of the puer.

I have emphasized fire as a central image in the life and task of the puer. Thus, naturally, disturbances in relation to fire pertain to this age, whether pyromania, the obsessive fascination and possible sexual arousal with fire, or pyrophobia, an excessive fear and avoidance of fire. In either case, the individual's unconscious is likely to absorb the meaning of fire.

## Narcissism

*Narcissism* is a distinct pathology of the puer, and indicates archetypal identification. Thus, primary narcissism is essential, since it enables the developing ego to feel its significance, being rooted in a greater Self and its own archetypal sense of divinity. Lacking primary narcissism, the child's feeling of grandeur, the person comes to experience him or herself as inadequate and unlovable, constantly lacking and a gnawing sense of emptiness. Narcissistic energy enables the ego to draw élan from its archetypal sources.

However, in the course of growing-up, the sense of divinity and archetypal wholeness has to be dismembered, in order to enable parts and portions of it to be adequately brought into the ego. This is the teleological task of the complex.[247] In narcissism, the ego is in identification with the archetypal—fascinated by its grandiosity, enchanted by its beauty, in the grip of its totality. *"The narcissistic character structure,"* writes Schwartz-Salant, *"is a pattern that is a link between the personal and the archetypal realms."*[248] Narcissism dies at age sixteen—like the seer Tiresias told Leiriope, Narcissus's mother, that her son was to live a long life, on condition that he never comes to know himself. That is, ego and consciousness, to know oneself, enforce necessary limits to narcissism.

---

246  Erik H. Erikson, *Identity: Youth and Crisis*, p. 28.
247  *The Complex*, p. 22ff.
248  Nathan Schwartz-Salant, *Narcissism and Character Transformation*, p. 26; italics in original.

'Know thyself,' as the Delphic dictum proclaims, has to do with identity, to what one is able to know about oneself. In narcissism, one does not know oneself, one's *identity*. Rather, in narcissism the individual *identifies* with the Self and with divinity. This is an inevitable aspect of a stage, in which the main task is to preserve divinity, Self and archetypal energy, and bring them into the realm of living reality. It becomes pathological when, on the one hand, the ego is inflated, unable to withdraw its identification with the Self and the archetypal world, or, on the other hand, when the ego, as one's conscious sense of identity, is experienced as an empty void, and in a constant state of emergency. The ego may then attempt to affix itself to the grand archetypal forces of the Self. This is the characteristic condition of highly talented but narcissistically wounded persons, who feel worthless if not for their intellectual accomplishment or artistic performance. The brief moment of applause becomes an all too short instant of transient narcissistic gratification.

Dorian Gray, for instance, wants to be more Dorian, that is, a gift of the goddess, than the Gray of earthly reality. As stated, the puer task, just like the complex, is to enable the complicated transition from the archetypal to the personal. No wonder youth is the time when complexes are on fire! In narcissism, earthly, adult reality is resisted. Therefore, when Dorian can no longer reject the inevitable transition of time, he becomes all too drastically exposed to old age, to the senex, and dies.[249]

Adira, a fifty-two-year-old woman, may serve as a brief illustration.[250] She felt close affinity to her father, strongly identifying with his charismatic personality and youthful energies. Yet, she was equally afraid of the manic elements of his character, leading him to frequent "brilliant" but impulsive business ventures, most of which ended in catastrophe.

Adira was a painter, claiming significance beyond her talent, surrounding herself with an aura of prominence. While critics considered her art as mediocre, she was able to have several private exhibitions, paid for by her husband. She greatly enjoyed the vernissages, not concerned with sales or critics. Outwardly dismissing them, she was plagued by a constantly gnawing feeling of doubt.

From the beginning of their relationship, when both were twenty-two, her husband provided her with the paternal security she needed. Already when young he would tell her, "It will be nice when we grow

---

249  Cf. *Enemy, Cripple, Beggar*, p. 29f.
250  'Adir' means mighty, powerful.

old together." While he often found it difficult to cope with his youthful and flamboyant wife, he was attracted to her vivaciousness, and ambivalently waited for her to grow old as well. She, however, remained a puella, while he, seemingly born a senex, kept patiently waiting for her, and thus their lives continued ever after, with no change, to the joy and satisfaction, the pain and the anxiety of both.

Sa'ar[251] serves as a tragic example of puer pathology. Even at the age of forty, he spent most of his time in the youth movement. He was highly admired and, in fact, loved, by both boys and girls. They saw him as a caring father-friend, so different from many of their own much stricter and bourgeois parents. They were fascinated by and attracted to his playfulness, coupled with sharp intelligence and friendly provocations. He felt narcissistically gratified in their company, much more so than in his routine work in a government office, which he experienced as empty and boring.

Eventually, Sa'ar was charged with sexual harassment of both boys and girls, and, characteristically, he felt everything he was accused of had been done innocently and in good faith. His flirtatious behavior might have been typical for a fifteen-year-old in search of his or her identity, but considering his age and his position of authority, was abusive. He did not recover from the trial and prison term. From a charming youngster he became a broken old man.

The essence of narcissism is to preserve divinity in face of earthly challenges—the Dorian colors of the gods in the face of the Gray dullness of everyday reality. However, the lack of balance between spirit and matter, such as the ego's identification with the gods, results in pathology. The identification may be due to inflation or deflation. In the first case, the person truly identifies with the Self, with divinity and grandeur, and expects others to relate to him or her accordingly. The archetype of the Spirit is often characteristic of this person; as Schwartz-Salant says, this is the "excess libido" that Jung speaks of, or "the 'neutral-energy' [which] Freud identifies with narcissism."[252] This is the spirit that we need for being fully alive. It is the essence of divinity that has to be brought into personal living; if lost, we have 'lost the spirit,' and become narcissistically deflated and depressed. The great fear of the narcissistic person is that the day may come and he will *lose* the spirit; therefore, he/she needs constant gratification to be convinced that it is still there. This person may have been related to as truly

---

251 Tempest, storm.
252 *Narcissism and Character Transformation*, p. 35.

special, he may have been immersed in and then driven out of Paradise, simultaneously having introjected an experience of parental rejection, envy or dislike. Such a person may permanently defend himself against the experienced threat of coming to know himself, rather relying on collective projections.[253]

The second case of narcissistic disturbance is more severe; the person is convinced of having already lost the spirit, experiencing an inner emptiness, 'knowing' the divine spirit but not feeling it. The ego will seek out that other who can feed him (with the divine spirit he yearns for), or reject the object that has nothing to give. Kernberg describes this disorder when he writes,

> People may appear to him either to have some potential food inside, which [he] has to extract, or to be already emptied and therefore valueless. ... it is the image of a hungry, enraged, empty self, full of impotent anger at being frustrated, and fearful of a world which seems as hateful and revengeful as the patient himself.[254]

## Tristia and Hilaria

The vertical axis along which the puer lives his life may be disrupted, imbalanced and disintegrated. We find what Hillman calls "the labile mood and the dependency of the spirit upon moods ... (heights and depths, glory and despair) and we hear echoes of the festivals for Attis called *tristia* and *hilaria*."[255]

The bipolarity of mood and affect, *hilaria* and *tristia*, that is, mania, too much fire, too strong passion, exaggerated self-esteem, alternating with melancholia, the lack and the loss—the lack or loss of fire, of spirit, of the loved one, of youth and vitality—is a distinct pathology of the puer-archetype. It must emphatically be underscored that this refers to archetypal images rather than chronological stages, even though the onset of affective disorders, such as cyclothymic disorder, usually occurs in early adult life. Particularly, the viewpoint presented here does not refer to distinct psychiatric diagnostic entities, such as affective disorder, but rather to the idea and the axis of mood and its pathology.

---

253  Bela Grunberger, 'On Narcissism, Aggressivity and Anti-Semitism,' *Int. Forum Psychoanal.*, 2, p. 239.
254  Otto Kernberg, *Borderline Conditions and Pathological Narcissism*, p. 233.
255  *Puer Papers*, pp. 24-25.

This vertical axis of mania and depression, of Babel-like towers of hubris reaching towards heaven, and broken ruins plunging into the depth of the abyss, is an archetypal axis of life. It brings the colors of affect that impede the monotonous death by constancy and regularity. However, when the colors are too bright or too dark, the polarized affect may burn to death or annihilate the subject.

Like Prometheus, the hero may challenge the gods above, and like Perseus he, or she, may fight the monsters below. Like Icarus, he must try his wings to rise toward the sun and dive towards the sea, with perpetual danger of coming too close, whether too high or too low, and dying too young. Psychologically, youth of course must die at a young age, some of its spirit lost in hope that has fallen to the ground, some of its spirit retained to provide for the fire that may burn an entire life.

The vertical axis is a progressive development of the very initial state of the child, of passing through the abyss, with the added spiritual dimension, which elevates from mere horizontal existence. The transformative aspect of death and rebirth, as reflected in mythical ideas such as the Messiah being born the very moment of the Temple's destruction, is not a linear, but a vertical process, of the new being born from the depths of destruction.

Consider the following dream by Yariva,[256] a fifty-year-old woman,

> A group of young people sits around the bonfire. Suddenly a platoon of the tsar's soldiers arrives. They ride on horses, as if it is a hundred years ago. One of the girls gets up and starts fighting against them, as if she was Joan of Arc; she is the only one who dares.
>
> She asks the soldiers why they are violent. They say the reason is that the young revolt against the emperor. The soldiers throw most of the young into the fire and burn them. She continues to fight, but knows it is all lost. She sacrifices herself, but hides one of the friends so that someone will survive.

In her comments to the dream, Yariva identifies with the female hero, or, rather,

> the kind of person I would have liked to be. I am always scared. I never revolted against my parents, did everything to please them, even as an adult, even now at fifty. On the one hand, it meant they were always pleased with me, and I always benefitted from being their favorite, but I never

---

256 Yariv, Biblical name meaning 'God Defends,' also 'adversary.'

really got anywhere, I never became myself, truly, independently, doing what really is right for me. I didn't sacrifice
anything, and that way I perhaps sacrificed myself. I never
did anything to the edge, no extremes, but therefore perhaps lost a sense of meaning, or passion, and also in a way
came to see my parents as powerful tyrants, just because
they always were so nice and good to me.

In mania, the ego bursts and bubbles, full of mana-energy,[257] while
in depression the ego is drained and tired. This is Dionysus, or Bac-
chus, the manic-depressive god.[258] He is a god of dualities, and has two
separate, yet related origins; he is god of wine, vegetation and fertility,
and he carries the features of mystery religions: ecstasy, relief from the
everyday world through intoxication, and initiation into secret rites.
He was, as well, twice-born: one myth tells us he was born from Zeus'
thigh, since his mother Semele was killed by father Zeus' lightning bolts
while she still carried Dionysus in her womb. In another account, while
Dionysus remains the son of Zeus, he was born by Persephone.

It is often told how Dionysus enters the city, is resisted, and then
destroys those who oppose him. Particularly in Euripides's play the *Bac-
chae*, we find Dionysus and the worship of him destructive and dangerous; his power causes earthquake and collapse of the Palace, and a burst
of flames from his mother Semele's grave. Semele, a daughter of Cadmus and Harmonia, burned to death when she saw Dionysus's father
Zeus in his godly shape.

Dionysus appears and disappears, comes and goes, creates and destroys, causes joy and suffering, excitement and death.

Clinically, we may then say that manic-depression represents a fal-
tering ego-Self relationship. The archetypal world is still very much at
work—as it is and should be in the puer. An ego has developed, and in
this sense, there is no psychosis. Yet, a unitary ego-attitude has not separated from the Self, the archetype of unity. The ego relates to the innate duality and bipolarity of the archetypal world inconsistently and
is easily propelled into mania or depression, flight or impasse, a feather
in the air or unbearable heaviness, endless space or suffocating imprisonment, rapid change or eternal immobility, unending possibilities of
creation or the destruction of hope and meaning, burning passion or
extinguished fire.

---

257  *Puer Papers*, p. 40.
258  Cf. Jole Cappiello McCurdy, Manic-Depressive Psychosis - A Perspective, *J.
   An. Psychology*, 1987, 32, 309-324.

In manic-depression, the development from archetype to ego, which takes place by means of the complexes, has not constellated adequately. Rather than the multi-facetted complexity ensured by the archetypal breakdown via complexes, existence remains archetypally bipolar, with splitting and fusion, as in the following dream. The dreamer was a forty-year-old man, a single child whose parents, both survivors of Auschwitz, had divorced when he was still an infant,

> In the dream, my wife has suffered trauma. I get an idea, to fill up a bucket with water, and she sits staring at her mirror image in the water. Afterwards I myself, her husband, put my head under the water and watch the sun through the water from below.
>
> Then I am a woman who enters the house of that man's wife. She, his wife, is in fact, 'bigger than life,' kind of 'earth mother,' seems not to have suffered trauma at all, that's my feeling anyway, but how do I know? I find she has money in a drawer. Since I need money, I consider taking, but for some reason I refrain—don't know, perhaps I am just afraid. I then see that there are cameras that would have detected me.

While the dream can be contemplated from a diagnostic point of view, for instance as regards this person's sense of gender identity, prospective elements of healing are present, as well. There is a need for primary narcissistic mirroring; however, the fusion between the archetypal and the personal dimension, as in the head watching the sun through the water from within the bucket, must be disentangled before the elements can be healing. Likewise, energy is available in the earth mother's drawer. However, it is not available to the conscious personality. For this person, the obstructing cameras may protect him from the otherwise all too unmediated exposure to archetypal energies.

The transition from youth to adulthood requires the assimilation of aspects of the puer into consciousness, so that archetypal energies will be adequately available to the ego, for the tasks ahead.

IV

# The Adult

## As the Moved to the Mover

Commonly, we assume that our conscious sense of identity comprises our entire personality. However, Jung's basic attitude to the psyche was that the personality revolves not around the ego, but, as Whitmont says, "rotates around the unconscious center, the Self."[259] It is painful to realize that earth is not the center of the universe, but orbits around the sun, which provides the energy required for life on earth. Jung writes,

> The ego stands to the self as the moved to the mover, or as object to subject, because the determining factors which radiate out from the self surround the ego on all sides and are therefore supraordinate to it. The self, like the unconscious, is an *a priori* existent out of which the ego evolves. It is, so to speak, an unconscious prefiguration of the ego. It is not I who create myself, rather I happen to myself.[260]

From this *unconscious prefiguration,* the ego unfolds in stages and evolves through life. However, never is the ego as powerful and almighty as in adulthood. "The sense of the 'numinous' tends to be lost," says Whitmont.[261] Essential to adulthood is a reasonable adaptation to reality rather than the passionate poetry that blossoms from the wellsprings of the soul. The barrier erected by the ordinary adult and by ego-consciousness "against the world of collective images is so high that, generally speaking, it can only be surmounted with difficulty," writes Adler.[262]

---

259  Edward C. Whitmont, *The Symbolic Quest,* p. 265.
260  Jung, *Psychology and Religion,* CW 11, par. 391.
261  *The Symbolic Quest,* p. 278.
262  *Studies in Analytical Psychology,* p. 125.

Yet, without ego, the waters may inundate the land, or the earth be set on fire; without ego, there can be no sustainable human existence.

## King on Earth

In adulthood, ego, consciousness and conscious identity—I, Me, Mine, I want, my will-power, the Promethean characteristics that were molded and solidified during the thirty thousand years he was bound to the rock—become the *ruler on earth*. The king in fairy tales often represents the dominant function of consciousness, the collective ego and the "central and dominant symbolic content of collective consciousness,"[263] the norms and rules of society. Marie-Louise von Franz clarifies,

> To be accurate you would therefore say that the king does not represent the main function but is the archetypal basis of that function in the sense that he is that psychological factor which builds up the main functions in all people.[264]

The youthful hero brings something new, similar to the way Prometheus brings the fire that inspires human consciousness and ignites acculturation. In contrast, the king *rules*. He rules and sets the rules. In society, he formulates the customs, is a manifestation of etiquette and *comme il faut*, the appropriate and correct behavior. In the individual, he shapes the ingrained habits that we often have such a difficulty realizing we are in the grips of, not to mention how hard it often is to break away from. The ego and personal consciousness stand between the pressures from the instincts and the unconscious on the one hand, and the pulls of the norms and ethics of collective consciousness on the other hand. The ego is the regulator between id and superego, fantasy and reality, internal and external. A well-functioning ego is necessary for the tasks of adulthood, such as becoming autonomous and self-supporting, and "letting go of childhood illusions and infantile attachments and dependency needs, forgiving one's parents, accepting them as limited fallible human beings like oneself."[265]

Ego and consciousness are always at risk of being flooded by the forces that rise from the depth of the unconscious, or being stifled under the commands of collective consciousness. However, a stable, yet flexible and dynamic ego-consciousness, is open to the symbols of the

263   Marie-Louise von Franz, *Interpretation of Fairytales*, p. 39.
264   *Interpretation of Fairytales*, p. 40.
265   John-Raphael Staude, *The Adult Development of C. G. Jung*, p. 39.

unconscious, as well as to the order, the structure and the signs of collective consciousness, of the requirements of the superego and society.

The archetype of the Father represents the world of the ego, of adult reality and obligations, particularly well. The ego, when too strongly aligned with the persona and the collective consciousness of norms and rules, comes under the authority of the Spiritual Father archetype. Edinger writes,

> As the great mother pertains to nature, matter and earth, the great father archetype pertains to the realm of light and spirit. It is the personification of the masculine principle of consciousness symbolized by the upper solar region of heaven.[266]

One prominent image of the Spiritual Father pertains to social rules and norms, i.e., collective consciousness, and attributes such as law and order, discipline and conventions. The elders of the tribe, the judge, priest and rabbi, carry aspects of the archetypal image of the Father.[267]

As I have elaborated elsewhere, Saul, first of the Hebrew Kings, had expelled all the mediums and the wizards from the land, because there is no place for mediums and magicians in the realm of a rational ego.[268] The prophet Samuel, who anointed Saul and made him king, warned the people that an earthly king would exploit the sons and the daughters of the people, lay claim to their fields and olive presses, and would charge taxes. But the people did not listen to him. They wanted to be like other nations. This is the common desire to be like others, to adjust to the way things are done, to adhere to collective consciousness. The people wanted a king who would judge them, go before them, and fight their battles.[269] The rabbis made a clear distinction between human and divine governance, saying that, "To an earthly king, a person goes full, and returns empty; to God, one goes empty, and returns full."[270] It is easier to let oneself be abused collectively by the ego's kingly rule than to attend to the prophets' harsh voice of warning—many or most of the Hebrew kings abused their power.

---

266 Edward Edinger, An outline of analytical psychology, *Quadrant*, 1, p. 6.
267 Cf. *The Origins and History of Consciousness*, p. 186ff.
268 *Enemy, Cripple & Beggar*, p. 60f.
269 1 Samuel 8:11-20.
270 *Pesikta Rabbati* (a medieval Midrash), 44:9.

## Boundaries of Reality

In adulthood, one's capacities and talents unfold in actual reality by means of ego-functions, by will-power, consistency and determination.

The essence of ego-consciousness is its *boundary*. The adult puts boundaries and limitations on the child's oceanic divinity as well as the libidinal fire of youth—otherwise the child would drown, and the young might set the world on fire. The father, says Jung, "represents the world of moral commandments and prohibitions, ... the spirit, whose function it is to oppose pure instinctuality."[271]

The boundaries of the ego enable and constitute the basis for consciousness, because they separate and differentiate between what is in and what is out, what is assimilated into conscious identity, and what is discarded in the shadow. This is why *rationality* pertains to the ego—rationality, as well as ratio, is relative and rationed, it is defined and limited. Nemesis, goddess of measure and retribution for undeserved good fortune, sets boundaries when man is caught up in hubris, mistaking himself for the gods, forgetting his limits and limitations.

The Self's reflection in the human world, in the realm of the ego, is possible due to the very boundaries and limitations that constitute the foundation of the ego. There is no *totality* in the adult world of the ego. Whenever a choice or a decision is made, something is by necessity excluded, relinquished or left behind. Totality pertains to Self and the unconscious, to the archetypal dominion of the gods. Thus, when Aphrodite told the young maiden Psyche to bring water from the river of life, she, being a goddess, did not understand the idea of limitation as it pertains to the world of mortals. Consequently, she was convinced that (the human) Psyche would fail, because as a god or goddess you take it all. She assumed that Psyche would have to bring *all* of the water from the river of life. As an archetype, life is total. Nothing is left out. However, in actual, human life, we are necessarily limited. In her vessel, Psyche could bring the water of life, but only as much as the body of her urn could hold and contain. We can only carry as much of the river of life, as can be contained within our body-ego-boundaries. Nancy Furlotti describes how Aphrodite's dark shadow is the experience of many, who have searched for and that have been seduced by her

---

271  CW 5, par. 396.

"life-giving gaze," only to be "left alone with [the] unfulfilled dreams [of Hollywood]."[272]

Concomitant to the formation of ego, our shadow constellates. When we define what pertains to our conscious identity, the shadow comes to comprise what remains outside the boundaries of the ego.[273] If the ego's foundation and boundaries are too weak, the city of the ego may be inundated by the sea, its buildings and institutions burned by the fire, or its inhabitants swept away by too strong winds. On the other hand, the adult ego's rule on earth may be such, that the ego becomes disconnected from the sea, the fire and the wind. Without the playful child, the earth dries up; without the spirit of youth, adults become burned-out; without the depth and introspection of old age, vision is blurred and there is no soulful wisdom blowing in the wind. The result is fatigue and loss of vitality.

One woman dreamed, simply but poignantly, that she is walking up-hill, on a very steep, difficult, muddy path, and next to her, the water, even if dirty, streams strongly down the river. She felt it as the conflict in her life between the youthful 'dirty' puella, and her hardworking, always responsible and upward struggling adult.

King Saul got rid of the sorcerers from the land, throwing them into the shadow in the typically rational belief that one can build the rule of the ego on pure rationality, without interference of the unconscious, the magic, and the irrational. But then, when the moment of crisis arrives, he himself turns to the witch of Ein-Dor. By then, however, he has already become the victim of the prophet Samuel's ghost, whom the witch stirs up from the underground.[274]


## Celestial Jerusalem—Terrestrial Jerusalem

The adult ego is, from an archetypal perspective, the Self's manifestation in consciousness and the realm of personal reality. This is the ancient idea of 'as above, so below.' The divine becomes human, the Self unfolds into the Ego, archetypal images become complexes in the reality of living people, the wholeness of ideas and the idea of wholeness become the separation and differentiation of concrete reality.

---

272  Nancy Furlotti, 'Angels and Idols: Los Angeles, A City of Contrasts,' in *Psyche and the City*, p. 243.
273  *Enemy, Cripple, Beggar*, p. 81ff.
274  *Enemy, Cripple, Beggar*, p. 88.

Beyond the realm of personal reality, mankind's phylogenetic ego and adulthood manifest in man-made artifacts and replications of the self. The material world is like a mirror which reflects the spiritual realm, says the *Zohar*, the *Book of Splendor*. The grand achievements of human consciousness lie in the constructive application and development of *self-principles*, combined with the *differentiating* function of consciousness: *creation* becomes creativity, inventiveness, art and science; *nature* is shaped into culture; and nature's *order*, as expressed for instance in the beehive or ant colonies, become human organizations. Furthermore, sexual and genetic *reproduction* turn into artifacts of production, re-production and mass-production.

The science of biomimicry, for instance, is inspired by, and tries to replicate designs and solutions that can be found in nature and in natural organisms. As Michael Pawlyn says, referring to its application in architecture, it means "treating nature as mentor when addressing our own challenges," learning from the principles that lie behind natural forms, because "for every problem that we currently face ... there will be precedents within nature that we can study."[275] Thus, rather than destroying the ego's basis in the greater Self, it means learning from it, possibly to the extent that the Self is enhanced by its manifestation in the man-made world.

*Celestial Jerusalem* is a prominent symbol of the Self as center of wholeness, as the whole center. She dresses herself in many names, such as City of Joy, Praise, Justice and Righteousness, or Beautiful, Comely and Beloved.[276] The seventy or more names that legend tells us she wears, bear witness to the extent to which Jerusalem is pregnant with archetypal imagery and projections of wholeness and proximity to Divinity. Earthly Jerusalem, however, far from always mirrors her Heavenly Sister's image of completeness and redemption. The concrete world of stones and trees, houses and people, *Terrestrial Jerusalem*, must not be confused with Jerusalem as symbol and archetypal image. "In its often shabby garb, terrestrial Jerusalem seems to want to shake off its celestial glory."[277] In so far as the 'below,' the realm of the human ego, manages to reflect a grain of what shines from above, it unavoidably does so in a mirror scratched by rough reality.

---

275  Michael Pawlyn, 'Biomimicry,' in Ken Yeang and Arthur Spector (Eds.), *Green Design: From Theory to Practice*, pp. 34, 40.
276  Jeremiah 49:25; Isaiah 1:21, 26; Song of Songs 6:4; Psalms 84:2; see also 'Jerusalem: Human Ground, Archetypal Spirit,' in *Psyche & the City*, p. 283f.
277  *Psyche & the City*, p. 280.

While necessarily separating from the Self, the ego of the adult is fully alive only in so far as its roots reach into the Self. As Jung says in his *Red Book*, "in that I accepted myself, I divided myself into two, and in that I united myself with myself, I became the smaller part of myself ... but precisely because of my smallness I can be conscious of the nearness of the great."[278] The ego becomes inflated, overgrown and malignant when *identifying* with the Self and the world of archetypes. We see this in narcissism, and in the particular grave dangers posed by tyrants and dictators. When the ego is archetypally identified, the shadow is denied. As a result, the projected shadow may grow into a wicked enemy, who threatens one's sense of wholeness. The hostile adversary must then be fought, and so conflict is escalated and aggravated.

## Athena and the Craftsman's Ego

The essence of the ego, reaching its peak in adulthood, is its distinction from the world of the gods and the archetypes. Yet, even ego and adulthood have their representative among the gods on the Olympus, since inevitably 'as below, so above.' However, the gods represent archetypal energies and structures, not their personal unfolding. Often *the hero* is thought of as symbolizing the ego, but I understand the hero-image rather to represent the *transformation* of Self *into* ego, and that aspect of the ego that searches for the treasures of the Self. The hero carries on his back, or in her bag, the complexes that enable the transformation of archetypal core into ego matter, while I take the *king* to represent the possible *manifestation* of Self *in* ego. Kings were supposedly appointed as God's representatives on earth. Marie-Louise von Franz has written extensively on the role of the King as representing the rule of collective consciousness, which certainly resonates in the adult world.[279] As we look back in history and around in the world, and when we scan our own psyche, we may easily become embarrassingly aware how the throne of royal rule corrupts, that is, ruptures the connection with the other/s.

The archetypal nucleus of the ego is *the notion of consciousness*, the idea of a known, separate, defined and partially independent center in which the Self, the image of the divine, can unfold. Just like everything else, the ego has an archetypal essence. Thus, we should be able to find a god or a goddess that may serve as an archetypal image of the ego.

---

278 *The Red Book*, p. 304.
279 *Interpretation of Fairytales*, p. 37ff.

I believe *Athena* is well suited to represent adult ego-consciousness. She is *born* an adult. She springs forth from her father Zeus' *forehead*. She is not born from her mother, "the wisest among gods and mortal men,"[280] Metis's uterus, but emerges from the head. She thrives in the patriarchal principle, forever loyal to patriarchal consciousness. She functions by means of purposeful thinking, planning and execution, strategy and practicality. While the Fates weave the web of destiny, Athena is a weaver of the world.[281]

If we consider civilization as the expression of the collective ego and consciousness, we cannot fail to notice that the origin of Western civilization is in the city of Athena. Here we find the podium of discourse, democracy, and aesthetics.

Athena was the protector of cities and patron of military forces, two separate but distinct expressions of the ego—the city as organized society constructed by man, and the warfare necessary to establish and defend a differentiated identity (which does not justify it being acted out in the atrocities of war). "The cultic places of Athene," says Kerényi, "exist mostly as shrines of a fortress and city Goddess ... she protects cities and ... holds her hand outstretched over cities and covers them with her golden shield." She is associated with "the working of wool and with the harnessing of horses ... the arts of weaving and of pressing oil from the olive," and, as Kerényi says, she,

> teaches men how to manufacture the plow, how to yoke oxen, and how to loosen up the hard ground with the rake. From her mankind receives the materials for all the arts that beautify life, and from her the metal workers and the armsmiths, the housewives and the weavers, receive their skillfulness.[282]

As Pallas Athena, the goddess holds the dual aspects of masculine and feminine. "The meaning of Pallas," writes Kerényi, "was once the name for robust maidens and implied the meaning of the masculine word *pallas* ... 'robust young man.' A distinct masculinity seems to adhere to this word even in its feminine form."[283] She is characterized

---

280  Hesiod, *Theogony*, 887, (In Hesiod, *Theogony and Works and Days*, translation by M. L. West, p. 29).
281  *An Illustrated Encyclopedia of Traditional Symbols*, p. 190.
282  Karl Kerényi, *Athene: Virgin and Mother in Greek Religion*, pp. 15-18.
283  *Athene: Virgin and Mother in Greek Religion*, p. 41.

by "clear-eyed sagacity, intelligence directed toward practical, concrete goals."[284]

Athena is well equipped with spear and shield, owl and helmet. She sends forth and equips heroes. For the hero to go forth and struggle with the horrors of darkness and the awe of lightning, he needs ego-tools and ego-defenses, such as the shield Athena gave to Perseus. Thus, he was able to dissect the monsters of the unconscious by reflection, which is a fundamental asset of consciousness, necessary when approaching the dark forces in one's shadow. In fact, it was Athena, who cast Medusa into the unconscious, after she had made love with Poseidon in the Palace of Athena. Once a beautiful nymph, Perseus challenged the petrifying gaze of the now monstrous Medusa, defeating her by the protective reflection that Athena's shield provided.

The weakness of Athena may be her adherence to the patriarchal principle. That is, she may become conventional and lose her innovative capacity. The ego may then have separated from the Self, from its deeper resources, and instead adapts excessively, clinging to the persona of collective consciousness. Athena defends "the prerogatives, the interests, the spirit of the Father, 'father-interests' as [Kerényi] terms it."[285]

Athena was patron of warriors but also of artisans and the crafts. Her name Athena may be taken to mean "the vessel of the sacred fire."[286] This may be the adult who is able to contain the passionate fire of adolescence, but perhaps also the Hephaestian fire in the potters' quarter,[287] so essential to the crafting of civilization.

I see *the craftsman* as a central image of the archetypally rooted adult ego, in the sense that the Self unfolds in the ego. The hero, who serves as a bridge between the archetypal and the individual realms, has frequently both a divine and a personal father. The latter is often a craftsman. For the hero to set out on his journey into the depths and the vast lands of the unconscious, he or she needs to be ignited by the very sparks of the beyond as they manifest in ego-consciousness. Jung writes,

> The hero's father is often a master carpenter or some kind of artisan. According to an Arabian legend, Terah, the father

---

284  Murray Stein, 'translator's afterthoughts,' in *Athene: Virgin and Mother in Greek Religion*, p. 109.

285  *Athene: Virgin and Mother in Greek Religion*, p. 112.

286  *Athene*, p. 48.

287  *Athene*, p. 47.

of Abraham, was a master craftsman who could cut a shaft
from any bit of wood, which means in Arabic usage that
he was a begetter of excellent sons. ... Joseph, the father
of Jesus, was a carpenter, and so was Cinyras, the father of
Adonis, who was supposed to have invented the hammer,
the lever, roof-building and mining. ... In fairytales, the
hero's father is, more modestly, the traditional woodcut-
ter.[288]

The original *Red Book* of Jung's is a masterpiece not only of his, but
of bookbinder craftsmanship as well. Sonu Shamdasani writes, "After
completing the handwritten *Draft*, Jung had it typed, and edited. ...
The first section of the work ... was composed on parchment. Jung then
commissioned a large folio volume of over 600 pages, bound in red
leather, from the bookbinders, Emil Stierli."[289]

While Jung's active imaginations, the fantasy material that forms
the basis of his interpretations and elaborations, preceded their inscription in *The Red Book*, the ego's sublime craftsmanship may be required
for the heroic descent into the darkness of the unknown. The impres-
sively bound pages of the red leather-covered tome hold and contain
the inscription of Jung's remarkable descent into the archetypal depths
of the unconscious. The masterfully bound book is like the crafted ego
that enables the hero's journey. "It is the creation of the alchemical vessel that invites the soul into dialogue and union to bring forth the divine. The carefully crafted and beautiful Red Book honored the process
and contents as a container for Jung's transformation."[290]

The craftsman replicates the divine on earth by means of his skill,
patience, carefulness and hard work. The prominent craftsman in the
Bible was Bezalel, whose name significantly means 'in the image, or
shadow of God.' As said in Exodus 31:3, he was filled with the "spirit
of God, in wisdom, and in understanding, and in knowledge, and in
all kinds of workmanship." He built the Tabernacle, the tent set up by
Moses, in which the Ark of the Covenant—a chest of acacia wood holding the stone tablets of the Ten Commandments—was carried through
the wilderness. Thereby he replicated creation. Bezalel "knew the com-
binations of letters with which heaven and earth were made," [that is,
the letters of God's name], and thus was able to build the Tabernacle,
which was considered "a complete microcosm, a miraculous copy of

---

288  CW 5, par. 515.
289  'Introduction,' *The Red Book*, p. 203.
290  Nancy Furlotti, personal communication.

everything that is in heaven and on earth."[291] He thus created an *imago mundi*, a crafted replica of the universe, wherein, like in a temple, the divine can dwell on earth.

In the following, a dream by Amalia,[292] a woman in her mid-forties, we identify the archetypal image of the old and wise craftsman,

> I am in front of a building. People carry posters and banners about all kind of things. When I go behind the house, a man that I know of, who always appears to "do the right kind of thing," has put a very heavy iron bed there—it is ugly, cold, metallic—nothing intimate. I get upset, and decide to go inside the building. I go up the stairs, many stairs. I get to a small, dark room. Behind a wooden desk sits an old man. He carves God's name (YHWH) on a small piece of wood, with great skill and patience.

This dream reflects a significant inward journey, from the banners and the posters at the façade of the building to its interior chambers. It is noticeable that the distortion caused by the representative of collective consciousness, the man who always does "the right kind of thing," who has placed a cold and ugly bed, which normally is an intimate piece, in the wrong place, serves as the instigating adversary, causing the dreamer to go inside. In the symbolism of the dream, the persona of collective consciousness which initially, and usually, appears as the front, in the open, the visible banners and slogans and 'correct' behavior, has been deposed into the shadowy backyard, whereby its cold and un-intimate quality becomes perceptible. In contrast to its superficial appearance when in its usual location, in the shadow it evokes affect and instigates toward movement.

What aspect of the psyche does the old craftsman represent? My assumption is that an ego that is well enough attuned to the Self and in this sense Self-related, which I refer to as *the craftsman's ego*, has absorbed the Wisdom of the Old, the wisdom of the objective psyche, which we attain by combining study and learning with an openness to the Self. Edinger considers the archetype of the old wise man to be a personification of the ego-Self axis.[293] Thus, the old craftsman is an inward aspect of the ego, who carefully relates to the god-image in one's soul. In the individuation process, an on-going dialogue between ego and Self is carried out. Sometimes there is ego-Self separation, some-

---

291  Gershom Scholem, *On the Kabbalah and its Symbolism*, p. 166f.
292  Amalia, means 'the labor of God.'
293  *Ego and Archetype*, p. 118.

times ego-Self union, depending on the archetypal stage we are passing through.

## The Ego between Pathos and Logos

Jungian psychology does not deal much with defenses, because in comparison to Freudian psychoanalysis, it is less of an ego-psychology.

The ego protects and defends itself and its conquered territory against the child, the puer and the senex. As a matter of fact, its defenses are an axiomatic aspect of the boundaries and limitations that constitute the ego's very essence. The ego must have a firm hold on the ground to protect itself against the ocean, the fire and the cold winds. However, as mentioned previously, if the ego is disconnected from all these, it becomes lifeless and dried-up. From the ego's point of view, "if you enter into the world of soul, you are like a madman."[294]

The ego's defenses are characteristically obsessive, compulsive, phobic and repetitive. Consequently, the overly defensive ego is reluctant to change, and may identify with the norms and conventions of collective consciousness. The outbreak of neurotic symptoms may in fact sometimes signify the egress from neurosis. "Neurosis," says Jung, "is really an attempt at self-cure, just as any physical disease is part an attempt at self-cure."[295]

Bina,[296] a forty-seven-year-old single woman, had worked in the same government office for over twenty years. Seemingly by chance she noticed one day that her salary had, without explanation, been lowered. She became furious, and set out on a frantic crusade, phoning clerks and colleagues. She yelled and intimidated whomever she was able to reach, personally or over the phone. "They are only out to get you, to screw you; you can't trust anyone. I know that they don't do this intentionally, there's no conspiracy, but you just can't rely on anyone." While not paranoid, she was clearly driven by a powerful complex, constellated around feelings of mistrust, which had been triggered. "For months I did not recognize myself," she said, commenting on her behavior. As it turned out, her salary had been readjusted, after Bina had mistakenly been overpaid for the past six years. At that point, she was inundated by anxiety. She wondered how she would be able to pay back the money. She thought of quitting her job, and thus possibly

---

294  *The Red Book*, p. 238.
295  CW 18, par. 389.
296  In Hebrew, Bina means 'understanding.'

avoid repaying her debt. Bothered by her conscience, she decided to speak to her superior and the bookkeeper. A decision was made to raise her salary, but to implement it only a few months later. Thus, she was not required to return what she had earned, feeling both moral and financial relief.

Following the incident and a period of several months during which she had been in the grips of her anxiety, fury and mistrust, she was able to trace the roots in a childhood complex. She had not previously acknowledged the extent to which she, on the one hand, was overly compliant and forthcoming to others, while on the other hand would not let anyone close to her, and was unable to form intimate relationships. She went through a period of mourning her unlived life, after which she felt satisfied with her moral decision, and grateful for her boss's support. "I feel like I have behaved like a captain whose ship is always in danger of hitting a reef and sinking, as if the waters and the weather are stormy, even if it's a calm summer's day." Her mistrust turned into a sense of honesty and a feeling of humbleness vis-à-vis both herself and others.

The case seems to illustrate Jung's position on neurosis as an opportunity for change toward healing, as "an attempt ... of the self-regulating psychic system to restore the balance, in no way different from the function of dreams—only rather more forceful and drastic."[297] The outbreak of a neurosis may prompt a change in the structure of the neurotic defenses.

When consciousness is the grand-all and be-all, its pathological symptomatology manifests by archetypal possession, and we find ourselves in the grip of a complex. When more severe, ego and consciousness may *identify* with an archetypal essence or an unconscious content, leaving little possibility for consciousness to find its way in. We may discern overlapping, yet distinct categories of possession:

**Possession by the Spiritual Father archetype.** This leads, as Erik Erikson has said, to adherence to the law according to the letter rather than the spirit.[298] In society, this may lead to a shrinking of the individual ego and independent thinking and initiative, to the mass ego, and to fascism. The Voice, the inner authority, may consequently be projected onto the external collective and the leader; at its worst, carried by Il

---

297  'The Tavistock Lectures,' CW 18, par. 383.
298  This pertains to the stage of 'Autonomy vs. Shame & Doubt,' see for instance *Childhood and Society*, p. 226ff.

Duce or Der Führer. In the psyche of the individual, the ego, caught up in collective consciousness, shrinks, becoming detached from shadow and Self.

Possession by the Spiritual Father archetype also leaves little room for the anima, for the feminine. The soul is lost, and the earth, dries up. The Biblical story about Ruth can be interpreted in this manner. Often the fairy tale kingdom is in need of soul and renewal, whereby the hero goes searching for the anima.

**Possession by defenses.** The ego protects and defends itself and its con-quered territory against the child, the puer and the senex. It must have a firm hold on the ground to protect itself against the ocean, the fire and the cold winds. The ego's defenses are characteristically *obsessive-compulsive* and *repetitive*. When pathological, the defenses lose their meaningful essence, and trap the individual in meaningless activity of mind or ritual. This happens for instance when obsessively intruding and anxiety-provoking thoughts are combated by repetitive and com-pulsive acts, or in *phobic* avoidance of or flight from (a specific) mean-ing.[299]

While this may reflect aspects of the personality, the midlife adult may defend him or herself against the change required at this stage, as old patterns of behavior become obsolete.

**Possession by the persona.** We find here the as-if personality, who is a high organization borderline personality.[300] The ego is not anchored in the Self, but glued to the shell of external appearance and behaviors.

**Possession by conversion.** The hysterical symptom, or conversion, re-veals that there is a secret life behind the repressions of (collective) consciousness. By means of hysteria, Freud found his way to imagine the unconscious. Symptoms of conversion, such as hysteric blindness or limping, are attacks on ego functions.


## The Emperor's New Clothes

A wonderful example of pathology that combines overvaluation of the Father archetype, imprisonment in the costumes of the persona of col-

---

299 'Phobos' implies flight in fear, see for instance Homer, *The Iliad*, 9.1-2: "... the Greeks to flight were giv'n, The feeble consort of cold fear..." (p. 139).

300 Vance R. Sherwood and Charles P. Cohen, *Psychotherapy of the Quiet Border-line Patient: The As-If Personality Revisited*, p. 51ff.

lective consciousness, and the ensuing loss of integrity and individuality, is Hans Christian Andersen's tale from 1837 about *The Emperor's New Clothes*. In so far as hysteria is an imaginary illness, *the* illness of imagination, we find in this tale of marvel several signs of histrionic behavior. The defensive need of compliance with the decrees of the king is, as well, rather visible:

> Many, many years ago lived an emperor, who thought so much of new clothes that he spent all his money in order to obtain them; his only ambition was to be always well dressed. He did not care for his soldiers, and the theater did not amuse him; the only thing, in fact, he thought anything of was to drive out and show a new suit of clothes. He had a coat for every hour of the day; and as one would say of a king "He is in his cabinet," so one could say of him, "The emperor is in his dressing-room."
>
> The great city where he resided was very gay; every day many strangers from all parts of the globe arrived. One day, two swindlers came to this city; they made people believe that they were weavers, and declared they could manufacture the finest cloth to be imagined. Their colors and patterns, they said, were not only exceptionally beautiful, but the clothes made of their material possessed the wonderful quality of being invisible to any man who was unfit for his office or unpardonably stupid.
>
> "That must be wonderful cloth," thought the emperor. "If I were to be dressed in a suit made of this cloth I should be able to find out which men in my empire were unfit for their places, and I could distinguish the clever from the stupid. I must have this cloth woven for me without delay." And he gave a large sum of money to the swindlers, in advance, that they should set to work without any loss of time. They set up two looms, and pretended to be very hard at work, but they did nothing whatever on the looms. They asked for the finest silk and the most precious gold-cloth; all they got they did away with, and worked at the empty looms till late at night.
>
> "I should very much like to know how they are getting on with the cloth," thought the emperor. But he felt rather uneasy when he remembered that he who was not fit for his office could not see it. Personally, he was confident that he had nothing to fear, yet he thought it advisable to send somebody else first to see how matters stood. Everybody in the town knew what a remarkable quality the stuff possessed, and all were anxious to see how bad or stupid their neighbors were.
>
> "I shall send my honest old minister to the weavers," thought the emperor. "He can judge best how the stuff looks, for he is intelligent, and nobody understands his office better than he."

The good old minister went into the room where the swindlers sat before the empty looms. "Heaven preserve us!" he thought, and opened his eyes wide, "I cannot see anything at all," but he did not say so. Both swindlers requested him to come near, and asked him if he did not admire the exquisite pattern and the beautiful colors, pointing to the empty looms. The poor old minister tried his very best, but he could see nothing, for there was nothing to be seen. "Oh dear," he thought, "Can I be so stupid? I should never have thought so, and nobody must know it! Is it possible that I am not fit for my office? No, no, I cannot say that I was unable to see the cloth."

"Now, have you got nothing to say?" said one of the swindlers, while he pretended to be busily weaving.

"Oh, it is very pretty, exceedingly beautiful," replied the old minister looking through his glasses. "What a beautiful pattern, what brilliant colors! I shall tell the emperor that I like the cloth very much."

"We are pleased to hear that," said the two weavers, and described to him the colors and explained the curious pattern. The old minister listened attentively, that he might relate to the emperor what they said; and so he did.

Now the swindlers asked for more money, silk and gold-cloth, which they required for weaving. They kept everything for themselves, and not a thread came near the loom, but they continued, as hitherto, to work at the empty looms.

Soon afterwards, the emperor sent another honest courtier to the weavers to see how they were getting on, and if the cloth was nearly finished. Like the old minister, he looked and looked but could see nothing, as there was nothing to be seen.

"Is it not a beautiful piece of cloth?" asked the two swindlers, showing and explaining the magnificent pattern, which, however, did not exist.

"I am not stupid," said the man. "It is therefore my good appointment for which I am not fit. It is very strange, but I must not let anyone know it;" and he praised the cloth, which he did not see, and expressed his joy at the beautiful colors and the fine pattern. "It is very excellent," he said to the emperor.

Everybody in the whole town talked about the precious cloth. At last the emperor wished to see it himself, while it was still on the loom. With a number of courtiers, including the two who had already been there, he went to the two clever swindlers, who now worked as hard as they could, but without using any thread.

"Is it not magnificent?" said the two old statesmen who had been there before. "Your Majesty must admire the colors and the pattern." And then they pointed to the empty looms, for they imagined the others could see the cloth.

"What is this?" thought the emperor, "I do not see anything at all. That is terrible! Am I stupid? Am I unfit to be emperor? That would indeed be the most dreadful thing that could happen to me."

"Really," he said, turning to the weavers, "your cloth has our most gracious approval;" and nodding contentedly he looked at the empty loom, for he did not like to say that he saw nothing. All his attendants, who were with him, looked and looked, and although they could not see anything more than the others, they said, like the emperor, "It is very beautiful." And all advised him to wear the new magnificent clothes at a great procession which was soon to take place. "It is magnificent, beautiful, excellent," one heard them say; everybody seemed to be delighted, and the emperor appointed the two swindlers "Imperial Court weavers."

The whole night before the day on which the procession was to take place, the swindlers pretended to work, and burned more than sixteen candles. People should see that they were busy to finish the emperor's new suit. They pretended to take the cloth from the loom, and worked about in the air with big scissors, and sewed with needles without thread, and said at last: "The emperor's new suit is ready now."

The emperor and all his barons then came to the hall; the swindlers held their arms up as if they held something in their hands and said: "These are the trousers!" "This is the coat!" and "Here is the cloak!" and so on. "They are all as light as a cobweb, and one must feel as if one had nothing at all upon the body; but that is just the beauty of them."

"Indeed!" said all the courtiers; but they could not see anything, for there was nothing to be seen.

"Does it please your Majesty now to graciously undress," said the swindlers, "that we may assist your Majesty in putting on the new suit before the large looking-glass?"

The emperor undressed, and the swindlers pretended to put the new suit upon him, one piece after another; and the emperor looked at himself in the glass from every side.

"How well they look! How well they fit!" said all. "What a beautiful pattern! What fine colors! That is a magnificent suit of clothes!"

The master of the ceremonies announced that the bearers of the canopy, which was to be carried in the procession, were ready.

"I am ready," said the emperor. "Does not my suit fit me marvelously?" Then he turned once more to the looking-glass, that people should think he admired his garments.

The chamberlains, who were to carry the train, stretched their hands to the ground as if they lifted up a train, and pretended to hold something in their hands; they did not like people to know that they could not see anything.

The emperor marched in the procession under the beautiful canopy, and all who saw him in the street and out of the windows exclaimed: "Indeed, the emperor's new suit is incomparable! What a long train he has! How well it fits him!" Nobody wished to let others know he saw nothing, for then he would have been unfit for his office or too stupid. Never had the emperor's clothes been more admired.

"But he has nothing on at all," said a little child at last. "Good heavens! listen to the voice of an innocent child," said the father, and one whispered to the other what the child had said.

"But he has nothing on at all," cried at last the whole people. That made a deep impression upon the emperor, for it seemed to him that they were right; but he thought to himself, "Now I must bear up to the end." And the chamberlains walked with still greater dignity, as if they carried the train which did not exist.

There seems to be nothing really to add to this succinct exposure of the naked truth except, perhaps, that as visible as truth appears to the reader of the tale, it may remain equally invisible when we are prisoners of the collective aspects of our consciousness. The king, the prominent image or the dominant of collective consciousness, is possessed by his persona and his appearance.

As Hermetian tricksters, the swindlers are able to tear asunder the inflated persona, by weaving a garment of invisibility for the person unfit for his office. But as the story tells us, integrity is not a requirement or a prominent attribute in a persona-possessed psyche. Rather, compliance, conformity and obedience, which delude one to see the splendid colors of mendacity, are compulsory requirements for office in autocracy. How often have not peoples and minds been deceived by the false appearance of treacherous leaders! Thus, paradoxically, the naked truth becomes hard to see, since it requires the integrity of the child, who finally can give voice to the Self. Were it not for the transformative aspect of the swindler-tricksters, the voice of the child may never have been raised, and the king and his advisors would have lived happily ever after.

## Father and His Shadows

Moshe[301] may illustrate the person who is possessed by the father archetype. He is strong and powerful, leaving little or hardly any space
for those around him, especially his sons. He sets the rules, and there
are no other rules than his. He is not the kind of person who comes to
therapy. His wife might, or perhaps his children. Therapy and analysis
entail looking into the mirror, into the shadow, into one's own weak-
nesses and shortcomings, shame and guilt. The Spiritual Father archetype as carrier of the collective consciousness, whether in society or
in one's private soul, is as antithetical to the shadow as are the bright
colors in the emperor's inflated delusions.

Moshe was married, with four sons. He was a successful lawyer, who
knew how to interpret the law so that it would suit the purposes of
his clients. Not even during his studies was he a *student* of the law; he
was always its *master*. Characteristically, he always represented the big
against the small—the bank or the big company against its customer.

Moshe was born and raised in a cooperative settlement. He experienced his father as a weak, simple and earthly man who had found
himself on the farm "because he would not have coped on his own."
In contrast, his paternal grandfather had been a respected rabbi and ad-
judicator of religious law, after whom Moshe was named. As compared
to his negative opinion about his father, he greatly admired his strong
and powerful, pioneer mother; "she was the only man in the house."
Moshe was proud of her persistent fights with the neighbors, when for
instance she would encroach upon their gardens.

During his teens, he was the natural leader of his group. Later he had
served as an officer in the army, experiencing fierce battle. He dismissed
post-trauma as revealing "the true face of a chicken."

No one would doubt the strength of his ego and his capabilities, or
question his authority. Arrogantly, he often told his sons self-aggran-
dizing stories, replete with statements such as "tell your school-mates
that I am a hundred times more intelligent than all the other parents
together." He always knew best. There could be no questions, and no
doubt.

---

301  Moshe (Moses) means to draw out, i.e., from the water. As leader and law-
giver, the code of religious laws are called the Law of Moses. There are fathers
from whom the sense of watery flow seems to have been extracted, leaving
them with the harshness of their laws and their surrounding in constant fear
that at any moment he may break the stone tablets in fits of authoritarian
rage.

Moshe's oldest son was an all too typical first-born to a strong father.[302] He worked in his father's law firm, attempting to be and behave
like his father, but often ridiculed by the employees when clumsily trying to impose his authority. He lacked his father's intelligence and authoritarian personality. Rather, he lived *the imitated life*, which makes
one lose the key to one's own destiny. Imitation is the very opposite of
being oneself, to consciously search for one's center, as a manifestation
of the individuation process.

The second son wandered astray, unable to find himself, experiencing himself as *homeless*. Without a sense of home, he worked as a
traveling salesman of cheap paintings in Japan, employed by a fellow
landsman, who held him in a firm grip, and most likely exploited him.
Running away from home, he ended up repeating his relationship with
an abusive father.

When growing up, the third son expressed his need for attention
in many different ways. As a teenager, his behavior became *antisocial*.
He was involved in criminal activities such as car thefts, often caught
in the midst of burglary. Repeatedly, his furious father had to come to
his rescue, to release him from custody. Besides being enraged, Moshe
detested the ease with which the police caught his son. He did not have
a clue as to the psychological riddle behind his son's revenge.

The youngest son became an *anarchist* and animal rights activist.
In sharp contrast to his father, he declared, "meat is murder," collect-
ing wounded dogs that he brought home to his not so animal-loving
father.

One way or another, all four sons lived out of their father's pocket,
either in subservience or in rebellion, but never free. As a consequence
of their father's identification with the spiritual father archetype, the
four sons responded each one in his respective way—imitation, wandering, anti-social behavior and anarchism. The mother's efforts at protecting the sons were met with ridicule and hostility from Moshe. She
was too frightened to leave or to stand up against him.


## The King who Refuses to Die

A key pathology of adulthood, pertaining as well to the archetype of
father, is *the old king who refuses to die*. Essential to the resolution of
the midlife crisis is the ability to let the king die. The known ways that

---

302  Cf. *The Hero and His Shadow*, p. 138f.

probably have served the person well, may now become obsolete. Some thoughtful kings will be open for change, while others will have to be dethroned. That is, some of our patterns of behavior will respond to the request for change, while certain habits will stubbornly resist. John-Raphael Staude speaks about what he calls "Jung's conversion experience at mid-life" to his "religion of the archetypes," in which "Psychology became Mythology. Libido became Eros. Parental imago figures became archetypal structures. Beyond and behind the personal phenomenal world lay the eternal forms, the Platonic Schopenhauerian Idea."[303]

At midlife, the adult ego has likely gained a foothold in society and established itself internally as the conscious and regulating faculty of the psyche. The ego has conceivably adapted to the persona of collective consciousness, to norms and collective principles. However, a time comes when the king must die. He must regenerate, and let a new generation, new guiding principles take over. There comes a time and the spirit of the old idea, of a myth, which has generated the current rules of collective consciousness, loses its libido, its fire. The wise king, the clever ego, presents his sons with a challenge or a riddle. He thereby allows new complexes to arise along the horizon of one's mind. He lets a new fire burn, allowing a new consciousness replace the old one. But it is often difficult to renounce one's earthly powers and assets and accomplishments, and so the young hero may have to overthrow the king, whether in society at large, or as an aspect of the individual personality.

The ego is afraid to die, especially if it strongly identifies with collective norms. To many, the threat of death may seem most terrifying in midlife. The old, often unexamined myths by which one lives one's life must die, to be replaced by a new guiding myth. As Staude says regarding Jung, that out of his midlife passage, he "discovered the Self as a new integrating center of the personality beyond the ego."[304]

For example, Hadara[305] was forty-nine-years-old when she experienced waves of anxiety, fearing imminent death. She had always been well-controlled, often telling people with pride how as a baby, the oldest of four siblings, all born less than two years apart from each other, she was toilet trained before she was a-year-and-a-half. Mother had been the dominant parent, while her father was sickly, cared-for and well protected. From an early age, the children had to be quiet at home, not

---

303  *The Adult Development of C. G. Jung*, p. xxi.
304  *The Adult Development of C. G. Jung*, p. 46.
305  The name means grandeur as well as citrus fruit. Hadar was a king of Edom.

to disturb their father and aggravate his illness. Furthermore, Hadara was born after years of infertility, for which the mother had blamed herself. Her aging but always active and healthy mother, now paralyzed by illness, shared with her daughter her ontological guilt of having survived, while most of her relatives had been murdered in the camps.

Hadara had always been strict with herself. She was competent and successful in her field. Men would be attracted to her, but she had difficulty imagining herself doing "anything wrong." Her anal, controlling defenses began to break down at midlife. As her strong and dependable mother was facing death, the internalized image of mother shattered as well, and the underlying death anxiety broke through. However, confronting the symbolic death, her personality could free up beyond the strict and regulated boundaries that had been her lot. She now felt entitled to "pick the fruit of my own desire."

A life-stage transition and the initiation into a new stage in life by necessity entail sacrificing the archetypal core of the previous stage. The previous life stage loses its energy and its hold. In the rites of passage, we encounter what has previously lingered in the shadow. The essence of the midlife crisis, I believe, is the encounter with *stagnation* and *mortality*, often experienced as loneliness and loss. Midlife is the entrance into hell, claims Campbell.[306] These may have been repressed into the shadow, as long as ego remains the adult's strong and undisputed ruler. *Avoiding* the encounter with stagnation and mortality, however, *causes* that very stagnation and feeling of death and depressive impasse. That is, the midlife crisis holds the healing potential of the malaise at its core, often requiring the recognition and acceptance of a process of enantiodromia, of great reversal, based on the soulful search for one's personal sense of substance, to become what one is, as among others Pindar said. "[T]he seeds of psychological renewal and of possible future directions for life lie hidden within [the shadow]," as Murray Stein says[307]—the shadow which hits us strongly at midlife.

For example, we usually blame the parents for our complexes. But parents serve, as well, as objects onto which we can conveniently project our complexes. Thus, the death of one's parents entails a concurrent removal of the objects of projection of the parental complexes. Sometimes the inheritance left behind and the strife among the siblings dividing the inheritance serves as transitional object for the projection of parental complexes, evoking feelings of anger, jealousy, neglect or

---

306  Joseph Campbell, *The Hero with a Thousand Faces*, p. 21.
307  Murray Stein, *In Midlife*, p. 83.

being favored. Complexes may also be transferred onto siblings, accusing each other for being like that parent or the other, or, in case of a positive parental complex, for *not* being like the deceased parent, not respectful of his or her memory, acting in contradiction to the deceased parent's will and wish, etc.

The dealings around inheritance, often in midlife, may be a profitable and maturational transition, of withdrawal of the projection of complexes. It then becomes part of healthy mourning and a mature internalization of the parents.

Ellenberger speaks about the creative illness at midlife of both Freud and Jung. He characterizes it as a "polymorphous condition that can take the shape of depression, neurosis, psychosomatic ailments, or even psychosis."[308] However, Ellenberger stresses its creative potential, mentioning for instance "[t]he strange malady that Sigmund Freud underwent between 1894 and 1900,"[309] that is, between age thirty-eight and forty-four, which terminated with the publication of his *The Interpretation of Dreams*. Likewise, Jung emerged from "the long night," his six troublesome years between 1913 and 1919 (again, age thirty-eight to forty-four!), experiencing that "the process in which he had been engaged had an aim; it led the individual to the discovery of the most intimate elements of his personality, the self."[310] With the publication of Jung's *Red Book*, the *Liber Novus* in 2009, we now have a unique insight into his confrontation with the unconscious and his discoveries.

Sometime in the middle of our life, the credit that most of us have been fortunate enough to have been given, comes to an end. What previously could be spent without too much concern, will now require conscious attention. Both Freud and Jung showed a remarkable capacity to delve into the shadows of their own reflection.

## The Parched Earth

If the ego's rule is too exclusive, leaving out and denying the child-Eros, the puer-spirit and the senex-soul—or, let us call it water, fire and wind—then the *earth dries up*, and it becomes a *dried-up, soul-less ego*. A soul-less ego is an ego without anima, without the feminine element. It is the strict, rational, unreflective, soul-less male ego, whether in a man or a woman.

---

308 *The Discovery of the Unconscious*, p. 447.
309 *The Discovery of the Unconscious*, p. 447..
310 *The Discovery of the Unconscious*, p. 672.

Nechama,[311] a particularly well adapted fifty-year-old woman, had the following dream,

> I stand inside a house, looking out. On the outside, there is a tree with a thick trunk, without branches. The crown of the tree has upward pointing leaves, very orderly, everything symmetric. But the tree is not grounded, and there are no roots. The water company has announced they will completely stop supplying water to the tree soon, and I know that I will have to water it with bottles of mineral water.

Neurosis cuts the lifeline, splits-off from its source in the Self, causes dryness and stiffness. This dream portrays the danger of drying up, and it moves toward compensation. In the dream, this woman has moved inside herself, looking out at her usually extraverted personality, represented by the tree without roots, in need of the nourishment of life from within the earth, from her more grounded feminine self. The bottles of mineral water may serve as an emergency procedure, but they cannot supply life-giving water for long. However, they clearly call the ego into urgent action.

Even as an adult, Nechama tended to rely on her parents for advice, such as, "whatever happens, always stay at your job, so that you ensure your pension rights." She had remained in her job as a secretary even though she felt that, as she said, "I die every day of boredom." This is neurotic suffering, in contrast to the suffering that is often an instrumental part of the healing-process. Neurosis means being disconnected from oneself, from both the conscious aspect of one's life as well as the experience of life.

After hesitant attempts and painstaking deliberations, and after she had the following dream, she decided to resign from her secretarial job, and find ways to earn a living from her awakening creativity,

> I live in a fortress with a high, rotting wall around. I have to dig around the wall in order to clean it up. Surprisingly, the wall doesn't fall but its shape changes. It becomes more open, green with birds.

Dreams that pertain to ego-pathologies may either truthfully and often painfully reflect back into consciousness the condition of the ego, or show the way by bringing forth valuable alternatives—if the ego and consciousness are willing to listen. The unconscious senses the pres-

---

311  Nechama means 'comfort.'

ence of an attentive ego, for which it may be worthwhile to produce fertile symbols. When the ego is inattentive and too rational, then the self-regulatory function of the psyche may be blocked. It is as if the psyche dries up because the self has no partner, when the symbols it creates are not attended to.

## The Limping Ego

Yoram[312] was a fifty-one year old physician. When driving his son's car, he was suddenly overcome by incapacitating weakness in his legs. The weakness was so powerful that he "could not continue [driving]." He was convinced the cause was an oxygen deficiency because of carburetor malfunction. The "looseness of his limbs" was so strong it held him in its grip for weeks. His (erroneous) self-diagnosis was *Bends disease*, or *decompression illness*, which may be caused by diving, and can be characterized by symptoms such as pain in the joints of arms or legs, extreme fatigue, numbness or paralysis, headache, confusion and double vision. He turned to several physician colleagues of increasing specialization; from internist, cardiologist and neurologists, to a specialist in diving and air pressure. Yoram was sent for increasingly specialized examinations, convincing some about his diagnosis, and nearly persuading his doctors to treat him in a high-pressure chamber.

Yoram had never fully 'made it.' He never became head of the ward where he loyally had been working since his internship. He had never developed a private practice, and because of his mortgage, had lately run into financial straits, to the extent that he had to sell his own car. This was the reason why he had borrowed his son's car. His symptoms expressed his feeling of being unable to stand on his own, the ground shaking, or as he—though unaware—expressed it himself, he was unable to continue. They also expressed his feelings of humiliation of no longer driving his own car but his son's, of not being master of his own life. Since his ego, his conscious identity, was unable to acknowledge the humiliating condition, his psyche turned around in the opposite direction, expressing itself by means of somaticized conversion (i.e., 'opposite direction') symptoms. The hysterical symptom expressed what was 'really' taking place behind the intact persona. Only when

---

312 Yoram means 'exalted,' often short for Yehoram ('God is exalted'), king of Israel after the kingdom had split. According to the texts, nobody regretted his passing, and while buried in Jerusalem, he was not laid to rest in the tomb of the kings.

facing his soul rather than merely keeping his face to the world, in pain and honesty, could he transfer the suffering and the meaning of his symptoms from his legs to his psyche.

The DSM states, "The definition of this disorder [hysterical neurosis, conversion type] is unique in this classification in that it implies specific mechanisms to account for the disturbance." The DSM then continues to describe these mechanisms. According to one of them, the person achieves "'secondary gains' by avoiding a particular activity that is noxious to him," for instance the soldier who cannot fire the gun with a "paralyzed" hand. That is, the symptom is *purposeful*. According to the other mechanism the person achieves "'primary gains' by keeping an internal conflict or need out of awareness." The symptom is said to have "a symbolic value that is a representation and partial solution of the underlying psychological conflict."[313]

That is, speaking about hysteria, the phenomenological classification of the DSM becomes psychodynamic (implying an underlying conflict), symbolic, teleological and almost imaginative.

Furthermore, to really make hysteria *the* illness, the DSM acknowledges that under certain circumstances "the conversion symptom may enhance the development of a chronic sick role." That is, the suffering soul gets trapped in the embodiment of the sick, suffering and ailing character—which otherwise may suffer repression in the backyard of the shadow.

And to finally convince us that it is, as well, the pathology of the medical and therapeutic mind, the DSM ascertains that unnecessary "diagnostic or therapeutic medical procedures may themselves produce disfigurement or incapacity."

## The Empty Shell

Helen Deutsch formulated the concept of the as-if personality in the early 1940s.[314] It is essentially an identity disorder, belonging to the spectrum of borderline personality disorders. Sherwood and Cohen aptly defines as-if pathology as "imitative, a way of life built on an endless series of transient identifications"[315] that replace each other, instead

---

313  *Diagnostic and Statistical Manual of Mental Disorders*, p. 244f.
314  Helen Deutsch, 'Some forms of emotional disturbance and their relationship to schizophrenia,' *Psychoanalytic Quarterly*, 11, pp. 301-321.
315  *Psychotherapy of the Quiet Borderline Patient: The As-If Personality Revisited*, p. xiii.

of being integrated into a stable sense of identity. The as-if personality may give the impression of an adequately developed ego, that appears as-if well-functioning. However, it is a "persona-ego," behind which the person suppresses feelings of weakness and avoids conflict with the environment. He or she adjusts swiftly to the requirements of the situation, changing colors like a chameleon. In the as-if personality, relatedness is not authentic, but often seems as if it is. Pseudo-affectivity and the capacity to wear personae according to the roles required by the momentary situation reflect an avoidance of intimacy and the lack of an integrated identity. The as-if person does not really feel alive.

The person with a frozen persona, or empty shell, suffers from a lack of stable identity behind a seemingly well-adapted persona, with which he or she identifies. However, here the persona is not flexible, but stiff and frozen. The whole personality seems invested in compliance to others and the external situation, in a seemingly rigidified courtesy. The individual seems to be entirely invested in the persona, so that we do not manage to trace hints of a genuine person behind the appearance. We may often observe features of dissociation, which is characteristic of psychic trauma.

Eva,[316] born in Berlin in 1928, may serve as an illustration of 'the empty shell.' She was the second of three sisters, in a rather typical, assimilated, and bourgeois Jewish family. They considered themselves "Germans, of Mosaic descent."

Her parents married shortly after the First World War, and her father established a small chain of hardware stores. He was formal, strict and severe, with a dry sense of humor. Eva's mother was more of a 'butterfly;' petite and proper, energetic and vivacious, including frequent extra-marital affairs.

Eva's eldest sister, Gertrude, was a copy of her father, serious and perfectionist. She never married, and had only had one close female friend, who was murdered in the Second World War. Her younger sister, Bernadine, was a copy of the mother, a flamboyant puella.

Especially after Hitler's rise to power, the family emphasized being "good Germans." Eva herself was extremely well behaved and compliant. She felt her mother's joie-de-vivre was reserved for others, especially her sisters, while no matter how good Eva was and how pleasing she tried to be, she would not gain her mother's love and appreciation.

Practically the only memory Eva claimed she could recall from her childhood was from Crystal Night, November 1938, when she had

---

316  Eva, from the Hebrew 'Hava,' means 'life.'

just turned ten. The father had been warned that the Gestapo might be looking for him. Rather than leaving the flat, he sent his wife and daughters out, and stayed behind to protect the home. Fortunately, the secret state police did not turn up. However, Eva wandered the streets of Berlin during the night, together with her mother and sisters. She recounts these events without recalling any details, and without a trace of affect.

Her father, who had opposed leaving the country since he considered himself German, stating, "I am more German than that Hitler, who with all his shouting is not of this culture," was finally convinced, and the family emigrated to the United States.

In America, soon after finishing high school, Eva married a young American Jewish man, who in retrospect may have been post-traumatic from his war experiences in Europe. They gave birth to a son and a daughter, both of whom left home at a very young age, moving to the Midwest, retaining very little contact with either parent.

While initially Eva may have married because she wanted to get away from her parents, particularly her mother to whom she felt a lifelong intense but restrained hatred, she soon felt controlled and imprisoned by her husband. After a year, she asked for a divorce, whereupon he made a suicide attempt. Eva never raised the issue again. She spent most of her days away from home, often aimlessly walking in the streets. She never made the connection to Crystal Night, even rejecting this understanding. She would spend time alone in cafés, sitting and staring, and whenever someone came up to her, she would put on a smile and enter into superficial conversations.

As regards to her children, she felt unable to cope with her first-born daughter. Eva found her extremely difficult, "born aggressive and without feelings." The son, she said, was "easy and quiet," but the birth of a second child made her give up any fantasy of divorce. It seems that in his teens he became somewhat of her son-lover, perhaps temporarily relieving her frozen depression. When he left for college, she felt angry and betrayed; "he didn't care about me any longer . . . he never told me anymore about his life, and his little 'adventures.'"

All through her life, a deep sense of loneliness and neglect dominated her self-image. The neglected and abandoned child remained a childhood fixation, leaving Eva passively angry and internally bitter. As a child, she may have coped with her strict senex-father and swift puella-mother by futile attempts at compliance. Walking the streets during the dark night of shattered glass may have frozen her façade and fortified her inability to relate to herself, to her inner core, which is often symbolized by the child, and manifests by a sense of being alive.

Eva was obsessively preoccupied with her feelings of neglect, aggressively withheld anger and bitterness, turning her appearance into a cold and lifeless persona of meticulously correct, but empty, cliché-like behavior. She felt she had no real friends, not understanding that her superficial ways prevented intimacy. She desired "one friend who is like me and understands me," unaware that that friend could only come into existence if she would befriend her Self.

An emptied soul and a neglected Self amount to an existence of meaninglessness. The Self is the archetype of meaning; there can be no experience of meaning if the core of one's personality is not related to. An ego that cuts its roots in the Self, or that has lost its dynamic and vital connection to the soul's universe as if there were no stars and no planets, no depth of the sea, neither the fire and the spirit, nor soul or wind, is a neurotic ego, living the meaningless life. Midlife provides an opportunity to pass through the agony and anguish, into the search for meaning, seeking the Self. Humility, self-reflection and craftsmanship may serve us well in a healing process of individuation.

# V. i.

# The Senex

---

That time of year thou mayst in me behold
When yellow leaves, or none, or few, do hang
Upon those boughs which shake against the cold,
bare ruined choirs where late the sweet birds sang.
In me thou seest the twilight of such day
As after sunset fadeth in the west,
Which by and by black night doth take away,
Death's second self, that seals up all in rest.
In me thou seest the glowing of such fire
That on the ashes of his youth doth lie
As the death-bed whereon it must expire,
Consumed with that which it was nourished by.
    This thou perceiv'st, which makes thy love more strong,
    To love that well which thou must leave ere long.

—William Shakespeare; sonnet 73[317]

## Fate and Destiny

From birth, we count the days and the years, the yearly birthdays of growth and progression. But we can register the data along the timeline of life, as they unfold in the datum of death, with equal accuracy, only that they are all put in place the moment we "yield to fate,"[318] that is, when the Angel of Death arrives to fetch our soul, as in the following legend,

A man dreamed that he saw someone bending over him with a sword. "Who are you, my lord," he asked, frightened.

---

317  Sonnet 73, in *The Oxford Shakespeare: The Complete Works*, p. 788.
318  'Death's Messengers,' in *The Complete Grimm's Fairy Tales*, pp. 718-720.

"I am the angel of Death," said the swordsman, "and I have come to fetch your soul."

"Have pity on me," begged the man. "I am poor, and have nothing to leave my children." Please wait and come back when I have put away something for them."

The angel of Death had pity on him, returned the sword to sheath, and said, "This time I'll let you off. But the next time that I come for you, your excuses will be of no help."

The man thanked him, but asked the Angel of Death to send a messenger before he comes back, so that he could prepare himself, without living in constant fear. The Angel of Death felt compassion, and agreed.

When the man woke up, he understood it was only a dream. He got up, went to work, and rather soon forgot about his dream of death. In the course of time, he grew rich, and married all his sons and daughters, until at last he grew old and fell fatally ill. Again, the Angel of Death arrived, and stood before him with his drawn sword. "Why do you come like this without warning? Did you not promise to send me a messenger first?" asked the man in anger.

"O man," said the angel, "I sent you not one, but seven messengers."

"Where were they?" asked the man, I did not see a single one of them."

The Angel of Death laughed grimly and said, "They are all here with me, all seven of them. The first was your eyes, which used to be sharp and grew dim. The second was your ears, which became so deaf that you could not hear even a trumpet blast. The third was your teeth, which once could grind stones and then fell out of your mouth. The fourth was your black hair that turned white. The fifth your stature, for once you were straight as a palm tree, and now you are bent like a bow. The sixth was your legs, now you need three, because without the cane you cannot walk. The seventh was your appetite – how once you loved to eat, and now everything has lost its taste! Those are the seven messengers I sent you!"

The man could not argue with the truth spoken by the Angel of Death, and let him take his soul.[319]

The similarity with the Grimm Brother's story about *Death's Messengers*, and other versions from around the world, reflects the impact of old age and death, and a universal inclination to repress the autumn-aches of our life, and deny its inevitable turn into winter. As an old saying bluntly tells us, age is a sickness from which everyone must die.

---

319  'The Angel of Death's Seven Messengers,' a Jewish legend from Yemen, in *Jewish Folktales*, pp. 180-181.

From the very first day of our life, we move backwards as well as forwards, just like Hermes, who the day he was born, deceived his brother Apollo by walking backwards, when stealing his cows. We often do not notice this movement in reverse. While reason and rationality pertain to the clear, empirical, evidence-based vision of the adult ego, the intuitions, the signs and the signals that seem to be concerned rather with fate and destiny, pertain to this reversed counting of life, to death as the mirror-life. We recognize them for instance after someone has died, when in retrospect we realize the hints that were there, but which we hardly noticed, and were unable to grasp. It refers to the wisdom of the senex, the old man and woman, with a profound awareness of soul, spirit and non-matter, and a sense of proximity to death, no matter what his or her chronological age might be.

Shortly before Zehavah,[320] a sixty-two-year-old married woman, stopped working after more than thirty years in the same public health fund, she dreamed,

> I go to visit a friend (not anyone I know from real life). She is exactly my age, but she lives alone. She lives in a very poor neighborhood, in an old and shabby building. She stands in the backyard, cooking on an old stove. She says she cooks for an old woman, who seems to be very sick. Cockroaches walk all over, and a rat almost jumps into the pan. I tell her we must contact the authorities, but she insists on cooking for the old woman. I feel terror. Then, I go down to the cellar. There sits the old woman. She doesn't look as sick as my friend had implied.
>
> I ask her what she thinks about impulsiveness. After much thinking—she is really not impulsive!—she says, that if she wouldn't have relied on her impulse, she would have lost the best years of her life.

In her dream, Zehavah visits an unknown, yet friendly side of her. While they are similar, of exactly the same age, this inner friend lives alone, in poverty and neglect. However, precisely there, in her neglected shadow, dwell the care and the cooking. A caring attitude is cooking in the backyard of her soul, which is necessary to approach the fears of old age.

In her ruminations following the dream, Zehavah reflected on the connection between impulsiveness, impulse and pulse. The dream, which she dreamed at the passage into life as a pensioner, opened the door to conscious reflection on the darker aspects of old age, behind

---

320 Zehavah means 'golden.'

which she could attend to the subtler meanings that she had previously avoided. She was aware how she had suppressed the poverty, illness and loneliness that may come with old age, having become blind by seeing too much of the weak and sick passing by her counter at work. But old age, discarded into the darkness of denial, had also lost its pulse of life. The old woman in the dream, ostensibly and at least potentially sick, needed to be attended to. She needed someone to prepare her food, to be identified in the dark so that she may emerge from her underground dwelling in the cellar, and by thoughtfulness feel the pulse of life.

## The Burning Fields

Old age means approaching death and departure. Loss and separation are an integral aspect of the age at which integration, oneness and ego-Self union constitute the essence of the opus.

Sacrifice for the greater purposes of the collective may character-ize youthful devotion, but is, likewise yet differently, a central feature of the wisdom in the Japanese story *Inamura no Hi*, 'The Burning Rice Fields' by Tsunezo Nakai. In his greater and genial wisdom, the old hero is willing to suffer personal loss for the survival of the villagers. This is how the story is told:

> Long ago, there lived in Japan an old man whose name was Hama-guchi. His farmhouse stood on the edge of a plateau, a flat, open space on the side of a mountain. Behind, the mountain rose in lofty wooded peaks. In front, it sloped gently down to the sea. At the foot of the mountain along the shore was the little village, made up of a hundred or more thatched houses and a great temple.
>
> One afternoon in late summer, Hamaguchi sat on the balcony of his house and watched the people in the village below. With him was his grandson, a lad of ten. The rice crop had been very fine, and the villagers were holding their harvest festival. All the shops were closed and the streets were gaily decorated with ropes of straw and paper lanterns. The villagers in bright-colored clothing were about to join in the harvest dance.
>
> Beyond the village, Hamaguchi could see the vast blue sea, wrinkling under the bright afternoon sun. Suddenly there came a slight shock. The house rocked three or four times and then stood still. Hamaguchi had felt many earthquakes in his time, and he was not at all frightened until he looked toward the sea.
>
> The water had become dark green and very rough. The tide had suddenly changed—the sea was running swiftly away from the land! The villagers stopped their dancing, and ran to the shore to

watch. None of them knew what this strange thing meant. But the old man on the mountain had seen one such sight as a little child. He knew what the sea would do. There was no time to send a message to the village, nor to ring the big bell in the temple, and yet the people must be warned.

"Yone!" he called to his little grandson. "Light a torch! Quick!"

The boy was puzzled, but he asked no questions. He kindled the torch at once. The old man ran to the fields, where hundreds of rice stacks stood awaiting sale. It was all his wealth. He ran from one stack to another, applying the torch to each. The dry stalks caught fire quickly, and soon the red flames were shooting upward, and the smoke was rising in great columns to join the wind clouds in the sky.

Yone ran after his grandfather, shouting and crying, "Grandfather! Grandfather! Why? Why are you setting fire to the rice?"

The old man had no time to answer, but ran on, igniting stack after stack. The high wind caught the sparks and loose brands and carried them farther, until the fields were all ablaze.

The watchman in the temple saw the fire, and set the big bell booming, and the people turned from the sea to look. In Japan, everyone in the village must give help in time of fire. No sooner did the people see that Hamaguchi's rice stacks were on fire than they began to run. Like a swarm of ants, they climbed the mountain—young men and boys, women and girls, old folk, mothers with babies on their backs, even little children joined in the race to put out the fire.

But when they reached the plateau, it was too late. The flames had already consumed the stacks of beautiful rice.

"It is too bad," the people exclaimed. "How did it happen?"

"Grandfather did it," cried Yone. "With a torch he set fire to the rice. He is mad."

In amazement, the people stared at Hamaguchi. "You did this thing!" they cried. "You set fire to the rice fields!"

"Look toward the sea," said the old man, "and know my purpose."

The people turned and looked. Far out they saw a great wall of water sweeping toward them more swiftly than a bird flies. It was the returning sea!

The people shrieked, but their voices were lost in a great sound, deeper than thunder, as the wall of water struck the side of the mountain. The hills shook, and were drenched in a great burst of foam.

When the cloud of spray had disappeared, the people saw a wild sea raving over their village. Great angry waves seethed and tumbled above the house-tops. They rolled away roaring, tearing out houses and trees and great rocks, and bearing them off. Again, the wall of water struck, and again and again, with less force each time. At last, it fell back once more in its former bed.

The people stood speechless on the side of the mountain. The village was gone; the temple was gone; the fields had been torn away. Nothing was left of their homes but a few straw roofs that floated on the water. But every man and woman and child was safe on the mountain side.

Then the people knew why old Hamaguchi had set fire to the rice. There he stood among them, as poor as any. And they fell on their knees to thank him.[321]

We have since learned the Japanese word for a large ocean wave, literally 'harbor wave,' after the devastating *tsunami* in 2004, then catastrophically repeated in 2011. This story makes us dramatically aware how insufficient it is to rely solely on rational consciousness. While wisdom does not guarantee survival under extreme duress, the stories of survival from the 2004 Indian Ocean tsunami can roughly be divided into three categories:

First, there were those whose instincts told them to follow the animals; then those who are accustomed to states of emergency, their ego in a constant state of vigilance, who therefore reacted immediately to the retreating sea, recognizing the abnormality. Finally, there were those who knew to draw upon the accumulated knowledge and wisdom, the tales and the lessons of the ancestors, recognizing the signs and the patterns that emerge as phenomena in the world of appearance. The wisdom of the old man, virtuous and steeped in self-sacrifice—the antidote of evil—makes us aware what we fail to notice if we do not honor old age.

The wisdom of Hamaguchi may be the external manifestation of the introverted process of Self-knowledge, as reflected in the dream of the old man carving God's name on a piece of wood (p. 121). The wise old person may be a representative of that psychological function, which enables the ego to relate to the Self. We would like to see the elderly more well-respected in society, but we might equally say that being fully an elder is to *respect*, as an internal, meaningful act of depth and ensoulment. This entails looking again, respection, looking back, to consider one's life, to grant it value and meaning. Perhaps it entails, as well, awareness in depth of the archetype of the shadow, which limits

---

321  Adapted from Sara Cone Bryant, *The Burning Rice Fields* (no page numbers), based on the story about Goryo Hamaguchi, who saved his fellow villagers when Hiro-Mura was struck by a massive tsunami in 1854.

and restrains the youthful conviction that "new, faster and easier" is always better.

## What Has Been Gathered Will Be Dispersed

Developmentally as well as archetypally, old age entails loss of ego-functions, the loss of which can be replaced or compensated for by ego-Self integration. When given the same piece to read, the young remembered the text better than the elderly, but the latter understood more of what was written.

Mara[322] was a seventy-two-year-old woman. Her husband had died ten years earlier. She remained in mourning, depressed, with occasional anxiety attacks and intrusive images of disaster. She still refused to touch any of his clothes and other belongings, leaving his possessions exactly the way they had been when he died. She did not want to make any changes that would interfere with a sense of his physical presence at home. However, this in no way fulfilled her desire to keep her deceased husband alive. The result was, rather, that she was increasingly stifled into becoming a zombie.

After two years in therapy, her deceased husband finally appeared in a dream, telling her that he was leaving,

> In the dream, I see him leave. He is in another place, but not with another woman. I can't reach him there, but I send friends of mine, people I can trust, to send him gifts from me, and to speak to him and ask how he is. He is fine. I am surprised that I am not angry that he has left, I feel he couldn't do otherwise, and I feel a warm feeling of love and longing for him.

The dream helped this woman to experience loss and love simultaneously, both the sadness of appropriate mourning and bittersweet taste of desire that cannot be fulfilled. Previously, she had relied on an unbearable split between life and death, poorly dealt with by the denial of death, with the result that her life also became extinguished. As in Mara's dream, it is the symbolic function of the psyche, which enables us to heal and unite what to our conscious mind seems impossible.

---

322  Mara means 'bitter' in Hebrew. When Naomi (which means 'my pleasure') returns from Moab, entering Bethlehem, she tells the people, "Do not call me Naomi, call me Mara, for the Almighty has dealt very bitterly with me" (Ruth 1:20).

In our world today, there is little celebration of old age and the old person. We need the idea of the old wise man and woman, but he/she seems to be present in fairy tales rather than in our post-modern society. The wisdom of the old is not easily valued in an era of hi-fi and Wi-Fi, hi-tech and hi-speed in which the young, beautiful and ambitious are the emperors. However, as Erik Erikson and others have stated, a society that does not value its elderly cannot grow healthy children.

Old age is often *exclusion* and *invisibility*. The senex as shadow, as the negative of the coping, capable and well-functioning adult ego is often repressed and denied. In today's world, old age no longer seems to indicate the unfolding of the senex-archetype in its meaningful aspect of *ego turning toward self*, of the ego's acceptance of its limitations and insignificance, which paradoxically are necessary, at this age, to gain a sense of meaning. We want nothing of ugliness and sickness, and so we put it away or silence it by an abundance of *pills*, today's life elixir in old age, fooling ourselves there is no aging, only prolonged youth.

The tale about 'The Old Man and His Grandson' is told around the world, and appears as well in *Grimm's Fairy Tales*:

> There was once a very old man, whose eyes had become dim, his ears dull of hearing, his knees trembled, and when he sat at the table, he could hardly hold the spoon, and spilt the broth upon the tablecloth or let it run out of his mouth. His son and his son's wife were disgusted at this, so the old grandfather at last had to sit in the corner behind the stove, and they gave him his food in an earthenware bowl, and not even enough of it. And he used to look towards the table with his eyes full of tears. Once, too, his trembling hands could not hold the bowl, and it fell to the ground and broke. The young wife scolded him, but he said nothing and only sighed. Then they bought him a wooden bowl for a few halfpence, out of which he had to eat.
>
> They were once sitting thus, when the little grandson of four years old began to gather some bits of wood upon the ground. "What are you doing there?" asked the father. "I am making a little trough," answered the child, "for father and mother to eat out of when I am big."
>
> The man and his wife looked at each other for a while, and began to cry. They then took the old grandfather to the table, and henceforth always let him eat with them, and likewise said nothing if he did spill a little of anything.[323]

In an Asian version, the father makes a basket, intending to throw the Grandfather into the river, since he has become a financial burden

323   *The Complete Grimm's Fairy Tales*, tale 78, p. 363f.

on the family. One of his children, however, asks him to bring back the basket, "because one day we will need to use it for you."

We often want the old person silent and invisible, without realizing that we then fail to hear the wisdom and see the insights of life's experience. A patient of mine, very much a puer in search of the elixir and confirmation of youth, was harshly confronted with the old man in him, when at the age of fifty-five he contracted cancer. He described his feelings of terror as he walked slowly, frightened and vulnerable along the hospital corridors, scared he would be run over by doctors and nurses and visitors rushing along, whom he felt did not see him, not only as a person with a life and a history, but even physically; "It seems I am a cancer, with a hint of a human being loosely attached to it." In one of his last dreams, he dreamed that,

> I have to take care of the big boss's fireplace. I cut the branches of the tree outside my window, to put them in the fire. I wake up very scared, realizing that I try to cut the branches of the tree so that the serpent of death shall not enter through my window.

Who is the big boss? Is it Life that he tries to keep burning? Is it Death whom he must serve? Is it the paradoxical condition of burning the tree of life in order to prevent the serpent of death from entering, yet letting it enter because the stuff that life is made of, life's energy, is being burned up? "[S]ince the snake cleaves to the darkness of the earth," writes Herzog, it expresses "the uncanny character of the Death-Demon."[324]

Is God, whether in life or in death, the Big Boss? If so, *what* is God? Is it the projected image of the Great Father, as in the monotheistic religions, or is it the God of Einstein and Spinoza? Spinoza said, "I believe that, if a triangle could speak, it would say, in like manner, that God is eminently triangular, while a circle would say that the divine nature is eminently circular. Thus each would ascribe to God its own attributes, would assume itself to be like God, and look on everything else as ill-shaped."[325] We hear the echo of Spinoza resound in Einstein, who said that the religious attitude is the "knowledge of the existence of something we cannot penetrate, of the manifestations of the profoundest reason and the most radiant beauty." Einstein expressed his belief in the God of Spinoza "who reveals himself in the orderly harmony of what exists, not in a God who concerns himself with the fates and

324  Edgar Herzog, *Psyche and Death*, p. 56.
325  In a letter to Hugo Boxel, 1674.

actions of human beings."[326] These are senex-questions, pertaining to meaning and metaphysics, Self and transcendency. The person's actual age is of minor importance; Spinoza was forty-two, and Einstein fifty-years-very-old, when they respectively expressed these views.[327]

As Gerhard Adler writes, it is the senex within us that makes us realize that, "[t]he whole of nature rests upon the double principle of growth and decay ... Just as in the life of a plant the first stage is governed by the principle of unfolding and expansion, so the second stage is one of in-folding and concentration."[328]

Differently stated, traditional Buddhist Scripture tells us,

> What is born will die,
> What has been gathered will be dispersed,
> What has been accumulated will be exhausted,
> What has been built up will collapse,
> And what has been high will be brought low.

Facing death, dispersal, exhaustion, collapse, and sinking low, are aspects of the senex's lot. When balanced with infolding and concentration, meaning can be found in death and dispersal. But if one-sided, the old person is fettered to the hellish netherworld of undying misanthropy.


## Tia Miseria

The misery of misanthropy reflects the unintegrated death in life, the Death that kills the joie de vivre of the playing child. Without passion and desire, life may seem to have been extinguished long before physical death puts out the flame. Death in life evokes terror in the heart of Youth, who with its spirit tries to provoke and destroy this misery. The mischievous boy is sometimes a manifestation of the inner playful child, threatened by the petrification of misanthropy. 'Tia Miseria,' a folk tale from Puerto Rico, tells us exactly this story:

> Once upon a time, in a faraway town, lived an old woman. The people in the town had forgotten her name, but they called her Aunt Misery, since she never had a kind word to say to anyone. She

---

326  Albert Einstein, responding to Rabbi Herbert Goldstein, who asked him if he believes in God, 1929.
327  See also *Requiem: A Tale of Exile and Return*, p. 42.
328  *Studies in Analytical Psychology*, p. 137.

never ever spoke to her neighbors, except when the naughty children would come and steal the pears from her beloved tree.

The fruit of her pear tree was the only joy left in her life. And so, when those mischievous boys sneaked in to her garden and climbed the pear tree, she would shout at them and curse them, but they would quickly run away, their mocking laughter ringing painfully in the ears of Aunt Misery.

One time, the only pear the boys had left behind was one that had fallen to the ground, half spoiled. Tia Miseria picked it up anyway and brought it inside, to prepare for her dinner. As she cut the pear, she heard a knock on the door. There stood a stranger, asking for shelter for the night. She invited him in, and prepared a bed. She gave him a plate with the only slice of food she had: a piece of bread, and the ripe half of the pear. The stranger nodded in gratitude, and ate the food hungrily.

The next morning, as he prepared to leave, he revealed himself, and told her he was a visitor from heaven. "As a reward for your kindness, I will grant you a wish; anything your heart desires."

Poor old Aunt Misery needed no time for reflection; she said, "I wish that whoever reaches up into the branches of my pear tree, shall remain there until I give my word."

"So be it," said the stranger and disappeared.

When the tree blossomed again a year later, and again brought forth fruit, then, with the fruit, came the mischievous boys. When she heard them coming, she peeped out the door and, for once, she smiled when she saw them sitting on the branches of the tree. When they saw her, they shouted "Witch! Witch! Tia Miseria!" but now she just laughed mockingly at them, "Steal my pears, will you?" and she reached up with her cane and struck the legs of the unfortunate boys who could not climb down.

When her arm grew tired, and the boys' curses and cries grew quieter, and turned to promises never to take another pear, never to set foot in the yard again, and never to steal anything from anyone, she finally had mercy with them. "I want you to paint my fence. And I want a roasted chicken every week," she told them and as they promised her, she let them come down from the tree, and they painted her fence and brought her chicken every week. So the life of Tia Miseria grew quiet, and she alone enjoyed her beloved pears, and you would believe that here ends the story.

And the years passed, and the tree grew old, very old and twisted and bending low because it was so old. Then one day, another stranger appeared and knocked at her door, and she asked him what he wanted.

"I am Death, and I have come to take you with me," said the stranger.

He looked so old and thirsty and weary that she offered him a glass of water. She gave him bread, and roast chicken. And Death was pleased, because rarely was he treated with such hospitality on his travels. But when he finished his meal, he said, "It is time; time is up."

Well, said old Aunt Misery, "we need some nourishment for our journey, right? The pears in my tree are truly delicious. But since I am too old to reach the ripe pears at the top of the branches, perhaps you would be so kind to climb up and get us some?"

And Death was only glad to do her a favor, so he climbed up— and got stuck in the tree. It seemed as if Death himself came alive: He cursed her, he yelled and screamed, he tried sweet talk, he tried to charm her and to persuade her, but nothing helped, she would have none of it. She left Death in the tree, and each day visited him and asked to hear stories of his many travels, but she would not let him go.

And the years went by, and because Death was stuck in the tree, he could not make his usual rounds, so no one died.

Soon Aunt Misery started to receive new visitors, who all came to her to complain; the doctors and the pharmacists, the undertakers and the priests. "Business is terrible," they complained. And the old who were tired of life, and those who have suffered injuries and are in pain, they all came to beg old Aunt Misery to release Death.

So she made a bargain with Death, telling him, "I will release you, on condition that you never bother me again." Death had no choice but to agree—truth is, choice and free will have never been prominent traits of Death.

So she freed him from the tree, and Death returned to the world. And he has kept his word and never returned to the garden of Tía Miseria, which is why Misery remains forever alive in this world.

The pathological senex-misery we are concerned with here pertains to being miserable because of not living one's life, of not relating affirmatively to one's life experiences. It is a condition in which "Everything is desouled, every particle of warm blood has been chilled, events unroll in icy egoism. ... there is nothing pleasing, nothing refreshing, nothing hopeful, but only things that are grey, grisly, gruesome, or pathetic, tragic, ironic, ..."[329] Lacking a sense of meaningful destiny, external objects as well as one's internal world become a disruption.

Without a sense of meaning, the psyche's energy becomes cathected to, or invested in misery, whether seemingly caused by others or by the cruelty of one's fate. The psyche is, then, not grounded in the Self, the archetype of meaning. In this sense, misery prevents the experience of

---

329  This is how Jung describes Joyce's *Ulysses*, CW 15, par. 169.

rebirth. Joan Borysenko describes the death-rebirth connection beautifully; sitting at her dying mother's bedside, she had a vision,

> In the vision[,] I was a pregnant mother giving birth, and I was also the child being born. Conscious of being in two bodies at once, I had a deep knowing that all people are interconnected, a part of one another. Both mother and child were enduring a dark night of the soul, a deep pain that was the harbinger of rebirth.[330]

Ego-Self reunion, preparation for dying and coming to peace with one's own death, becomes a possible route for the senex. However, the old man or woman may be overwhelmed by decline and the loss of friends as well as ego-capacities, and surrender to gloom and despair. As a sixteen-year-old senex, Jung pondered about God's creation of this world "out of His satisfaction." When Jung looked out at the small world of the village in the country, "where there are few people and nothing much happens," and "old age, disease, and death are experienced more intensely," he wondered how God could be satisfied.[331]

Simone de Beauvoir mentions how jealousy, "profoundly rooted in sexuality," is inflamed by age. She exemplifies,

> The hairdresser whose business is failing readily persuades himself that his wife is deceiving him and makes terrible scenes. And since old age is a time of generalized frustration it begets a general resentment that may take the form of jealousy.[332]

Old age confronts us with the inconceivable polarity of wholeness and annihilation. These were, in fact, our two initial images, pertaining to the child, of the life cycle. We find the struggle of this senex-polarity for instance in Freud's late life, on the one hand passionately vital, on the other a morbid pessimist. The Self of Meaning is, unlike the Original Self from which the ego is born, no longer an image of Wholeness, but a coniunctio of Wholeness and Division, Wholeness and Annihilation.

Approaching the otherworld of soul may be experienced as death in life, loss of meaning, loss of power and of narcissism. When bodily and other ego-functions decline, and the inner world is uninhabited, there seems to be no refuge from the experience of emptiness—in contrast to

---

330 Joan Borysenko, *A Woman's Book of Life*, p. 250.
331 *Memories, Dreams, Reflections*, p. 58.
332 Simone de Beauvoir, *Old Age*, p. 351.

the young person, who sometimes may compensate an inner emptiness with physical appearance, attraction and attractiveness.

The core pathology of the senex is *catatonic depression* of the netherworld, of Hades, the petrification of encountering the Gorgons in the condition of death, the stalemate of the soul, without even an attempt to fight the monsters. The wind does not blow, the air is heavy. It is like living in a deadening hell. In Egypt, the poet and philosopher Ptah-Hotep (500 BCE) wrote,

> How hard and painful are the last days of an aged man! He grows weaker every day; his eyes become dim, his ears deaf; his strength fades; his heart knows peace no longer; his mouth falls silent and he speaks no word. The power of his mind lessens and today he cannot remember what yesterday was like. All his bones hurt. Those things which not long ago were done with pleasure are painful now, and taste vanishes. Old age is the worst of misfortunes that can afflict a man. His nose is blocked, and he can smell nothing any more.[333]

Nathan,[334] a sixty-seven-year-old dentist, had decided to retire in the near future, "so that I can finally have some fun in life, after forty years of work, work, work. Who really likes to spend his entire life drilling holes and then filling them, just for the sake of paying bills that only grow the more you earn?" he wondered sardonically. He was not sure what he intended to do with his life as a pensioner when he retired, besides "getting out of my clinic." The following was his initial dream in a brief analysis,

> I am at my clinic. The last patient of the day has just left. I walk out to the car, but it is not there. It is dark already, and I keep walking in the street as if I was homeless. I find a bench to sleep on. Before daybreak, I hurry away so that no one I know will see me. I get to a backyard called "the place where the dead live." Worm-like rats creep over the body of a dying dog. It is the 'dog of hell'—it is completely black, limping, and has a dog's body but the face of an old man. Its face is pale, white, staring without expression in his eyes, more dead than alive. I don't know if I should rescue it, or just let it die. I then have to enter a house at the center of the place where the dead live, where I have to

---

333  In *Old Age*, p. 92.
334  Nathan, 'he gave,' was a prophet and adviser to King David. God revealed to him in a dream that not David, but his son Solomon was to build the Temple.

fetch something. A distant relative of mine who died many years ago, and who was a very bad person, sits there. He is dead also in the dream, but faints when he sees me.

With paradoxical vividness, the dream gave expression to Nathan's depression, which may have been lingering latently during all those years of what he described as boring work and his sense of "a dog's life." As he rid himself of his false persona, of his jovial façade, he opened up and confronted the underlying depression. Only then, after acknowledging his depressive sense of deadness, was he able to explore ways in which he could experience a sense of meaning. He discovered an interest in archeology, and felt that "drilling in people's teeth for forty years was merely a preparation for digging in the ground under the guidance of people who can share with me so much knowledge of history."

# V. ii.

# Homage to Sophocles

## From Thebes to Colonus

*Oedipus at Colonus*, which Sophocles wrote at the age of ninety, shortly before his death in 406 BCE, is a masterpiece of old age. It is an homage to the creativity of the old person, a celebration of the inward journey.

The play was first performed posthumously in 401 BCE at the Dionysia in Athens. Produced by Sophocles' grandson, his namesake Sophocles, son of Ariston, the play won first prize.

There is little movement in the play, but as A. E. Haigh wrote in 1896, "in scenes of pensive beauty it shows us the calm tranquil, and not inglorious close of a stormy and disastrous life."[335]

Oedipus at Colonus is the mirror story, reflecting the reverse image of Oedipus, the hero, the complex and the king, ruler of Thebes. In *Oedipus Rex* we follow young Oedipus, the hero who is unluckily born to Laius and Jocasta in spite of the oracle's fateful prophecy. She had warned Laius that he will be killed by his son, who will also sleep with his mother, Jocasta, wife of Laius. This triggers the hero's journey, which begins with Oedipus' miraculous survival when thrown out in the dark and cold night outside the city boundaries by his father. He then grows up as the easily enraged, redheaded adopted son at the court of the king of Corinth.

After being teased that he is not truly the born son of mild king Polybus, Oedipus sets out to inquire with the Oracle at Delphi whether the king and the queen really are his parents. When he hears her prophesy, he does not wait for the oracle to finish, but reacts the way we do when someone steps on our 'oedi-pus,' our swollen foot, that is, when some-

---

335   Arthur Elam Haigh, *The Tragic Drama of the Greeks*, p. 198.

one steps on our complexes. We become infected by exaggerated and disproportionate affect, burst out in anger or withdraw, wounded to the bones. Terrified by the oracle's answer, predicting his parricide and mother-incest, Oedipus does not await the answer to his own question about the parents of his living reality—from this we understand that the whole story does not deal with his real parents, i.e., the couple in Corinth that has adopted him, cared for and educated him. Rather, the complex drives him away from them, toward the acting out vis-à-vis the parents of his archetypal fantasies.

Thus, in blind fate, he aims toward Thebes.

On the way, at the godforsaken three-way crossroad, he meets his father. As La Fontaine says, "Our destiny is frequently met in the very paths we take to avoid it."[336] The impulsive, complex-ridden young man he is, Oedipus gets into a quarrel and kills his father, the king, unbeknownst to him.

However, Oedipus is, as well, a clever young man. When he arrives at the gates of Thebes, he knows the right answer to the Sphinx's riddle. The Sphinx, that dreadful monster with a woman's head and breasts, the body of a lion, and the wings of a bird, had settled on the walls of the citadel, the city's protecting fortress. She killed the Thebans one by one, strangling them to death.

Before killing her victims, the Sphinx asked them her riddle:

> There is a two-footed creature on the earth, and a four-footed one called by the same name, and also a three-footed one. It alone of all living creatures that dwell on the earth, in the air, and in the sea changes its form.

The Thebans would be freed from this plague once the riddle would be answered to the satisfaction of the Sphinx. Oedipus gave his well-known answer:

> Man is what you mean, since after he is born he crawls around on the earth and is four-footed, walks upright in his prime, but when he becomes old, he bears a crooked neck under the load of old age and leans on his staff for the third foot.

Thus, he became King of Thebes, marrying Jocasta, 'the shining moon,' his father's widow, the Queen, his mother.

---

336 Jean de La Fontaine, 'The Horoscope' (Book VIII, fable 16), *The Original Fables of La Fontaine*, p. 30.

Jung has warned us that Oedipus's answer is too simple—or, rather, the *riddle* is; Jung says, "the complex whose symbol is the Sphinx ... cannot be disposed of by solving a childish riddle. The riddle was, in fact, the trap which the Sphinx laid for the unwary wanderer."[337]

Perhaps the riddle *is* relevant for the first half of life, but merely knowing the cycle of life may not be sufficient for the second half of life, in search for greater, or deeper meaning. Jean-Pierre Vernant pertinently says,

> Oedipus, Oidipous, guesses the riddle; he himself is the di-pous, the man with two feet. But his error, or rather the effect of the curse that effects his lame lineage, is that, through solving the riddle ... he also returns to his place of origin, to his father's throne and his mother's bed. Instead of rendering him like a man who walks straight in life ... his success identifies him with the monster evoked by the Sphinx' words: the being who at one and the same time has two feet, three feet, and four feet, the man, who in his progression through life, does not respect the social and cosmic order of the generations but instead blurs and confuses them. Oedipus, the adult with two feet, is the same as his father, the old man who walks with a stick, the three-footed one ...; he is also the same as his children who crawl on all fours ...[338]

Froma Zeitlin points out that in the Oedipal drama, the progression of time has collapsed. She asks, "Is not incest ... the quintessential act of return: ... the paradigmatic act that destroys time by collapsing the necessary temporal distinctions between generations."[339]

When autonomous complexes burst, they invade, affect, infect, take command of conscious identity, and cause epidemics in consciousness; thus, tragedy ensues. This is the case with King Oedipus, when the consequences of his act of father-killing and mother-sleeping throw their shadows onto the city of Thebes.

Eventually, when Oedipus realizes his fate, he blinds himself in an act of self-castration, and realizes that, "ever since my own body's eyes through my own hand took away the world of appearance, I think I have actually begun to see."[340] It is in midlife, that the rule of the ego

---

337   *Symbols of Transformation*, CW 5, par. 265.
338   In Joseph Wilson, *The Hero and the City*, p. 13.
339   *The Hero and the City*, p. 12.
340   *Oedipus Variations*, p. 71.

ends, which sometimes requires that the ego be overtaken by illness of epidemic dimensions.

Tiresias the seer has told Oedipus, "One must stop seeing the world to gaze upon god."[341] This marks the beginning of the story of *Oedipus at Colonus*, the senex part of his life. He is no longer the furious young man who, driven by anxiety, tries to escape his fate, merely to fall into his complexes. He is no longer the man who became king because he knew the answer to the seemingly simple riddle of life, that man passes from infancy through adulthood to old age. Driven by his complex, Oedipus remained ensnared by archetypal fate, thus failing to become master of his own destiny. Now an old and blind, wandering beggar, leaning on his faithful daughter Antigone, Oedipus leaves Thebes, and arrives at Colonus.

As they arrive at the sacred grove, the townspeople at Colonus ask him to disclose his identity, to tell them *who he is*—which cannot be easy if you are an aging Oedipus! In a way, arriving at the sacred grove of our life, we need to leave much of our conscious identity behind, even if it has not been stained by acting out, neither by incest nor by parricide. Initially, the country folks at Colonus want him expelled, but he insists fate has brought him. His fate, he claims, is now to die at Colonus whereby the land will be fertilized.

Theseus, king of Athens and Colonus, is summoned. Oedipus tells him that he has come to die and to be buried in Colonus. By his death he will bring peace to the land. Consequently, Theseus offers him protection.

But Creon, king of Thebes, brother of Jocasta, and thus Oedipus's uncle as well as his brother-in-law, arrives, and pleads to Oedipus, "Cover our shame, come back to your father's city."[342] Uncannily, the Thebans as well seek protection by Oedipus after his death, by burying him close to, yet outside the boundaries of the city—just like Laius had discarded the infant outside the city. Oedipus, however, rejects King Creon's request.[343]

When Creon accuses Oedipus of parricide and incest, Oedipus responds by exculpating himself from guilt, and Creon has to return empty-handed.

---

341  *Oedipus Variations*, p. 71.
342  *The Theban Plays*, p. 94.
343  As for instance Kerényi points out, the Aeschylean Oedipus died and was
     buried in Eteonos, outside Thebes (*Oedipus Variations* p. 26).

Next in line to ask favors from Oedipus is Polynecis, his son, who wants his father's blessing in his war against his brother Eteocles, who had dethroned him. What he receives from his father Oedipus is, however, nothing but curses. Without a trace of compassion, Oedipus calls his son his worst enemy. Oedipus repeatedly distances himself from his sons, who eventually kill each other, while he expresses love and gratitude to his daughters.

The play reaches a dramatic peak when Oedipus pleads not guilty for his fate, which, as he says, was determined before he was born, so how can he be blamed? Is a person free to determine his or her destiny, or is fate predetermined by the gods? We may ask to what extent are fate, destiny and guilt intertwined?

The play ends with the death of Oedipus. The messenger returns to inform the people of Colonus that "the life of Oedipus is ended." The chorus inquires if it was "by some act of God, was it? And with no pain?" whereupon the messenger answers that "it was wonderful," followed by a detailed, awe-inspiring description of Oedipus's departure.[344] The Chorus then declares,

> This is the end of tears:
> No more lament.
> Through all the years
> Immutable stands this event.

Thus ends this play, which Cicero considered to be the most tender of poems.

## The Crossroads Revisited

The story begins at the psychological crossroads between Thebes and Colonus. Regarding Oedipus, this indicates the interface between the first and second half of life. This is not necessarily a chronological issue, but refers to the 'twice-lived life,' paraphrasing the saying that a book, which is not worth reading twice, is not worth reading once. The life that is not related to, in which the spaces between the lines are empty, holds less feeling, meaning and sense of being experienced. The unrelated life is like an unread book, and "a dream which is not interpreted is like a letter which is not read."[345]

---

344  *The Theban Plays*, p. 119ff.
345  R. Hisda,Talmud, Ber. 55a.

The metaphorical crossroads between Oedipus, King of Thebes, and Oedipus at Colonus, is the turning point between being the actor on the stage of one's life, and struggling to understand it; of living our life, sometimes as driven by our complexes, and relating to it in a meaningful way, vitally nourished by the source of our Self.

As stated previously, if the crossroads are not related to appropriately, if not paid due respect, the threshold experience provided by the crossroads of life becomes insignificant, trivial. Joshua,[346] a twenty-nine-year-old man dreamed,

> I enter a dark alley. A woman, whose face I cannot see, stands in the dark, at the entrance to a house in front of me. She asks me from where I have arrived, and where I am going. I tell her, "I came to ask you where I can find my key." She gives me a key and says, "This is your key, but now you have to find your way." I am not sure if she emphasizes *find*, or *your*, or *key* or *way*, but I continue onward until I arrive at a small place, like a checkpoint, where I have to wait before I can continue to the other side. The key consists of quite a big ring of gold, with an elongated arrow or sword of silver across the ring, extending further at one end. I need to figure something out before I can cross over to the other side, but I wake up before I manage to figure it out.

The crossroads in this man's dream do not pertain to the ego's conscious decision-making processes, the way we may experience standing at the crossroads, when contemplating important decisions to be made. The anima with the face that cannot be seen, standing invisible in the darkness of the soul, asks the young man a seemingly simple, yet important question: whence and whereto. His answer is, as well, rather simple: to find his key. But the anima does not provide easy directions, but soulful guidance for the one who is willing to ponder. Even with the key, there is a need to find one's way, which leads to the very next crossing, and perhaps the one after that as well. The dreamer is still young, not merely because of his chronological age. He must learn to wait. He needs to get old. While his waiting needs neither be interminably for Godot, nor a Kafkaesque trial, it does require the patience of the old person, the reflection that emerges while patiently waiting.

---

346 Joshua, 'God is salvation,' son of Nun, succeeded Moses as a leader of the Israelites, and led them into the Land of Canaan. The fall of Jericho was brought about by silently circling the city for seven days.

On the way, Joshua must also discover the nature and the qualities of his key, in order to find the possibility of shaping a personal destiny in conjunction with the guidance from the self.

The key combines gold and silver, sun and moon, the ring and the sword, masculine and feminine. It reminds us of the Ankh, which is an image of a cross and a loop, a Crux Ansata, the looped cross. Combining the erect male organ with the female, it is a sexual symbol of fertility, uniting the opposites; a distinct image of the Self.

The Ankh is a hieroglyph, that is, a sacred imprint, meaning *life*. It also pertains to life after life, or eternal life. It has been observed, that the Ankh looks like the shadow of a person with outstretched arms – we may perhaps say, that the shadow of a person stretches out towards the transcendent essence of life.

The Ankh is sometimes called *the key of life* and the word ankh means *mirror*, as well. Thus, the key that opens the lock to the unknown that lies ahead, is coupled with the mirror that reflects our image and soul, which enables us to reflect upon ourselves, as von Franz says.[347] Jung relates the crossroads to the duality of 'mother,'

> Where the roads *cross* and enter into one another, thereby symbolizing the union of opposites, there is the "mother," the object and epitome of all union. Where the roads *divide*, where there is parting, separation, splitting, there we find the "division," the cleft—the symbol of the mother and at the same time the essence of what the mother means for us, namely cleavage and farewell.[348]

In his poem "The Road Not Taken," written in 1916, Robert Frost brings us not only the dilemma as we arrive at the crossroads, but the "sigh" of complexity, sadness and satisfaction as we reflect upon the road not taken, having taken the road less travelled:

> Two roads diverged in a yellow wood,
> And sorry I could not travel both
> And be one traveler, long I stood
> And looked down one as far as I could
> To where it bent in the undergrowth;
>
> Then took the other, as just as fair,
> And having perhaps the better claim,
> Because it was grassy and wanted wear;

---

347  Marie-Louise von Franz, *The Way of the Dream*, p. 132.
348  CW 5, par. 577.

Though as for that the passing there
Had worn them really about the same,

And both that morning equally lay
In leaves no step had trodden black.
Oh, I kept the first for another day!
Yet knowing how way leads on to way,
I doubted if I should ever come back.

I shall be telling this with a sigh
Somewhere ages and ages hence:
Two roads diverged in a wood, and I—
I took the one less traveled by,
And that has made all the difference.[349]

As I have quoted earlier, Kerényi says, "The crossroads themselves are the fate."[350] Approaching the crossroads along the path of my life, I have the opportunity to contemplate my way and my direction, from where I come and what I leave behind, whereto I am heading and what I need to carry. At the crossroads, I need to find the questions to ask, and contemplate the weight of the responsibility that I am obliged to carry, as a consequence of my choices and my answers. These are not merely the decisions of consciousness, but conscious decisions in lieu of my fate.

## The Holy Grove at Colonus

After long wanderings, Oedipus, the blind old wanderer, leaning on his faithful daughter Antigone, arrives at a place of rest, along the road from the sea and the country towards Athens. A rocky path leads to a thickly-wooded grotto, and a stone figure of Colonus on a horse becomes visible. Oedipus is not familiar with this place. That is, this is a place beyond personal knowledge and identity.

He has arrived at a sacred precinct, a Temenos, that Antigone vividly describes as "overgrown with laurel bushes, olive and wild-vine" and "full of the voices of many nightingales." She pleads, "You have come a long way, father," and begs him to sit down on a "seat of natural rock."[351]

---

349   Robert Frost, *The Road Not Taken*, p. 1.
350   *Oedipus Variations,* p. 11.
351   *The Theban Plays,* p. 72.

No longer the impulsive and complex-driven young man, Oedipus is now able to wait. "Three masters," he says, have taught him patience, "pain, time and the royalty in the blood."

The holy ground belongs to the Eumenides, the spirits or goddesses of earth and darkness. "It is not a place as famed in song and story," says a countryman who approaches Oedipus, "but its name is great in the hearts of those that live here."[352]

The sacred grove is not a place of earthly name and fame, but one of withdrawal into heart and soul. The Erinyes, "the angry ones," are the same as the Eumenides who at Colonus are called the "Allseeing Kindly Ones." The same feminine force of nature and godliness may be kind and caring, as well as angry and furious, and we may wonder, both men and women, when does the one strike us, and when does the other stroke us?

Ashera is the Canaanite goddess of the sacred grove. She is the mother of the twin brothers Shachar and Shalem, the morning star and the evening star. Her name holds the strange root *asher*, which has a variety of meanings. It can be understood as 'to confirm' and 'to verify,' or 'to praise' and 'to make happy.' It may, as well, mean, simply 'that which.' Strikingly, the same root appears as the middle word of the acronym for God, Yahweh—'ehyeh *asher* ehyeh.' Since the time of the Temple and the High Priest, nobody knows how to pronounce the Tetragrammaton of God's name, which can mean many different things, such as, 'I am that I am,' 'I am who I am,' 'I will be whom I will be,' 'I will be what I will be,' 'I will be where I will be,' 'I will be what I want to be,' 'I am he who was, am and will be.'[353]

The holy grove is a sanctuary, and Oedipus prays for asylum, for an end to his tormented days. He acknowledges having travelled the road to this sacred place by divine guidance, and asks to be granted "fulfilment and close of life," and that those who have received him, be blessed. He tells the people of Colonus that he has no home, and begs them not to ask his identity. We may wonder, what existence is reflected in being homeless, desiring one's identity not to be revealed? Is this the final stage, in which the ego's home and identity become the chains that bind and burden, to be broken free from so that we can stand in front of the empty nothingness that unites us with the world soul?

---

352  *The Theban Plays*, p. 73.
353  Exodus 3: 14: And God said to Moses, I AM THAT I AM; and he said, Thus shall you say to the people of Israel, I AM has sent me to you.

Oedipus tells King Theseus,

> Time, Time, my friend,
> Makes havoc everywhere; he is invincible.
> Only the gods have ageless and deathless life;
> All else must perish. The sap of earth dries up,
> Flesh dies, and while faith withers falsehood blooms.
> The spirit is not constant from friend to friend,
> From city to city; it changes, soon or late;
> Joy turns to sorrow, and turns again to joy.[354]

The chorus of elders tells Oedipus this is a place of silence; "speak where speech is lawful, or else be silent," they say, and ask of him to "make amends ... to the divinities."

What silence do the elders ask of Oedipus?

For many victims of the Shoah, silence has kept them frozen between unbearable memories and a post-War life that could not be fully lived. Silence may be a container for pain and fear, a vessel constantly threatening to break. It may hold both the fear and the instinctive warning, which Jung says we try to avoid by noise, since,

> Noise protects us from painful reflection, it scatters our anxious dreams, it assures us that we are all in the same boat and creating such a racket that nobody will dare to attack us. Noise is so insistent, so overwhelmingly real, that everything else becomes a pale phantom. It relieves us of the effort to say or do anything, for the very air reverberates with the invincible power of our modernity.[355]

There is, as well, the meaningful silence, which enables us to hear the "beating of the great heart of the world," the silence from the depth of which wisdom, Sofia, is born, the silence within the center.

Oedipus has to bring holy water from where a fresh spring flows, and bring it in clean hands. He is told that there are vessels "of delicate workmanship," whose edges and handles he has to cover with lamb's wool. Then, while facing dawn, facing East, Oedipus shall pour the drink-offering onto the sunless earth in three libations, the last containing water and honey.

Then, "with both hands thrice nine sprays of olive lay," that is, with both hands, Oedipus shall three times lay down nine olive branches.

---

354 *The Theban Plays*, p. 90.
355 Gerhard Adler, *C. G. Jung Letters: 1951-1961*, p. 389.

He should do this while simultaneously praying, without lifting his voice, to the earth goddesses, after which he must turn and go.

Oedipus has sought refuge and has sacrificed the sense of home and identity. He bows to the holy presence of the feminine forces of the sunless earth, the realm of the defeated gods, that is, where we renounce our godliness as well.

## Guilt, Fate and Destiny

Jung says,

> Individuation and collectivity is a pair of opposites, two divergent destinies [or destinations]. They are related to one another by guilt. ... Individuation cuts one off from personal conformity and hence from collectivity. ... [I]t means ... stepping over into solitude, into the cloister of the inner self. ... [S]ince the breaking of ... personal conformity would mean the destruction of an aesthetic and moral ideal, the first step in individuation is a tragic *guilt*. ... The accumulation of guilt demands *expiation*. ... Every further step in individuation creates new guilt and necessitates new expiation.[356]

In fact, "life itself is guilt," says Jung.[357] In what may be the central piece of the drama at Colonus, we hear Oedipus claim that he is the victim rather than the perpetrator. He pleads not guilty for having carried out what amounts to his fore-doomed fate,

> The gods so willed it—doubtless an ancient grudge
> Against our house. *My* life was innocent,
> Search as you will, of any guilty secret
> For which this error could have been the punishment,
> This sin that damned myself and all my blood.
>     Or tell me: if my father was foredoomed
> By the voice of heaven to die by his own son's hand,
> How can you justly cast it against *me*,
> Who was still unborn when that decree was spoken?
> Unborn? Nay, unbegotten, unconceived.
> And if, being born, as I was, for this calamity,

---

356 'Adaptation, Individuation, Collectivity,' CW 18, par. 1094-1099.
357 'The Personification of the Opposites,' *Mysterium Coniunctionis*, CW 14, par. 206.

I chanced to meet my father and to kill him,
Not knowing who he was or what I did—
How can you hold the unwitting act against me?
Likewise my mother—O shame, that you should force me
To speak as I must about your sister's marriage—
But you have broken all bounds of piety,
And I cannot be silent. She was my mother—
My mother, and knew not—neither of us knew
The thing we did—her shame!—she bore my children.
I know, I know it is you that take delight
In slandering her and me. To speak of it
Is as much against my will as was the doing.
Yet this I must say again! I am not condemned,
And shall not be, either for my marrying
Or for my father's murder, which your spite
Persists in casting in my teeth.

The chorus responds with compassion to Oedipus's exculpatory plea and declares, "Our guest is innocent, sir, though cursed by fortune. We cannot withhold our aid."[358]

Are we guilty of our foredoomed fate? Are we responsible for the genes that may cause our depressions, the constitution that influences our behavior, the geography that determines our residence, the times in which we were born? Personally, were I born a decade earlier, I may have been murdered as a child.

The Talmud says, "Everything is foreseen, and everything is laid bare, yet everything is in accordance with the will of man." Furthermore, "When an inner situation is not made conscious," says Jung, "it happens outside, as fate."[359] It is consciousness that enables us not to be bound entirely to the fate that the gods have pronounced, but to become, if not masters, at least guides toward our own destiny, that is, the place and the goal we are destined for. Jung writes beautifully when he says,

> Only the living presence of the eternal images can lend the human psyche a dignity which makes it morally possible for a man to stand by his own soul, and be convinced it is worth his while to persevere with it. Only then will he realize that the conflict is *in him*, that the discord and tribulation are his riches, which should not be squandered by

358 *The Theban Plays*, p. 101f.
359 'Christ: A Symbol of the Self,' *Aion*, CW 9ii, par. 126.

attacking others; and that, if fate should exact a debt from him in the form of guilt, it is a debt to himself. Then he will recognize the worth of his psyche, for nobody can owe a debt to a mere nothing. But when he loses his own values he becomes a hungry robber, the wolf, lion, and other ravening beasts which for the alchemists symbolized the appetites that break loose when the black waters of chaos— i.e., the unconsciousness of projection—have swallowed up the king.[360]

What guilt do I carry? For what? To whom? For what purpose? How do I pay for it? What retribution? What atonement? How does it lead me? How do I shape my aims and destiny? How do I tread my individual path allowing for the eternal images to become a "living presence?"

Guilt expresses the inevitable tension, conflict and balance between individual and collective, ignorance and knowledge, between predetermined fate and individual destiny.

## Fertilizing the Earth

As we draw to an end, we hear the chorus in an ode to old age and death,

> Show me the man who asks an over-abundant share
> Of life, in love with more, and ill content
> With less, and I will show you one in love
> With foolishness.
> In the accumulation of many years
> Pain is in plenty, and joy not anywhere
> When life is over-spent.
> And at the last there is the same release
> When Death appears,
> Unheralded by music, dance, or song,
> To give us peace.[361]

Oedipus hears the thunder, and understands that, "God is sending his voice across the sky to summon me to death." He then calls for Theseus, whom he takes aside, and tells him,

> Son of Aegeus, what I have now to unfold
> Is a thing that your city shall keep in its secret heart

---

360  CW 14, par. 511.
361  *The Theban Plays*, pp. 108-109.

> Alive to the end of time. Soon I shall take you,
> None guiding me, to the place where I must die;
> And no one else must know it. Tell no man
> The region where it lies concealed from sight,
> That it may be for you henceforth for ever
> A source of strength greater than many thousands
> Of yeomen shields or allied spears.

In death, Oedipus renounces all ego-narcissism; no one must know his burial place. His ego is sacrificed by means of secrecy, hidden, set apart, and can then become a source of strength for the land.

Hermes and the Queen of the Nether World lead Oedipus on his way to the sacred grave, the whereabouts of which no one except Theseus will know,

> Do not touch me.
> Leave me to find the way to the sacred grave
> Where this land's soil is to enclose my bones.[362]

The messenger then describes the thunder, the voice of the God of Earth; and the women, that is, his daughters, trembled and wept, and "for a long time they lamented loudly and beat their breasts. Pained at their outcry, Oedipus took them in his arms and said: 'my children, to-day your father leaves you. This is the end of all that was I, and the end of your long task of caring for me. I know how hard it was. Yet it was made lighter by one word—love. I loved you as no one else had ever done. Now you must live on without me.'"[363] Oedipus here repeats the renunciation of his personal identity, of "all that was I."

The messenger gives a breathtaking account of Oedipus's death,

> In what manner Oedipus passed from this earth, no one can tell. ... We know he was not destroyed by a thunder-bolt from heaven nor tide-wave rising from the sea ... May-be a guiding spirit from the gods took him, or the earth's foundations gently opened and received him with no pain. Certain it is that he was taken without a pang, without grief or agony—a passing more wonderful than that of any other man.[364]

The death we are dealing with here is not only the *termination* of one's life, but the *contribution* to our life, which our awareness of its lim-

---

362   *The Theban Plays*, pp. 117-118.
363   *The Theban Plays*, p. 120.
364   *The Theban Plays*, p. 121.

inality may bring us. Vladimir Propp says, "The scene of leave-taking [when Oedipus departs at the end of the play] is the most disturbing in all of tragedy, it is the moment of the birth of man."[365] As Edmunds says, for Hegel, "Greek tragedy was not a matter of the depths of the individual but rather of the destructive conflict of opposing forces." Hegel regarded Oedipus's "transfiguration in death [a]s his and our evident reconciliation in his own individuality and personality."[366]

How do I bring about an "inner reconciliation," for instance between guilt and life, individual gain and collective contribution, in order to "fertilize the earth?" What is the meaning with which I want to induce my life, the soil on which my life grows? What covenant do I sign with my life?

The anchor of identity in meaning, or ego in Self, is to me the meaning of the impregnated soil in which the soul of my life can grow.

---

365   Quoted by Lowell Edmunds in *Oedipus: The Ancient Legend and its Later Analogues*, p. 39.
366   *Oedipus: The Ancient Legend and its Later Analogues*, p. 40.

# V. iii.

# The Last Chapter: Self and Meaning

## Ancestral Roots

The nucleus of the senex is death, which does not merely mean absence of life and vitality, but psychologically entails an attitude of turning away from the ego-demands at the peak of adulthood. Old age is the inevitable sacrifice of body-functions and ego-strengths. Death is not only physical, biological death, but the ability to let go, to let things die, and to let go of the ego's one-sided domination. While the separations of everyday make us die a bit, enabling constant renewal, the death of body and consciousness signifies *the* separation. Now is the time for the ego to renounce its lead, to give up its firm hold in and on this world, to turn toward the Self.

In old age, the ego turns toward the greater Self, to the Big Boss, as in the dream related above (p. 149)—whoever that Big Boss is. It may be the attentiveness to an inner voice. While we need to renounce the primacy of the ego, we must not follow our inner voice uncritically, since if trusted too confidently, it may lead us astray. Just like the self-regulating processes help to rectify imbalances of the psyche, we need a regulating ego, so that the inner voice will not become limitless, psychotic or perverse. Even worse, we may project the Self onto an ideology that we follow blindly, and people or nations may be caught up in the fanatic worship of a leader. In the aftermath of the First World War, Jung wrote, "every individual needs revolution, inner division, overthrow of the existing order, and renewal," but rather than believing in the illusion of "victorious power," he suggests the cure to be "Individual self-reflection, return of the individual to the ground of human nature, to his own deepest being with its individual and social destiny."[367] This

---

367  '*From* Preface to the second edition,' (1918), CW 7, p. 5.

does not exclude social involvement on behalf of the individual, but may reduce the risk that the ego be swept away by collective forces.

The ego's changing attitude, particularly in old age, often takes the shape of a transcendent or religious approach, which, as Daryl Sharp says, is "an attitude informed by the careful observation of, and respect for, invisible forces and personal experience," indicating a subjective relationship to metaphysical and extramundane factors.[368] "[T]he term 'religion' designates the attitude peculiar to a consciousness which has been changed by experience of the numinosum."[369] This means as well the recognition of a sense of spirituality, "a hush that follows the storm, a reconciling light in the darkness of man's mind, secretly bringing order into the chaos of his soul," as Jung says.[370]

In this sense, religion has little to do with the obsessive-compulsive authoritarianism that often characterizes the collective consciousness of established and formal religious structures. All too often, religious authority replaces personal responsibility. The Self is sometimes projected not only onto the transcendent, but onto the God-image presented by the priests and the rabbis and the imams—that is, those who 'know' all too well what God wants, thinks, means and intends. The religious function, rather, refers to the linking back, respectfully and in reverence, to the ancestors, rather than submission to the formal authority of whatever collective consciousness. Ann Casement says succinctly, "The religious life is the one that follows its own destiny by separating from identification with the herd persona."[371] Consequently, past and present, inner as well as outer events in one's life, are 'linked-back,' reflected upon, so that their meaning can be identified and deepened. This is old age as an archetypal image, at whatever chronological age one finds oneself. That way, one's individual ego may take its modest place as a link in the chain of generations, and open its heart to hear the voices of the ancestors, thus gaining from their wisdom, yet preserve its individual destiny and vocation.

Shulamit[372] had been a successful scientist. She had spent her entire adult life doing laboratory research. For many years, she had felt driven by her parental expectations of success and upward mobility,

---

368  Daryl Sharp, *Jung Lexicon: A Primer of Terms and Concepts*, p. 117.
369  CW 11, par. 9.
370  'A Psychological Approach to the Trinity,' CW 11, par. 260.
371  Ann Casement, 'Persona,' in: Leeming D.A., Madden K., Marlan S. (eds). *Encyclopaedia of Psychology and Religion*. Vol. 2, pp. 670-72.
372  Shulamit means 'peacefulness.' She appears in King Solomon's (Heb. Shlomo, 'peaceable') Song of Songs. Later, Shulamit appears as Salome.

but eventually found satisfaction in her research projects. Now, at age sixty-eight, she realized she had spent too little time with her children, even though she had developed a rather warm and caring relationship with her grandchildren during the last few years.

Prior to coming for analysis, she had become interested in the interphase between psychology and physics. She had come across the writings of Jung and Pauli, and eventually began to write down her own dreams. In the process of freeing up her locked-in feelings, she had, as so often is the case, come to realize the all-too-many shortcoming of her parents, both who died at an old age during her years in analysis. Having gained a sense of being firmly anchored in herself, independent from her perceived parental expectations, she had the following dream,

> I am in my home. A childhood friend of mine, whom I always envied because she came from a large family with lots of warm feeling and delicious food, in contrast to the cold and superficial atmosphere at home, came to visit. We talk for a while, and then we go for a walk, and as if by chance, we arrive at the neighborhood where we grew up. I point at our house, though it has been rebuilt, and ask, "Do you remember?" She nods, and at that moment, my dead mother calls me, and asks me if I don't want to come for a visit. "I thought you were dead," I tell her, but she says she lives in a small house in the backyard. I try to get there, but it's like a labyrinth, and I have to pass by dark streets like the outskirts of town with closed store fronts and garages. After what seems like a long way, I finally get to the house in the backyard, and it seems completely closed, shabby, abandoned. But then, suddenly, I see my parents, they are tiny, weak, sick, seem to need my help, but they say they don't, just want me to come and see them, "and you'll meet your grandparents as well."
>
> I wake up sweating, anxious, feeling guilty that I probably didn't do what I should have done for them before they died.

Guided by her childhood friend, who more naturally and with less struggle could be whom she really felt she was, Shulamit returns to her childhood quarters, and arrives at her "rebuilt" childhood home, possibly repaired in the analytical treatment. This prepares her for taking a new direction, which in a way is the opposite road taken so far. While in the past she had had to find the way to her own separate and independent self, she now had to see the other side of her parental images, no longer the parents who burdened and imprisoned her in their powerful expectations, but the parents that she needed to meet on *their* ground. While the ancestors had gathered her parents to them in death, Shulamit now, approaching old age, needed to approach the ancestors, so that she could gather them to her. The capacity to feel guilt, to know the debt we need to pay, serves as a necessary corridor to the depths of one's soul, in which the forefathers and the birth-giving mothers come alive.

In old age, we often search our way back, recalling childhood memories, reconnecting with family background, a religion or a country left behind. We tend to return to where we came from. While the tasks of youth and young adulthood require breaking away from one's roots, and to establish a separate and individual identity, now comes the time of return—though sometimes the road Home, "to whence I come, was a much longer and more painful road than the departure..."[373] An interest in one's family genealogy is a common expression of this.

We return to our ancestors in order to heal our neurosis. As Jung says, if "man was still linked by myth with the world of the ancestors, and thus with nature truly experienced and not merely seen from the outside, [the neurotics] would have been spared this division with themselves."[374] Our deceased parents have become part of a lost world, which we explore in order to find our ancestral roots and the often lost voices of wisdom from the past.

## An Oak and an Acorn

The old wise man or woman is the *inward hero*, who does not bring into consciousness, but rather turns away from the ego and brings it in contact with the unconscious, that is, ego-Self union. It is neither the glory nor the spirit of youth, who tries to carry the sense of divine essence into the realm of adult duty and responsibility, but the soulful *quest for meaning*, beyond our social façade. Comparing life to drama, Zalman Schachter-Shalomi says, "Old age is the time when the meaning of the play becomes clear to us."[375] This is the quest for the Self in its manifestation as the archetype of meaning, and for a meaningful myth to live by. In his speech in celebration of Freud's eightieth birthday (May

---

373 See *Requiem: A Tale of Exile and Return*, p. 51.
374 *Memories, Dreams, Reflections*, p. 144.
375 Zalman Schachter-Shalomi and Ronald S. Miller, *From Age-ing to Sage-ing*, p. 17.

9, 1936), Thomas Mann said, "While in the life of the human race the mythical is an early and primitive stage, in the life of the individual it is a late and mature one."[376] As we find in integrated and individuated older men and women, the inwardness is not a turning away from the world around, but there may be a "convergence of societal history and individual development."[377] Social circumstances come to have a bearing on one's philosophy of life and independent, individuated outlook. Thus, turning inwardly may well be paralleled by openness towards others.

While the integrated old person is less likely to be overpowered by the "influence of external factors,"[378] individuation leads "to more intense and broader collective relationships and not to isolation."[379] However, in so far as the hero of youth brings the treasures of the soul and the fire of the gods into the realm of reality, the path of the senex departs from substance as corporeal matter toward focusing on what is *substantial*. Sub-stance is no longer what concretely 'stands under,' but the position of under-standing. Abandoning the emphasis on ego-reality, the matter and meaning that fertilize the ground on which the future can spring forth, now become substantial.

After a few months in analysis, Shulamit dreamed,

> I am walking along a boulevard with parallel rows of sixty-seventy-year-old trees, planted meticulously along each side of the street, at equal intervals, all looking exactly the same—tall, straight, meticulous, but with almost no branches and rather bare crown. I walk to the end, and then I ask, "what am *I* to do?" A man's voice tells me to proceed to the tree-planting ceremony—it must be Arbor Day. I go there, a small place set apart by very low bushes; one needs to tread carefully not to step on them, they are not very impressive, but serve a purpose. I look around and notice that I am the only one there. I then have to choose which sapling to plant. I choose an oak tree, drawn to it especially by the acorn.

Shulamit was departing on her old age journey by a sense of planting the seeds for a new life—her own, but also that of her off-spring. She had walked the straight and orderly road of life, having reached a

---

376  'Freud and the Future,' *Daedalus*, p. 374.
377  *The Seasons of a Man's Life*, p. 37.
378  'The Undiscovered Self,' CW 10, par. 511.
379  CW 6, par. 758.

holy place, that is, a place 'set apart,' where she could grow, by her very own and individual choice.

She realized that the perfection she had strived for in her scientific work had little value at this stage of her life. Individuation has nothing to do with perfection. What would we say about the life of Leonardo da Vinci? Certainly that it signified a magnificent achievement of all times. Could a life be culturally more individuated than his? Yet, his last words are supposed to have been, "I have offended God and mankind because my work did not reach the quality it should have."

Shulamit contemplated her compulsive need for perfection, which had served her well in her scientific endeavors, but considerably less so with friends and in family matters. "The oak tree will grow and live when I am no longer here," she said, "but just because I will only be able to *imagine* it full-grown, never see it like that in reality, just like my grandchildren, does not mean I shouldn't plant it, or not see them grow up, and tell them stories and listen to their little every-day stories that they want to share with me." She thought of herself as "the guard and the gardener of the garden." While we are not the creators of the garden, we need to guard and protect it, and tend to it.

When God appears to Solomon in a dream and asks, "What shall I give you?" Solomon answers, "An understanding heart to judge your people, that I may discern between good and bad."[380] The translations into English all speak of "an understanding heart" or "a wise heart," which reflects the essence of his request. In the original Hebrew it says lev shomea, that is, Solomon asks for a *hearing* heart. Wisdom comes from listening with your heart—not pure mind and intellect, but also not 'heart and nothing but heart.' Furthermore, *hear!* in Hebrew is shema!, the basis of mashmaot, which means *meaning*.[381]

After his dream at the sanctuary at Give'on, Solomon returns to Jerusalem. Two prostitutes, come before him, and one of them says,

> "O my lord, I and this woman live in one house; and I gave
> birth to a child with her in the house. And it came to pass
> the third day after I had given birth, that this woman also
> gave birth; and we were together; there was no stranger
> with us in the house, only the two of us in the house. And
> this woman's child died in the night; because she lay on it.
> And she arose at midnight, and took my son from my side,
> and laid it in her bosom, and laid her dead child in my

---

380  1 Kings 3:9.
381  The *Shema* is usually considered the most important prayer in Judaism, often said as the last words of a dying person.

bosom. And when I rose in the morning to nurse my child, behold, it was dead; but when I had looked at it closely in the morning, behold, it was not my son, that I had borne." Then the other woman speaks, and she says, "No; but the living child is my son, and the dead is your son."

Solomon asks for a sword,

And they brought a sword before the king. And the king said, "Divide the living child in two, and give half to one, and half to the other." Then the woman, whose son was the living child, spoke to the king, for her love was enkindled towards her son, and she said, "O my lord, give her the living child, but do not slay it." But the other said, "Let it be neither mine nor yours, but divide it."[382]

It was clear to King Solomon that the mother was the one who was willing to forfeit her son so that he may live.[383]

The name Solomon means *the peaceable*, from the same word as shalom, *peace*, and shalem, *whole*. A listening heart reflects the wisdom from the depths of the Self, that can guide us through what sometimes amounts to unbearable conflicts, limitations and divisions of the ego. When we transcend the boundaries of the ego, and plant a tree for the future—which may serve as a metaphor for caring for nature, psyche and soul in this world—ours becomes a listening heart, open to hear the call of our children.

## We Are All Beggars, Are We Not?

In old age, hearing becomes impaired and vision more blurred. For some, this provides an opportunity to open the senses to the pulsation of the soul, to hear the echoes of the sounds that arise from the depths, and perceive the reflection of the patterns that take shape under the sea.

This may be the transparency and the invisibility of not being seen by others, and the fear of being run over by the phenomena, the appearances of this world. However, as has been mentioned, it entails exchanging the reality-oriented ego-vision for the inward gaze—like Oedipus upon tearing out his eyes, and the seer Tiresias, or Samson. When

---

382  1 Kings. 3:17-26.
383  This can be compared to Abraham's willingness to slay his own son (see for instance Erel Shalit, 'Sacrifice of Isaac,' in *Encyclopedia of Psychology and Religion*, pp. 809-811).

blinded to this world of appearance, the inner world of transparent, invisible psychic substance may open up, to be sighted. This change in the ego-Self relationship marks a release of the ego from the persona of social roles. It is the invisibility of allowing oneself to be a beggar, a wanderer, or an old fool—not in the social, but in the psychological sense.[384]

In order to attain a sense of integrity in old life, rather than suffer severe despair, Erikson emphasizes the importance of reflection. The reflective instinct is specifically human, and determines "[t]he richness of the human psyche and its essential character," says Jung. *Reflexio*, which means 'bending back,' "is a turning inwards, with the result that, instead of an instinctive action, there ensues ... reflection or deliberation." "What youth found and must find outside," says Jung, "the man of life's afternoon must find within himself."[385] Jung calls reflection "the cultural instinct *par excellence*."[386] Reflection on one's life is instrumental at every developmental stage, unless it takes precedence over living one's life. In old age, the proportions alter, so that reflection on one's life becomes at least as important as merely living it.

When cut off from one's inner depths, the personality shrinks as the ego dries up and becomes limited. A reflective state of mind, however, enables the depths to be reflected in the mirror of one's Self and soul. Henry Miller tells us in *Colossus of Maroussi* that he did not know the meaning of peace until he visited the principal sanctuary of Asclepius at Epidaurus, where dream incubation began around 600 BCE. In the intense stillness and the great peace at Epidaurus "I heard the heart of the world beat. I know what the cure is: it is to give up, to relinquish, to surrender, so that our little hearts may beat in unison with the great heart of the world." Henry Miller makes it clear that Epidaurus, principally, is an internal space, "the real place is in the heart, in every man's heart, if he will but stop and search it."[387]

Reflection and imagination constitute the intangible substance of soul, which Hillman suggests refers "to that unknown component which makes meaning possible," and which he imagines "like a reflection in a flowing mirror."[388]

---

384  See *Enemy, Cripple & Beggar*, p. 197ff.
385  CW 7, par. 114.
386  CW 8, par. 241-243.
387  Henry Miller, *The Colossus of Maroussi*, p. 70f.
388  *Re-Visioning Psychology*, p. xvi.

Shulamit dreamed,

> I walk up to the holy city of Zefat (Safed), and walk through
> the narrow lanes to the HaAri synagogue.[389] I stop outside,
> turning my back to the wall. I just stand there, with my
> hand outstretched, holding a ball of air in my hand. A
> young man comes up to me. He believes I am a beggar and
> gives me a ½-shekel coin. I tell him we are all beggars at
> some stage in our life. He then leads me into the old syna-
> gogue. We just stand there, very quietly, and slowly he be-
> comes an old man, and I feel rather young, perhaps thirty
> or forty years old—or young! We stand in front of the holy
> ark, stretching out our hands to each other, and, floating in
> the air, there are thin transparent, slightly colored bubbles,
> like children's soap bubbles, in an incredible structure, like
> a DNA structure.

We sense the transparency of the incorporeal soul, and the simulta-
neous permanency of the DNA structure, which anchors the chain of
generations in individual corporeal manifestation.

The task of the senex is to reverse the direction of the hero, a reversal of the movement along the ego-Self axis. The issue is no longer the
emergence and development of the ego from the Self, and the ego so-
lidifying its rule on earth, stable on the ground of reality. It is no longer
a question of the hero searching the treasures of the soul, in order to
enrich the ego. Consciousness now pertains, rather, to the ego's self-
renunciation. It is the realization that the qualities one possesses are, in
fact, "manifestations of the gods,"

> Spirituality and sexuality are not your qualities, not things
> which ye possess and contain. But they possess and con-
> tain you; for they are powerful daemons, manifestations
> of the gods, and are, therefore, things which reach beyond
> you, existing in themselves. No man hath a spirituality
> unto himself, or sexuality unto himself. But he standeth
> under the law of spirituality and of sexuality.[390]

In 'The End of the Journey,' the final picture of the alchemical treatise *Splendor Solis*, "the sun shines above a muted landscape, with black-
ened tree stumps ... The sun's rays do not brighten the city..." Referring
to the image, Henderson and Sherwood say it tells us "that becoming

---

389  HaAri is the acronym for the Kabbalistic Rabbi Isaac Luria. Born in Jerusalem, 1534, he died in Zefat 1572, thirty-eight years old.
390  From Jung's 'Septem Sermones ad Mortuos' (Seven Sermons to the Dead),
in *Memories, Dreams, Reflections*, p. 387.

conscious does not result in a state of elation or bliss."[391] Consciousness pertains to knowing the suffering landscape that life provides, whether the landscape within the individual's private psyche, or the landscape of the soul and the matter in the world. Consciousness does not provide so much joy and pleasure, but rather for the depths, from which meaning and wisdom arise.

If the ego does not open up to the Self, the mirror of the soul will reflect the emptiness and loneliness of the narcissistic ego. However, if the ego is attentive, the voice will resound from within the soul and reflect the meaningful images and the symbols of the Self.

There may be more questions than answers blowing in the wind, but perhaps the answer is: blowing in the wind; to let the wind (in Hebrew: 'ruach') blow and to let the soul/spirit (also 'ruach') move. We are left with the questions blowing in the wind, to which the blowing in the wind, rather than the wind that has stopped blowing, may be the soul's main answer. "The wind is the pneuma hidden in the prima materia," says Jung.[392] Individuation entails the extraction of the spirit that dwells in one's raw material, of detecting, awakening and engaging the energy that may be trapped in the matter. But the answer may, as well, drift in the water, flare in the fire, and ripen on the ground.

## A Book in Order

After a year in analysis, during a period of several months, Shulamit came to feel guilt and regret about her shortcomings and failures in life, especially for not having attended to what she now felt to be most important. She did not know how she would be able to rectify her sense of wrongdoings. She said, "It will take more years than I have been allocated." She then had the following dream,

> I walk along the alleys of the old city in Jerusalem. Inside a small cave-like little shop with all kinds of paraphernalia, sits a very old woman. She is a story-teller, but no one listens any longer to her stories. In front of her is an old book with a spine of leather, pages having turned yellow-brown of age. The woman tells me, "Turn to the last page," which is very torn. One by one, I very carefully take the threads of the paper of the last page, and put them in order and glue

391  Joseph L. Henderson & Dyane N. Sherwood, *Transformation of the Psyche: The Symbolic Alchemy of the Splendor Solis*, p. 169.
392  CW 14, par. 15, note 103.

them together. When I finish, the old woman smiles at me and says, "Now the book is in order."

The alleys of the old city constitute the veins of the innermost kernel of Jerusalem, the significance of which has been elaborated elsewhere.[393] Within the within, within the dream in the heart of Jerusalem, in a cave-like opening, characteristic of many of the Old City shops, Shulamit finds the forgotten story-teller.

While the old woman was not necessarily celebrated in antiquity, and was accused of telling useless stories, fabula anilis, we should keep in mind that those are the stories of grandmothers, Bubbe Meises, as they are called in Yiddish. These are the crude and improper stories that would not be told by the more sophisticated senex-philosopher. But is it not the old and drunken woman, the *Anus*, who in the cave tells the story of *Eros and Psyche*, of the development of the human soul? We may not be able to know the value of our story, nor as measured "against the centuries," neither as "measured by the ideas of today."[394]

We may say that we then have come 'full circle.' Latin for ring and circle is anus. This is the root, as well, for those common words signifying year and years, such as annual and anniversary. Anile means, as well, senile, which seems to be no different between men and women— we may all become anile and senile. It also means 'like an old woman.' Anus is a woman who has come of age, a woman of many years, who knows to tell the often long-forgotten stories we need to hear. Without knowing where even the road less traveled leads us, we may only humbly strive for the senex's spirit of seniority and the anus's annual celebrations, rather than being overtaken by the senilities and anilities of old age.[395]

After her dream, Shulamit felt a great sense of relief, taking the dream as telling her that if she related carefully to 'the end of her book,' the damaged pieces in the puzzle of her life might fall into place.

Mircea Eliade, the historian of religion, wrote in his diary,

> I grasp the true meaning only after having gone through all the material. I would compare my immersion in the documents to a fusion with the material ... A descent to the center of dead matter ... Indirectly, the experience of

---

393  See 'Jerusalem: Human Ground, Archetypal Spirit.'
394  *Memories, Dreams, Reflections*, p. xii.
395  I am grateful to Vered Lev Kenaan, who informed me about the senex-anus syzygy (personal communication).

death. ... When I find myself again, when I return to life—I see things differently, I *understand* them.[396]

As much as we in old age reflect back upon what has been satisfactory in our lives, we need, as well, to bear our failures and foregone opportunities. Even if we have managed to walk our own individual path, having been fortunate to follow the road less traveled and found our way home to a sense of meaning in our personal quest, we need to carry the unanswered questions and unknown possibilities of the road not taken.

---

396  Mircea Eliade, *No Souvenirs*, p. 92.

# Bibliography

Adler, G. (1966). *Studies in Analytical Psychology*. New York: G. P. Putnam's Sons.

Adler, G. (1975). *C. G. Jung Letters: 1951-1961*. Princeton, NJ: Princeton University Press.

Aeschylus (1995). *Prometheus Bound*. Mineola, NY: Dover Publications.

Alighieri, D. (1984). *The Divine Comedy: Inferno*. New York: Penguin Classics.

American Psychiatric Association (1980). *Diagnostic and Statistical Manual of Mental Disorders*, Third Edition. Washington, DC: APA.

Anonymous & Payne, J. (2006). *The Book of the Thousand Nights and One Night*, Vol. IV. Middlesex, UK: The Echo Library.

Andersen, H. C. (1996). *The Complete Illustrated Works*. London: Chancellor Press.

Apuleius, L. (1996). *The Golden Ass*. Hertfordshire, UK: Wordsworth.

Archive for Research in Archetypal Symbolism (2010). *The Book of Symbols: Reflections on Archetypal Images*. Los Angeles: Taschen.

Ariès, P. (1962). *Centuries of Childhood: A Social History of Family Life* (translated by Robert Baldick). New York: Vintage.

Bachelard, G. (1983). *Water and Dreams: An Essay on the Imagination of Matter*. Dallas: The Dallas Institute of Humanities and Culture.

Beauvoir, S. de (1972). *Old Age*. (Translated by Patrick O'Brian). London: André Deutsch and Weidenfeld and Nicolson.

Becker, E. (1973). *The Denial of Death*. New York: The Free Press.

Bialik, H. N. & Ravnitzky, Y. H. (Eds.) (1992). *The Book of Legends: Legends from the Talmud and Midrash*. Translated from the Hebrew by William G. Braude, with an introduction by David Stern. New York: Schocken Books.

Biedermann, H. (1994). *Dictionary of Symbolism: Cultural Icons and the Meanings Behind Them*. Translated by James Hulbert. New York: Meridian.

Billström, J. (1941). *Människans Fyra Åldrar*. Stockholm: Hökerbergs.

Bolen, J. S. (1989). *Gods in Everyman*. New York: Harper and Row.

Boer, C. (1989). *Ovid's Metamorphoses*. Dallas: Spring Publications.

Borysenko, J. (1998). *A Woman's Book of Life: The Biology, Psychology, and Spirituality of the Feminine Life Cycle*. New York: Riverhead Books.

Bryant, S. C. (1963). *The Burning Rice Fields* (with pictures by Mamoru Funai). New York: Holt, Rinehart & Winston.

Buber, M. (2000). *The Way of Man: According to the Teaching of Hasidism*. New York: Citadel.

Buhler, G. (2009). *The Laws of Manu*. http://www.fordham.edu/halsall/india/manu-full.html

Caldwell, R. S. (1987). *Hesiod's Theogony*. Translated, with Introduction, Commentary, and Interpretative Essay. Newburyport, MA: Focus Classical Library.

Calvino, I. (1997). *Invisible Cities*. London: Vintage.

Campbell, J. (1968). *The Hero with a Thousand Faces*. New York: Bollingen.

Casement, A. (2010). Persona, in: Leeming D.A., Madden K., Marlan S. (eds). *Encyclopedia of Psychology and Religion*. Vol. 2, pp. 670-72. New York: Springer.

Cavafy, C. P. (1992). *Collected Poems* (Revised Edition). Translated by Edmund Keeley and Philip Sherrard. Edited by George Savidis. Princeton: Princeton University Press.

Cirlot, J. E. (1991). *A Dictionary of Symbols*. New York: Dorset Press.

Cooper, J. C. (1990). *An Illustrated Encyclopedia of Traditional Symbols*. London: Thames and Hudson.

Deutsch, H. (1942). Some forms of emotional disturbance and their relationship to schizophrenia. *Psychoanalytic Quarterly*, 11:301-321.

Dickens, C. (2001). *Bleak House*. Hertfordshire, UK: Wordsworth Classics

Davis, A. (1980). *Pirkei Avos: The Wisdom of the Fathers*. A new translation and anthology of its classical commentaries. New York: Metsudah Publications.

Drob, S. L. (2010). *Kabbalistic Visions: C. G. Jung and Jewish Mysticism*. New Orleans: Spring.

Edinger, E. (1968). An outline of analytical psychology, *Quadrant*, 1, 1-12.

Edinger, E. F. (1974). *Ego and Archetype: Individuation and the Religious Function of the Psyche*. New York: Penguin.

Edinger, E. F. (1994). *The Eternal Drama*. Boston: Shambhala.

Edinger, E. F. (1999). *The Psyche in Antiquity, Book One: Early Greek Philosophy.* Toronto: Inner City Books.

Edmunds, L. (1985). *Oedipus: The Ancient Legend and its Later Analogues.* Baltimore and London: The John Hopkins University Press.

Elder, G. R. (1996). *The Body: An Encyclopedia of Archetypal Symbolism, Vol. 2.* Boston: Shambhala.

Eliade, M. (1977). *No Souvenirs,* NY: Harper & Row.

Ellenberger, H. F. (1970). *The Discovery of the Unconscious: The History and Evolution of Dynamic Psychiatry.* New York: Basic Books.

Erikson, E. H. (1977). *Childhood and Society.* 2nd Ed. London: Triad/Palatin, Granada.

Erikson, E. H. (1983). *Identity: Youth and Crisis.* London: Faber and Faber.

Erikson, E. H. (1997). *The Life Cycle Completed.* Extended Version with New Chapters on the Ninth Stage of Development by Joan M. Erikson. New York: Norton.

Erikson Bloland, S. (1999). *Fame: The Power and Cost of a Fantasy.* www.theatlantic.com/issues/99nov/9911fame.htm

Freud, S. (1953-1973). *Standard Edition of the Complete Psychological Works.* 24 vols. London: Hogarth Press.

Frost, R. (1993). *The Road Not Taken and Other Poems.* New York: Dover.

Furlotti, N. (2010). 'Angels and Idols: Los Angeles, A City of Contrasts,' in Thomas Singer (Ed.), *Psyche and the City: A Soul's Guide to the Modern Metropolis.* Louisiana, New Orleans: Spring Journal Books.

Graves, R. (1985). *Greek Myths (Illustrated Edition).* London: Penguin.

Graves, R. & Patai. R. (1989). *Hebrew Myth: The Book of Genesis.* London: Arena.

Grimm Brothers (1972). *The Complete Grimm's Fairy Tales.* New York: Pantheon Books.

Grunberger, B. (1993). On Narcissism, Aggressivity and Anti-Semitism1. *Int. Forum Psychoanal.,* 2:237-240.

Haigh, A. E. (1896). *The Tragic Drama of the Greeks.* Oxford: Clarendon Press.

Hall, J.A. (1986). *The Jungian Experience: Analysis and Individuation.* Toronto: Inner City Books.

Hamilton, E. (1969). *Mythology: Timeless Tales of Gods and Heroes.* New York: Mentor.

Hannah, B. (1997). *Jung: His Life and Work.* Wilmette, IL: Chiron.

Henderson, J. L. & Sherwood, D. N. (2003). *Transformation of the Psyche: The Symbolic Alchemy of the Splendor Solis*. New York: Brunner-Routledge.

Herzog, E. (1983). *Psyche and Death: Death-Demons in Folklore, Myths and Modern Dreams*. Dallas: Spring Publications.

Hesiod (1999). *Theogony and Works and Days*. A new translation by M. L. West. Oxford: Oxford University Press.

Heraclitus (2001). *Fragments: the Collected Wisdom of Heraclitus*. (Translated by Brooks Haxton). New York: Viking.

Hillman, J. (Ed.) (1979). *Puer Papers*. Dallas: Spring Publications.

Hillman, J. (1989). *Facing the Gods*. Dallas: Spring Publications.

Hillman, J. (1992). *Re-Visioning Psychology*. New York: HarperPerennial.

Hillman, J. (1996). *The Soul's Code: In Search of Character and Calling*. New York; Random House.

Hillman, J. (2000). *Pan and the Nightmare* (New Revised Edition). Woodstock, CT: Spring Publications.

Hollis, J. (2003). *On This Journey We Call Our Life*. Toronto: Inner City Books.

Homer (2003). *The Iliad*. Hertfordshire, UK: Wordsworth Classics.

Jacoby, M. A. (1985). *Longing for Paradise: Psychological Perspectives on an Archetype*. Boston: Sigo Press.

Jaffé, A. (1979). *C. G. Jung: Word and Image*. (Bollingen Series XCVII:2). Princeton: Princeton University Press.

Jung, C. G. (1962). *Memories, Dreams, Reflections*. Pantheon Books.

Jung, C. G. (1953-1979). *The Collected Works*. (Bollingen Series XX). 20 Vols. Trans. R. F. C. Hull. Ed. H. Read, M. Fordham, G. Adler, Wm. McGuire. Princeton: Princeton University Press.

Jung, C. G. (2009). *The Red Book: Liber Novus*. S. Shamdasani (Ed.). M. Kyburz, J. Peck & S. Shamdasani (Trans.). New York: W. W. Norton.

Jung, C. G. & Kerényi, C. (1993). *Essays on a Science of Mythology: The Myth of the Divine Child and the Mysteries of Eleusis*. Princeton: Princeton University Press.

Kerényi, K. (1976). *Hermes: Guide of Souls*. Dallas: Spring.

Kerényi, K. (1978). *Athene: Virgin and Mother in Greek Religion*. Translated from German and with translator's afterthoughts by Murray Stein. Woodstock, CT: Spring.

Kerényi, C. (1991). *Prometheus: Archetypal Image of Human Existence.* Princeton: Princeton University Press.

Kerényi, K. & Hillman, J. (1995*). Oedipus Variations: Studies in Literature and Psychoanalysis.* Dallas: Spring.

Kernberg, O. (1975). *Borderline Conditions and Pathological Narcissism.* New York: Jason Aronson.

La Fontaine, J. (2006). *The Original Fables of La Fontaine.* Translated by FC Tilney. Cirencester, UK: The Echo Library.

Lacarrière, J. (1996). *The Wisdom of Ancient Greece.* New York: Abeville Press.

Laing, R. (1971). *The Divided Self.* Harmondsworth, UK: Penguin.

Larousee (1987). *New Larousse Encyclopedia of Mythology.* Introduction by Robert Graves. Twickenham, UK: Hamlyn.

Lev Kenaan, V. (2008). *Pandora's Senses: The Feminine Character of the Ancient Text.* Madison, WI: University of Wisconsin Press.

Levinson, D. (1978). *The Seasons of a Man's Life.* Ballantine Books.

Madden, K. W. (2008). *Dark Light of the Soul.* Great Barrington, MA: Lindisfarne Books.

Mann, T. (1959). 'Freud and the Future,' in *Myth and Mythmaking, Daedalus*, vol. 88:2, pp. 374-378.

McCurdy, J. C. (1987). Manic-Depressive Psychosis – A Perspective, *J. An. Psychology*, 32, 309-324.

Miller, H. (2010). *The Colossus of Maroussi.* New York: New Directions Books.

Mumford, L. (1989). *The City in History: Its Origins, Its Transformations, and Its Prospects.* New York: MJF Books.

Nehru, J. (1990). *The Discovery of India.* Oxford: Oxford University Press.

Neumann, E. (1963). *The Great Mother.* London: Routledge & Kegan Paul.

Neumann, E. (1971). *Amor and Psyche: The Psychic Development of the Feminine; A Commentary on the Tale by Apuleius.* Princeton: Bollingen/Princeton University Press.

Neumann, E. (1970). *The Origins and History of Consciousness.* Princeton: Bollingen/Princeton University Press.

Neumann, E. (1994). *The Fear of the Feminine: And Other Essays on Feminine Psychology.* Princeton: Princeton University Press.

Pawlyn, M. (2011). 'Biomimicry,' in Yeang, K. & Spector, A. (Eds.), *Green Design: From Theory to Practice*. London: Black Dog Publishing.

Plato (1997). *Symposium and the Death of Socrates*. (Translated by Tom Griffith, with an introduction by Jane O'Grady). Hertfordshire, UK: Wordsworth.

Rilke, R. M. (1986). *Letters to a Young Poet*, NY: Vintage Books.

Rycroft, C. (1972). *A Critical Dictionary of Psychoanalysis*. Harmondsworth, UK: Penguin.

Sadeh, P. (1989). *Jewish Folktales*. (Translated from the Hebrew by Hillel Halkin). New York: Doubleday.

Samuels, A., Shorter, B. & Plaut, F. (1986). *A Critical Dictionary of Jungian Analysis*. London: Routledge.

Sanford, J. A. (1995). *Fate, Love, and Ecstasy: Wisdom from the Lesser-Known Goddesses of the Greeks*. Wilmette, IL: Chiron.

Sardello, R. (1992). *Facing the World with Soul: The Reimagination of Modern Life*. New York: HarperPerennial.

Sardello, R. (2001). Archetypal Silence, *Oregon Friends of C. G. Jung Newsletter*. http://www.ofj.org/story/march-2001-newsletter-archive.

Schachter-Shalomi, Z. & Miller, R. S. (1997). *From Age-ing to Sage-ing: A Profound New Vision of Growing Older*. New York: Warner Books.

Scholem, G. (1969). *On the Kabbalah and its Symbolism*. New York: Schocken Books.

Schwartz, H. (2004). *Tree of Souls: The Mythology of Judaism*. New York and Oxford: Oxford University Press.

Schwartz-Salant, N. (1986). *Narcissism and Character Transformation*. Toronto: Inner City Books.

Segal, H. (1974). *Introduction to the work of Melanie Klein*. Basic Books.

Shakespeare, W. (2005). *The Oxford Shakespeare: The Complete Works* (2nd Edition). Oxford: Oxford University Press.

Shalit, E. (2002). *The Complex: Path of Transformation from Archetype to Ego*. Toronto: Inner City Books.

Shalit, E. (2004). *The Hero and His Shadow: Psychopolitical Aspects of Myth and Reality in Israel (Revised Ed.)*. Lanham, MA: University Press of America.

Shalit, E. (2008). *Enemy, Cripple and Beggar: Shadows in the Hero's Path*. Carmel, CA: Fisher King Press.

Shalit, E. (2010). Sacrifice of Isaac, in David A. Leeming, Kathryn Madden and Stanton Marlan (Eds), *Encyclopedia of Psychology and Religion*, Vol. 2. New York: Springer.

Shalit, E. (2010). 'Silence is the Center of Feeling,' in Robert and Janet Henderson, *Living With Jung: "Enterviews" with Jungian Analysts.* Louisiana, New Orleans: Spring Journal Books.

Shalit, E. (2010). 'Jerusalem: Human Ground, Archetypal Spirit,' in Thomas Singer (Ed.), *Psyche and the City: A Soul's Guide to the Modern Metropolis.* Louisiana, New Orleans: Spring Journal Books.

Shalit, E. (2010). Destruction of the Image and the Worship of Transiency. *Jung Journal*, Vol. 4, number 1, Feb. 2010, pp. 94-108.

Shalit, E. (2010). *Requiem: A Tale of Exile and Return.* Carmel, CA: il piccolo editions.

Shalit, E. (2011). *Will Fishes Fly in Aquarius – Or Will They Drown in the Bucket?* Carmel, CA: Fisher King Press.

Shalit, E. & Hall, J. (2006). The Complex and the Object: Common Ground, Different Paths. *Quadrant*, 36:2, pp. 27-42.

Sharp, D. (1991). *Jung Lexicon: A Primer of Terms and Concepts.* Toronto: Inner City Books.

Sherwood, V. R. and Cohen, C. P. (1994). *Psychotherapy of the Quiet Borderline Patient: The As-If Personality Revisited*, London, Jason Aronson.

Sophocles (1974). *The Theban Plays.* Harmondsworth, UK: Penguin.

Spitz, R.A. (1945). Hospitalism: An Inquiry Into the Genesis of Psychiatric Conditions in Early Childhood. *Psychoanalytic Study of the Child*, 1, 53-74.

Staude, J.-R. (1981). *The Adult Development of C. G. Jung.* London: Routledge & Kegan Paul.

Stein, M. (1983). *In Midlife.* Dallas: Spring.

Tatham, P. (1992). *The Makings of Maleness: Men, Women, and the Flight of Daedalus.* London: Karnac.

Tripp, E. (1974). *The Meridian Handbook of Classical Mythology.* New York: Meridian.

Von Franz, M.-L. (1995). *Creation Myths.* Boston: Shambhala.

Von Franz, M.-L. (1987). *Interpretation of Fairytales.* Dallas: Spring.

Von Franz, M.-L. (1994). *The Way of the Dream.* Boston: Shambhala.

Whitmont, E.C. (1991). *The Symbolic Quest.* Princeton: Princeton University Press.

Wilson, J. (1997). *The Hero and the City: An Interpretation of Sophocles'* Oedipus at Colonus. Ann Arbor: University Press of Michigan.

Winnicott, D.W. (1958). *Collected Papers: Through Paediatrics to Psycho-Analysis*. London: Tavistock Publications.

Winnicott, D.W. (1980). *Playing and Reality*. Harmondsworth, UK: Penguin.

# Index

Levinson, Daniel
 *The Seasons of a Man's Life* 8-11,
  16, 175, 187
libido 30-32, 35-36, 61, 68, 101,
  105, 131

# M

Madden, Kathryn Wood
 *Dark Light of the Soul* 80, 187
mana-energy 108
manic-depression 108-109
Mann, Thomas 6, 175
 'Freud and the Future' 6, 175,
  187
 'Myth and Mythmaking' 6, 175,
  187, 189
Mars 66
Medusa 119
Menoetius 96
mercurial 40
Mercurius 36
metaphysics 150
Metis 118
midlife transition 10, 15
Miller, Henry
 *The Colossus of Maroussi* 178,
  187
misanthropy 150
Mnemosyne 30, 77
Mother
 archetype 54, 60, 74
 Earth 27, 30
 Good 54, 88
 Great 60, 74, 77, 83, 90, 187
 Nature 77
 Terrible 54, 68, 74, 77, 82, 88
Mount Hermon 28-29
Mount Nebo 34
Mumford, Lewis
 *The City in History* 27, 187

# N

narcissistic energy 32-33, 103
Narcissus 29, 33-34, 103

Nehru, Jawaharlal
 *The Discovery of India* 27, 187
Nemesis 114
Neumann, Erich 11, 64
 *Amor and Psyche: The Psychic
  Development of the Feminine*
  187
 *The Fear of the Feminine* 98, 187
 *The Great Mother* 74, 187
 *The Origins and History of Con-
  sciousness* 10, 60, 67, 81,
  113, 187
Nyx 17

# O

obsessive-compulsive 79, 124,
  172
Oedipus 5, 18, 22, 45, 66, 74, 77,
  83, 95, 156-161, 163-170,
  177, 185, 187, 190
Oedipus at Colonus 5, 18, 156,
  159, 161, 190
Oedipus Rex 156
Oracle at Delphi 156

# P

Pan 28-29, 82, 186
Pandora 97-98, 101, 187
parental abandonment 84
patriarchal
 consciousness 118
 God 26
 principle 118-119
Pawlyn, Michael
 'Biomimicry' 116, 188
Persephone 94, 108
Perseus 59, 65, 107, 119
Phanes 64
pilgrimage 23, 43
Plato
 *Symposium and the Death of So-
  crates* 22, 33, 72, 92, 188
Plutarch
 "On the failure of the Oracles"
  29

# You might also enjoy reading these Jungian publications:

*Eros and the Shattering Gaze* by Ken Kimmel
ISBN 978-1-926715-49-0

*Becoming: An Introduction to Jung's Concept of Individuation*
by Deldon Anne McNeely
ISBN 978-1-926715-12-4

*The Creative Soul* by Lawrence Staples
ISBN 978-0-9810344-4-7

*Guilt with a Twist* by Lawrence Staples
ISBN 978-0-9776076-4-8

*Enemy, Cripple, Beggar* by Erel Shalit
ISBN 978-0-9776076-7-9

*Divine Madness* by John R. Haule
ISBN 978-1-926715-04-9

*Farming Soul* by Patricia Damery
ISBN 978-1-926715-01-8

*The Motherline* by Naomi Ruth Lowinsky
ISBN 978-0-9810344-6-1

*The Sister From Below* by Naomi Ruth Lowinsky
ISBN 978-0-9810344-2-3

*Like Gold Through Fire* by Bud & Massimilla Harris
ISBN 978-0-9810344-5-4

*The Art of Love: The Craft of Relationship*
by Bud & Massimilla Harris
ISBN 978-1-926715-02-5

Phone Orders Welcomed
Credit Cards Accepted
In Canada & the U.S. call  1-800-228-9316
International call  +1-831-238-7799
www.fisherkingpress.com

# The Philemon Foundation

*Preparing for publication the Complete Works of C.G. Jung.*

The Philemon Foundation has as its mission the publication of C.G. Jung's previously unpublished manuscripts, seminars, correspondence, and other works, in English and in German, adhering to the most rigorous standards of contemporary academic scholarship.

In the mission and spirit of the organization, the Philemon Foundation is the successor to the Bollingen Foundation, the foundation that originally made possible the publication of Jung's *Collected Works*. In this new era, the Philemon Foundation is in a unique position to have the support and contractual collaboration of the Stiftung der Werke von C.G. Jung, the charitable successor to the Association of the Heirs of C.G. Jung.

Given the volume of material yet unpublished in various public and private archives, the Philemon Foundation conservatively estimates that it will prepare for publication an additional 30 volumes to comprise the *Complete Works.*

Publications to date include
*The Red Book, Children's Dreams,* and *The Jung-White Letters.*

In order to bring to publication the critical, unpublished work of C.G. Jung, your support is needed.

Help us carry the mission forward.

**www.philemonfoundation.org**

Made in United States
Orlando, FL
25 June 2022

19162829R00115